# BIG BOOK OF
# BABY NAMES
## AND
# ANNOUNCEMENTS

Publisher: Rick Bailey
Executive Editor: Randy Summerlin
Editor: Judith Schuler
Art Director: Don Burton
Managing Editor: Cindy J. Coatsworth
Typography: Michelle Carter
Director of Manufacturing: Anthony B. Narducci

ISBN: 0-89586-295-6
Library of Congress Catalog Card Number: 82-82982
©1983 HPBooks, Inc.
Printed in U.S.A.
6th Printing

# TABLE OF CONTENTS

**Published by HPBooks**
**A division of HPBooks, Inc.**
P.O. Box 5367
Tucson, AZ 85703
(602) 888-2150

# ABOUT THE AUTHOR

Sandra Buzbee Bailey is the mother of four children and an avid researcher of names. Her interest in the subject began when she did a paper on the development of slang for a college class. She became intrigued with variations and derivations of words and names. This fascination led her to genealogy and an interest in incorporating names of past generations when naming new generations.

Before each of her children was born, Sandra read novels, baby-name books and genealogy records looking for the "just right" name. She created so many name lists and became so adept at research that it was natural for her to do the most complete book on the subject. But, all the work was worth it, says Sandra with a smile. Not one of her children has rejected his name—yet!

# ABOUT THE ILLUSTRATOR

Darcy Anne Tom moved to Tucson, Arizona, after she completed her education at the Kendall School of Design in Grand Rapids, Michigan. As an illustrator, she has been involved in many projects, including illustrating children's educational books. Darcy is married and recently had the occasion to name a baby—her own little boy!

ACKNOWLEDGMENTS

My sincere appreciation to my mother, Geraldine Buzbee of Herman, Nebraska, for her love and support during the production of this book. Thanks to Dr. Judy Mitchell, who provided valuable assistance in developing a pronunciation guide for the names. Thanks also to my children, Ryan, Elliott, André and Sasha, whose births prompted my search for new and interesting names.

# NAMING YOUR BABY

Jeremy
James
Jonathan

# ABCs Of
# Naming Your Baby

How many times in your life do you sign your name? If you sign it once a day and live to be 75 years old, you will have written your name 27,393 times. Many people hear or see your name. It represents you. People get an impression about you from your name.

Studies show a name reflects a certain image. To many people, Judy gives the image of an all-American sportswoman. Dawn gives the image of a sexy, beautiful girl. A name is like a nose—you're usually stuck with the one your parents gave you. And it's there for the world to comment on.

## SUCCESS OR FAILURE—IT'S ALL IN A NAME

Research on the psychological effect of a name indicates that it may help make you a success or failure. It depends on the way people react to your name. The sound or spelling alone could land you in jail, get you a job as a college president, or help you become a movie star!

Here's a case in point. A study by two psychology professors, Herbert Harari and John McDavid, suggests teachers are influenced by a student's name when they give out grades. Two groups of teachers were asked to mark essays. Some were told the essays were written by David, Michael, Lisa and Ann. Others were told that the same essays were from Elmer, Sebastian, Adele and Beatrice. The essays by the first group with common, popular names got consistently higher marks than those written by students with older, stodgier names. So if your child gets an *F* on a paper, perhaps you should blame it on the name you gave him, not his I.Q.!

Names that are too hard to pronounce or too offbeat may also doom a student to failure. Studies of 3,000 undergraduates at Harvard University show the highest proportion of dropouts was among those with strange or exotic names.

# A NAME IS WORTH A THOUSAND WORDS

The way you perceive a person often depends on his name. How much confidence would you have in a person named John Will Fail or Mary Christmas? They will be joked about and laughed at all their lives. How about uncommon names such as Dwight David Eisenhower, Rutherford Birchard Hayes and Ulysses S. Grant? What did people call these boys when they were young?

How about a name like Cardinal Jaime Sin? There really is a person with this name. He often relates in speeches how he enjoys inviting people to *the house of Sin*. Difficult or humorous names can be overcome—but it takes a lifetime of courage, thick skin and laughing in the face of ridicule. Don't force your child to endure it. Be careful and thoughtful when selecting a name.

Famous people can popularize a name, but be cautious of choosing a faddish name. Names like Tad, Rip and Bo may be in one year, but out the next. Basing a name on the year's most popular TV star or the latest song may seem clever, but the glow may fade later. Don't associate your child with a fad or craze. You don't want your child's name to date him unnecessarily.

# WHAT'S IN A NAME?

How significant is the meaning of a name? Meanings vary from one language to another. Often there is uncertainty as to the exact meaning. But you shouldn't assume that all names have lost their meanings, just that some have taken on different or more diverse meanings with the passing of time.

If you name your child Abraham, *Father of the multitude*, does it mean he will have 12 children? Will a girl named Doris, *From the sea*, automatically be a good swimmer? Of course not. The meaning of a name is as important as you want to make it.

In some native cultures, names are considered part of a man's soul. They have a personal effect on the child and how he is treated. In today's modern society, many people don't know the meaning of their names. But a name and its meaning can be important if we make it so. It can give us something to be proud of and something to pattern our lives after. The choice is yours and your child's!

**KAMEKO**—*Child of the tortoise*

# A LASTING LEGACY

One of the lasting gifts you give your child is his or her name. Take time to pick or construct a name that has the dignity, beauty and lasting qualities you want. The right name will bring both of you happiness.

In this book you will find more than 13,000 names, nicknames and variations—Oriental, Egyptian, Russian, Hebrew, European, Latin, Polynesian, American Indian, American, East Indian and Eskimo. Look through the names to find ones you like. Make a checklist and then eliminate them one by one. Another section in this chapter, How To Choose Or Create A Name, beginning on page 15, will help you further.

Take plenty of time deciding on the name to give your child. It will be a legacy he or she will appreciate for a lifetime.

# Where Names Come From

## HEY YOU THERE!

Thousands of years ago, before the development of formal language, how did one tribe member identify another? One native may have grunted to his neighbor, "Ugg," meaning "Hey you over there!," and that was the beginning of name identification.

History shows early names were coined from a variety of sources: from a circumstance of birth, a physical characteristic of the child or some hoped-for quality parents wanted their child to possess. Early names were borrowed from tribal gods. They were taken from animals, objects, stones and flowers. If the name caught on, it was handed down from one generation to another.

Along the way original meanings were forgotten or combined with other meanings. As nations mixed through trade or war, they borrowed names and added their own pronunciations and spellings. The result was a mixture of names. The trail is sometimes difficult to follow for someone who wants to discover the original meaning of a word or name.

## RELIGION DOES ITS PART

Christianity provided a remarkable change in the giving of names. In the Middle Ages, it was decreed by Christian law that a child's name had to contain the first name of a saint or martyr, or the child could not be baptized. The list of eligible names was taken from the Bible and included such names as Mary, Ann, Elizabeth, John, Nathan and James. For this reason, these names have been common in Christian cultures for centuries.

Different sects brought about trends in names. An example is the Puritans. They began using names as an indication of moral or religious worthiness. The outcome was a proliferation of names such as Repentance, Purity, Comfort, Faith, Hope, Charity and Mercy.

**GABRIELLE—**
*God is my strength*

# MADE IN HOLLYWOOD

In more recent times, the movie industry has done its share of creating trends or vogues in names. The influence of the silver screen has carried over into all aspects of people's lives, including what we name our children. Many children were given names because of a famous Hollywood namesake: Greta, Hedy, Myrna, Joan, Bette and Pearl; or Cary, Charlton, Rex, Boris, Ricardo and Marlon.

Television has been even more pervasive. It influences our thought and speech in more ways than we imagine. From soap operas, situation comedies and made-for-TV-movies, we have been deluged with popular names such as Jaime, Sonny, Erica, Constance, Jaclyn and Derek.

# WHICH SMITH?

Have you ever tried to count all the John or Mary Smiths in a big-city phone book? If so, you realize the importance of choosing the right first name to go with your surname. If you have a common surname, consider giving your child a unique and unusual first or middle name.

Another way to avoid problems with common surnames is to select three given names so your child will avoid identity mix-ups. Chinese and American Indians don't have this problem. These cultures frequently give as many as 10 names. But before you go to excess, remember that most application or registration forms provide a space for only three names.

The combination of first name and surname should sound pleasing together. Be careful that the combination doesn't create humor or discomfort. A child may get tired of living a lifetime with unfortunate combinations such as Lovey Good, Goodhue Red, Ham Burger, Lake Trout or I. M. Zamost.

# BOY OR GIRL?

There is a trend today to give a boy's name to a girl and, to a lesser extent, a girl's name to a boy. Examples are Terry, Chris, Jerry, Carrie and Billie. Most American-Indian and Polynesian names don't have this problem—their names can be used for both boys and girls. American culture is heading in that direction, possibly because of the equal-rights movement and the tendency for women to assert themselves in all areas of society.

Some names sound the same for boys or girls, but the spelling gives a clue to the sex. In the following names, the first spelling is feminine and the second version is masculine: Carol/Carroll, Leslie/Lesley and Claire/Clair. Unless you see the person, it is difficult to determine the sex. Such mistaken sex identity may prove troublesome to your child. Your son may get women's mail and your daughter may be drafted!

**WARREN**—*Protecting friend*

# NICKNAMES—A WAY OF LIFE

We have a tendency to shorten names. We may be too lazy or too busy to pronounce a complete name. When picking out a suitable name for your baby, consider the shortened form or nickname. If you pick William, be sure you don't mind friends or family calling your boy Bill or Willy. Barbara may sound beautiful to you—but you may dislike Babs or Bobi. You can't entirely predict nicknames, but remember that many people go through life answering to them.

Another shortened form of a name is a love nickname or pet name. Names of endearment are good therapy for everyone. A name that is special between two people helps their relationship. Often these names develop naturally and are difficult to predict. But if your son is named Teddy, don't be surprised if his baby name is Teddy Bear—especially if he's cute and cuddly!

# MY HERO!

"My boy is named after the most famous man in history, Abraham Lincoln," said a proud mother. Many cultures have been overly enthusiastic about naming their children after national heroes or heroines. Thousands, maybe millions, of children have been named after George Washington, John Kennedy, Winston Churchill, Joan of Arc, Florence Nightingale and Napoleon. There's nothing wrong with this if the name is not contrived and fits with your surname. Be careful of naming your child after people who are more infamous than famous. Such names as the following generate more negative response than positive: Adolf Hitler, Benedict Arnold and Lee Harvey Oswald.

In many families, it is traditional to name the first boy after his father or grandfather. If the baby is a girl, strange things may happen, such as changing James to Jamie. But is it fair to name only the first child after the father or mother and imply the other sons or daughters are not quite as good or important?

In our family we decided each son would bear his father's name, which is Rickard. So we gave each boy his father's name as a *middle* name. In naming our daughter, we decided on Sasha, which is a derivative of my name, Sandra. So, in our case, both parents' vanity is satisfied.

**SASHA**—*Helper of mankind*

Another problem may be grandparents or relatives. You can't please everyone. You may start a tug-of-war if you consult relatives about names. Make your choice of a name and then announce the happy news—it's less traumatic that way.

Some people want to pass on an ancestral or traditional family name. This often gives children a link with the past and helps you in your search for a name. A common practice is to give the wife's maiden name as a middle name, which helps in genealogical research. There is one caution: Don't settle on an out-of-date name that will be disliked by your child throughout his life.

## THE ARTS AT WORK

Books, plays, poems and music have provided many characters from which to draw names. Authors of fiction can create super heroes or heroines and choose names to fit them perfectly. The arts are a great source of names for your child. Remember some of the wonderful and lovable characters that you have enjoyed in reading, listening or viewing. Maybe one of these characters will provide the right name for your baby.

# How to Choose or Create a Name

Should your child share a name with anyone? Your boy or girl is unique—why saddle him or her with a common name like Mary or John? Some psychologists believe common names help a child become successful and uncommon names should be avoided. Other experts say the reverse. Some people feel special when they're the only Kaja in the class or school.

One woman confided it was difficult to live with her unusual name. But she said she would not trade it for a common name. It made her feel out of the ordinary—not just another Mary, Jane or Barbara. She also gave her children uncommon names.

The decision is up to you. This book offers you common and uncommon names. If you can't find the perfect name for your special child, use the following helpful hints to create your own.

# PRONUNCIATION + SPELLING = NAME

Names are tricky at best. Don't confuse the issue by making it hard to pronounce. Consider the whole name as a unit, not just the first name. The name should sound nice and melodious. How would you like to go through life with the name Chuck Stuck? Say it 10 times. Now do the same with Jonathan Stuck. One name is harsh and abrasive. The other flows smoothly.

Your child's name should sound pleasing. One way to accomplish this is to use the rhythm system. Most phonetic specialists agree that equal numbers of syllables in first and last names sound clipped and dead. Names like Pat Bond, Jeff Call or Stan Green are not nearly as rhythmical as Pat McDonald, Jeff Browerman or Stanley Green.

Next comes the problem of spelling. Have you ever looked at a person's name on paper and been afraid to pronounce it? It's helpful if names are spelled simply and close to the way they are pronounced.

"Teacher, my name is *juh-MEL-uh*. No, it's spelled J-A-M-I-L-A. No, it's not pronounced ja-MIL-a. No, it wouldn't be better with two E's!" By this time, the children in the classroom are all rolling on the floor with laughter. How embarrassing for your beautiful daughter! Maybe a more simple name—one that's easier to spell—would be less confusing and less irritating.

# SPELL IT OUT

A letter sent to Ann Landers points out the problem of initials. The man's name in the letter was J.B., with no other given name, just initials. He said not having a full-fledged name was the worst thing a parent could possibly do. Teachers called him a liar, insisting that he must have a first name. He had trouble with insurance companies, military service, voting and opening bank accounts. Giving your child initials for a name may lead him into countless arguments and problems. Friends will always think he's covering up a ridiculous first name!

Juniors or numbers after names can also cause problems. There is a trend away from this tradition. Would you like to be known as "little Bill" or "big Bill"? No one likes to live in someone's shadow. Do your child a favor—give him his own identity.

Consider what your child's initials will spell? If you name your son Peter Ivan Gordon, he will go through life with the initials P.I.G. Look at all aspects of a name before you make a final decision.

# YOUR NAME AND MEANING

Create a name with the meaning you want. You may find a name you like but the meaning is not quite right. For example, Katherine means *pure* and Kali means *energy*. By combining them, you can form the meaningful name, Kalerine. This might express your hope for the future—*pure energy*.

Now consider a boy's name. Homer means *promise* and Donald means *world ruler*. By combining and altering them slightly, you can create the name Maldon, possibly meaning *promised world ruler*.

This process can be used many times to develop your own names and meanings. Try different names together and see what you create.

# Famous Name Changes

During the last part of the 19th century and early in this century, immigrants to the United States often changed their names. People arriving in this country were encouraged to take new names to fit better into American society.

Today, the practice of changing names is most prevalent among movie stars, show-business celebrities and sports stars. Many hope a more appealing name—and one that's easy to pronounce—will help them attain popularity. It's all part of the art of selling yourself to the public.

Following is a list of people who changed their name to create a better public image or for personal or religious reasons. Their original name is listed opposite their professional name. See which you like best.

| PROFESSIONAL NAME | ORIGINAL NAME |
|---|---|
| Muhammad Ali | Cassius Marcellus Clay, Jr. |
| Woody Allen | Allen Konigsberg |
| Julie Andrews | Julia Vernon |
| Fred Astaire | Frederick Austerlitz |
| Lauren Bacall | Betty Joan Perski |
| Lucille Ball | Diane Belmont |
| Jack Benny | Joseph Kubelsky |
| Irving Berlin | Israel Baline |
| Yogi Berra | Lawrence Peter Berra |
| David Bowie | David Jones |
| Mel Brooks | Melvin Kaminsky |
| Yul Brynner | Taidje Kahn, Jr. |
| Bugs Bunny | Happy Rabbit |
| George Burns | Nathan Birnbaum |
| Ray Charles | Ray Charles Robinson |
| Chevy Chase | Cornelius Crane Chase |

| PROFESSIONAL NAME | ORIGINAL NAME |
| --- | --- |
| Cher | Cherilyn LaPierre |
| Mike Connors | Krekor Ohanian |
| Robert Conrad | Conrad Robert Falk |
| Joan Crawford | Lucille Le Sueur |
| Bing Crosby | Harry Lillis Crosby |
| Tony Curtis | Bernard Schwartz |
| Rodney Dangerfield | John Cohen |
| Doris Day | Doris Kappelhoff |
| Sandra Dee | Alexandra Zuck |
| John Denver | Henry John Deutschendorf, Jr. |
| Bob Dylan | Robert Zimmerman |
| Dale Evans | Francis Octavia Smith |
| Jamie Farr | Jaemeel Farah |
| W. C. Fields | William Claude Dukenfield |
| Redd Foxx | John Elroy Sanford |
| Greta Garbo | Greta Luisa Gustafson |
| Judy Garland | Frances Gumm |
| Crystal Gayle | Brenda Gail Webb |
| Cary Grant | Archibald Leach |
| Rex Harrison | Reginald Cary |
| O. Henry | William Sidney Porter |
| Bob Hope | Leslie Townes Hope |
| Rock Hudson | Roy Scherer, Jr. |
| Elton John | Reginald Kenneth Dwight |
| Boris Karloff | William Pratt |
| Diane Keaton | Diane Hall |
| Bert Lahr | Irving Lahrheim |
| Ann Landers | Esther "Eppie" Pauline Friedman Lederer |
| Michael Landon | Michael Orowitz |
| Gypsy Rose Lee | Louise Hovick |
| Jerry Lewis | Joseph Levitch |
| Peter Lorre | Laszlo Loewenstein |
| Bela Lugosi | Arisztid Olt |
| Paul McCartney | James Paul McCartney |
| Shirley MacLaine | Shirley Beatty |
| Karl Malden | Mladen Sekulovich |
| Dean Martin | Dino Crocetti |
| Groucho Marx | Julius Henry Marx |
| Meatloaf | Marvin Lee Aday |
| Ethel Merman | Ethel Zimmerman |
| Zero Mostel | Samuel Joel Mostel |
| Kim Novak | Marilyn Paul Novak |
| Hugh O'Brien | Hugh J. Krampe |

| PROFESSIONAL NAME | ORIGINAL NAME |
|---|---|
| Tony Orlando | Michael Anthony Orlando Cassivitis |
| Peter O'Toole | Seamus O'Toole |
| Satchel Paige | Leroy Robert Paige |
| Gregory Peck | Eldred Gregory Peck |
| Bernadette Peters | Bernadette Lazarra |
| Ginger Rogers | Virginia McMath |
| Roy Rogers | Leonard Slye |
| Mickey Rooney | Joe Yule, Jr. |
| Yves St. Laurent | Henri Donat Mathieu |
| Soupy Sales | Milton Hines |
| Sissy Spacek | Mary Elizabeth Spacek |
| Mickey Spillane | Frank Morrison |
| Ringo Starr | Richard Starkey |
| Sly Stone | Sylvester Stone |
| Robert Taylor | Spangler Brugh |
| Danny Thomas | Amos Jacobs |
| Rip Torn | Elmore Torn, Jr. |
| Twiggy | Leslie Hornby |
| Abigail Van Buren | Pauline Esther "Popo" Friedman Phillips |
| Nancy Walker | Ann Myrtle Swoyer |
| Mike Wallace | Myron Wallace |
| Muddy Waters | McKinley Morganfield |
| John Wayne | Marion Michael Morrison |
| Tuesday Weld | Susan Kerr Weld |
| Gene Wilder | Jerome Silberman |
| Flip Wilson | Clerow Wilson |
| Shelley Winters | Shirley Schrift |
| Natalie Wood | Natasha Gurdin |
| Cy Young | Denton True Young |
| Loretta Young | Gretchen Young |

# MIX IT UP!

# PUT LETTERS IN THE MIXER

One way to create a name is to combine mother's and father's names. Do this by taking the given name or maiden name of the mother and the first or last name of the father. Pick letters from each name to form a pleasant-sounding name. For example, Rickard and Sandra form Sandrin. The last name, Kelsey, and maiden name, Martin, combine to form Kelmar. You may want to go back as far as grandparents and great-grandparents for name combinations.

A meaningful word can be used to form a name. The letters in the word *earth* can be switched to Retha. Chastity can be altered to form Sachtity.

If all else fails, use the letter-bowl trick. Choose letters of the alphabet from names of ancestors, from your children's names, from famous people or from the alphabet. Put them in a bowl and mix them up. Make sure you have enough vowels. Play a game with your family by picking out letters to form the ideal name.


# ABSOLUTELY THE END

Adding certain suffixes or endings to a name can produce an interesting new name. Try the following endings on masculine and feminine names: *alie, ann, an, and, ana, ald, ane, lee, een, ella, elle, ena, ene, et, ette, etta, ey, ice, ie, illa, ille, ina, inda, ine, inne, itsa, sin, sy, isa, itka, is, ita, ley, lyn, y, yn, win, wina.* On a name like Sabra, drop the *a*, add *illa* and you form the new name, Sabrilla.

You can also modify a boy's name to give the desired touch. The ending *ie* can be added to Ross to form Rossie or turn Ron into Ronnie.

If you want to name a child after father or mother, but don't want to use a junior or second, add a suffix to form a slightly different name. Lew becomes Lewis or Lewan. Jean becomes Jeanene or Jeanetta. Many names in this book can be altered by adding such endings. Possibilities are limitless.


# ADD DASH TO THE MIX

Hyphenation is another way to create a name. A hyphen joins two names together and adds style to an otherwise bland name. John-Lee and Lani-Ann are two examples.

A trend today is to give girls their mother's maiden name as part of their name. The two names are connected by a hyphen, such as Mary Newton-Alison. This can be done with a boy's name. Robert Paul Martin-Black is more memorable than Robert Paul Black.

# A MISSING LETTER

With a little modification, family names are a source of new names. Grandma's or grandpa's name, minus a letter or two, can produce a favorable name. Harlow can be changed to Arlow and still put a twinkle in grandpa's eye. You may want to rearrange grandma's name to form a more modern and unusual name. Samantha becomes Manthas by dropping one letter and rearranging the others. This way you can give joy to grandparents without duplicating the same name. Think how interesting family reunions will be!

# MOTHER NATURE

Name combinations can be found everywhere you look, especially in nature. By using the first letters of Sky, Island, Volcano, Earth and Nature, you create Siven, a name for a child of nature. Use the opposites, Fire and Ice, to make the intriguing name, Firice.

This same approach works by combining letters or syllables. Try combining words from the title of your favorite song, book or poem.

Use any of these ideas to create a new name. Employ your imagination. Experiment and have fun. The most important points to remember while experimenting are:

- Make sure the name sounds pleasing.
- Be certain it's pronounceable.
- Spell it correctly and predictably.
- Be sure you like the name!

# Most Frequently Given Names

The American Name Society is a group devoted to the study of names. Representatives from this group recently conducted a poll to determine the most popular boys' and girls' names. The results of the survey are used here with the permission of Kelsey B. Harder, the Society's president.

According to the American Name Society, these are America's favorite names, in order of popularity:

| Top American Boys' Names | Top American Girls' Names |
|---|---|
| 1. Michael | 1. Jennifer |
| 2. Jason | 2. Mary |
| 3. Matthew | 3. Karen |
| 4. David | 4. Michelle |
| 5. Brian | 5. Jessica |
| 6. Christopher | 6. Katherine |
| 7. John | 7. Rebecca |
| 8. James | 8. Deborah |
| 9. Jeffrey | 9. Robin |
| 10. Daniel | 10. Megan |

# Astrology—Just Plain Fun

Astrology originated in 2000 B.C. in Babylonia. It began with the study of heavenly bodies to predict the future. Between 600 and 200 B.C., astrologers developed individual horoscopes.

Interest in astrology declined with the rise of Christianity. In the 1930s, a newspaper in England began publishing a horoscope column and interest in astrology picked up again.

Astrology is based on the belief that heavenly bodies form patterns that reveal a person's personality or future. Most scientists believe that astrology is not a science. Others regard it as fun and harmless. Whether you believe it or not, you can still have fun applying it to naming your baby.

## CAPRICORN (Dec. 22—Jan. 20)
Birthstones—Ruby, chalcedony
Flowers—Flaxweed, moss, rush, ivy, amaranth
Colors—Dark browns, green, black
Personality—The most conscientious children of the Zodiac
Zodiac Symbol—The goat

## ARIES (March 21—April 20)
Birthstones—Bloodstone, crystal
Flowers—Buttercup, daisy, starthistle
Color—Brilliant red
Personality—The most brilliant children of the Zodiac
Zodiac Symbol—The ram

## AQUARIUS (Jan. 21—Feb. 19)
Birthstones—Garnet, amethyst
Flowers—Daffodil, pansy
Colors—Mingled shades
Personality—The most loyal children of the Zodiac
Zodiac Symbol—Water-bearer or the sage

## TAURUS (April 21—May 21)
Birthstones—Sapphire, ruby, diamond
Flowers—Cowslip, daisy, goldenrod, violet
Colors—Red-orange, yellow, cream
Personality—The most popular children of the Zodiac
Zodiac Symbol—The bull

## PISCES (Feb. 20—March 20)
Birthstone—Amethyst
Flowers—Tuberose, water lily, lotus
Colors—Green-blue, shades of lavender, amethyst
Personality—The most imaginative children of the Zodiac
Zodiac Symbol—The fish

## GEMINI (May 22—June 21)
Birthstones—Agate, sapphire, quartz
Flowers—Marigold, fern, lily-of-the-valley
Colors—Silver-gray, blue
Personality—The most alert children of the Zodiac
Zodiac Symbol—The twins

## CANCER (June 22—July 21)
Birthstones—Emerald, cat's-eye
Flowers—Lily, white poppy, iris
Colors—Pearl, delicate greens
Personality—The most sensitive
  children of the Zodiac
Zodiac Symbol—The crab

## LIBRA (Sept. 24—Oct. 23)
Birthstones—Peridot, aquamarine
Flowers—Goldenrod, violet, cowslip
Colors—Blue, pale yellow, pastels
Personality—The most intuitive
  children of the Zodiac
Zodiac Symbol—The balance

## LEO (July 22—Aug. 23)
Birthstones—Amber, topaz, onyx
Flowers—Poppy, sunflower, red rose
Colors—Amber, deep orange
Personality—The happiest children of
  the Zodiac
Zodiac Symbol—The lion

## SCORPIO (Oct. 24—Nov. 22)
Birthstone—Topaz
Flowers—Thistle, hawthorne
Color—Deep red
Personality—The most thorough
  children of the Zodiac
Zodiac Symbol—The scorpion

## VIRGO (Aug. 24—Sept. 23)
Birthstones—Carnelian, jade
Flowers—Fern, azalea, morning glory
Colors—Yellow, gray-blue
Personality—The most ambitious
  children of the Zodiac
Zodiac Symbol—The virgin

## SAGITTARIUS (Nov. 23—Dec.
Birthstones—Emerald, topaz
Flowers—Holly, jessamine, carnation
Colors—Deep violet-blue
Personality—The most independent
  children of the Zodiac
Zodiac Symbol—The archer

# BIRTH ANNOUNCEMENTS & HANDOUTS

# Birth Announcements

First impressions count! Your baby made quite an impact on you. Use the announcement ideas in this chapter to make an impression on friends and relatives.

There are four categories of birth announcements: surnames, hobbies or interests, professions, and general ideas. Even though announcements illustrate a particular name, many can work for anyone by slightly changing the message. Announcements related to professions or interests may not coincide with your situation, but they may spark ideas or variations that work for you.

Materials for announcements are usually inexpensive and often found around the house. Most announcements can be made from poster board, wood, cloth, writing paper or construction paper. Use felt pens, colored pencils, acrylic paints or watercolors to add color to announcements. To help preserve your message, cover it with clear contact paper before cutting it. Grocery or craft stores carry contact paper and other items for making announcements.

Use the illustrations in this chapter as a guide for creating your announcement. If you want it to be the same size as shown, trace the illustration on transparent tracing paper. Use the edge of a pencil to rub graphite on the opposite side of the design and retrace the design on paper. Or use carbon paper to trace the design onto paper or cloth. If you want your announcement larger or smaller, measure key points on the illustration and enlarge or reduce them to scale on your announcement.

To involve the whole family in announcing a new baby, let older children help color, letter and draw the announcements. They'll enjoy helping announce their new baby brother or sister.

Use the illustrations and ideas in this chapter any way you want. Be creative and enjoy announcing your baby in style!

# Surnames

## LET'S GO FISHING

The surname Bass was the inspiration for this announcement, but the idea can be used for Trout, Pike, Fisher, Fishman, Finley and other names. Draw and cut out the announcement. Put in a fish representing each member of the family. The smallest diapered fish is the new arrival. Bubbles carry the data of the birth. Color fish gold, green or other bright colors. You can cut the fish, bubbles, fish house and vegetation from colored construction paper and glue them in the scene. This announcement goes over swimmingly with friends!

# A TOUCH OF ROYALTY

Here's an idea for surnames that contain the words King, Queen, Duke, Royal or Prince. The idea also works for any family with blueblood. Fold a sheet of paper in half. Cut three sides of the announcement as shown in the illustration above. Use blue, purple and gold to color the crown. Spread white glue on the gemstone and sprinkle with gold or silver glitter to add sparkle to the announcement. Write text in stylish script on the inside. The copy above shows you how to word the message. Now there's an announcement fit for a King—or his son or daughter!

**browns**
are announcing:

NAME _Brook Marie_
DATE _August 4, 1979_
WEIGHT _6 lbs. 9 ozs._
LENGTH _20"_
TIME _5:53 pm._

now we're going to color the town red!

# COLOR THE TOWN RED

A large, oversize crayon makes a clever announcement for surnames that contain a color—Brown, Black, Redman, Whitely and so forth. It also works well for any colorful family. Use colors appropriate to the name or choose any bright, bold color. You might add: "Now we're going to color the town red!" Maybe your friends will get the hint and join the party!

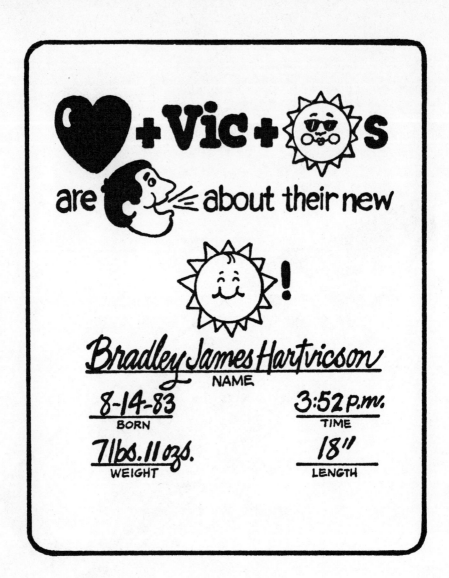

are ❤ about their new

Bradley James Hartvicson
NAME

8-14-83
BORN

3:52 p.m.
TIME

7 lbs. 11 ozs.
WEIGHT

18"
LENGTH

## HIDDEN MEANINGS

Analyze your surname and come up with a unique word puzzle for recipients to solve. For example, the name *Hartvicson* has several shorter words or sounds in it. *Hart* becomes the heart symbol and *son* becomes a friendly sun. Many longer surnames can be taken apart in the same way. Use an open mouth to tell or shout about your baby. The baby-face sun represents a new baby boy. Fill the lower half of the announcement with important information on the birth. Your friends will get the meaning soon enough!

# Hobbies Or Interests

There's a little racket at our house!

JAMIE JOHN JENKENS
SEPT. 15, 1982   10 lbs. 2 oz.
3:57 PM   18½"

We're busy playing with our new racket.
You are invited to come play with him too!

## WHAT A RACKET!

Avid tennis players can have fun with this announcement. Draw or cut out the message in the shape of a tennis racket. Use words that sound alike such as *racket* and *racquet,* or other tennis terms, to convey the idea of the new arrival. The same concept works using a baseball glove, golf putter or bowling ball for other sports. Score this announcement 40 LOVE!

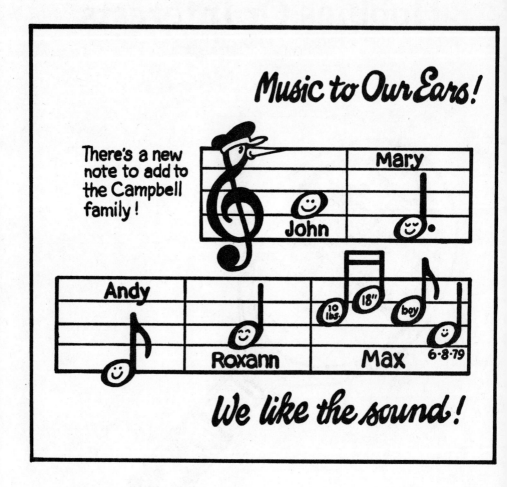

## NAME THAT TUNE

Here's an announcement for musicians or music-lovers. Make a sheet-music staff to carry the good tidings. The treble clef becomes the stork. Each note represents a member of the family. The last measure contains facts about the baby. Recipients will appreciate the sound of this announcement!

Steven Lee Stanford arrived just in time, on OCTOBER 6th, to weigh in at 10lbs. 4ozs. and 20" long.

HE WAS WEARING A BLUE DIAPER WITH A WHITE BLANKET ROBE. THE FIGHT WAS ROUGH BUT WE ALL WON!

## THE CHAMP

Fight-fans can help this new arrival box his way out! Pattern this announcement after a boxing glove. Use brown construction or craft paper for the glove. Punch holes with a hand punch for eyelets. Use short shoelaces to tie the glove. This announcement is a real knockout!

Meet
our future
quarterback

STANLEY JOHN BAKER

BORN 12·17·83    TIME 5:45 P.M.
WEIGHT 8 LBS. 2 OZS.
LENGTH 19"

PHOTO

## TACKLE THIS!

Here's the perfect announcement for football players, coaches or Sunday-afternoon quarterbacks. Cut out a helmet shape from colored construction paper or poster board. Use the colors or insignia of your favorite team to personalize the helmet. Make four diagonal slits as shown to hold a picture of the baby. Don't forget the vital statistics on your little bruiser.

**SEAN LYNN BARRET** dropped in on the Barret home on the night of Nov. 10th at 2 a.m. She weighed 6½ lbs. and was 17" long!

RIBBON →

# DROP IN

Skydivers or daredevils will enjoy sending this announcement. It's a welcome change from printed announcements. Cut out a round piece of cloth from remnants. Or sew together alternating panels of pink and blue cloth. Punch four to six holes around the edge of the cloth. Thread pink and blue ribbons through the holes and attach ribbons to a small plastic baby that can be found at most toy or craft stores. Write a cheery message on the cloth with permanent laundry markers. Mail the parachute in a large Manila envelope or small box. What a nice surprise to drop in the mail to friends or relatives!

# Professions

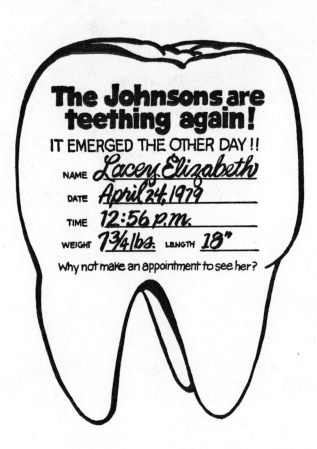

The Johnsons are
teething again!

IT EMERGED THE OTHER DAY!!

NAME *Lacey Elizabeth*

DATE *April 24, 1979*

TIME *12:56 p.m.*

WEIGHT *7¾ lbs.* LENGTH *18"*

Why not make an appointment to see her?

## TEETHING AGAIN

Dentists or dental hygienists appreciate this toothy way to present a new member of the family. Cut out the tooth shape from bright, white paper. Outline it in black, blue or bright pink. The sample copy gives you ideas on ways to word the message. This announcement makes a clever tie-in to your profession and may bring you several visitors—private and professional!

# WE LOVE HIM!

What a blooming-good idea! Present your new arrival as a pretty flower-child. Frame a picture of your baby with colorful yellow petals. Attach a straw to the flower and bright green leaves to the straw. Makes a great announcement for gardeners, florists or flower-lovers.

# IT ADDS UP!

One plus one doesn't equal two—but three—when you use a calculator to announce your baby. Bankers, loan officers, credit managers and other financial people can give an announcement that adds up to fun. In place of the numbers that normally appear on the calculator, put the date of birth, time born, weight and length. The baby's name reads on the digital display. It's all calculated to get your good tidings out to the world.

# PRINT OUT

Just the ticket for creative programmers or those who have access to a computer. Program the computer to print out a baby symbol such as a stork, bottle, rattle or diaper pin using X's. Let the X's also show vital statistics about the birth. If you're not adept at programming, use a computer or word processor to print the announcement in regular typeface. Box the information in lines or X's. This announcement will compute with technical friends.

# General Ideas

The Calls are ringing to tell you about the call they made to the doctor...

TIME 4:02 PM
DATE 3-2-79
WEIGHT 6½ lbs
Elizabeth Jane Call
18"
LENGTH

## ONE RING-A-DINGY

This toy telephone announcement works well for any family with a happy message to tell! Put vital statistics in the phone's finger holes. Color the announcement with felt markers or acrylic paints in bright, cheerful colors. Try blue eyes, red lips, pink cheeks, green wheels and a red receiver. This is one call your friends and relatives won't want to miss!

The Andersons Present

PHOTO

Mary Lee

APRIL
5
1983

12:07
a.m.

8lb.

21"

# HIGHEST RATINGS

Tune in for the debut of your newest TV star. Cut along the dotted lines at top and bottom of the TV screen to form tabs. Insert a cute photo of baby using the tabs as photo holders. Knobs give information on the date, time, weight and length. Make sure your friends don't miss the best show of the season!

## IN A WHIRL!

Here's a fast-moving way to announce your new baby. Tornado shape draws immediate attention when delivered in person to your friends or pulled from an envelope. Cut around the edge of the tornado to emphasize its shape. This is one announcement your friends will remember—as well as all the commotion it caused!

## BROTHERLY LOVE

Here's an announcement from a brother's point of view. Too bad the addition was a baby sister and not a new bedroom or playroom! If your family is larger than the one in the illustration, draw a larger house with more rooms. Use felt markers or color pencils to color the boy and the house. This is one way to remember everyone in the family when you announce your new arrival.

44

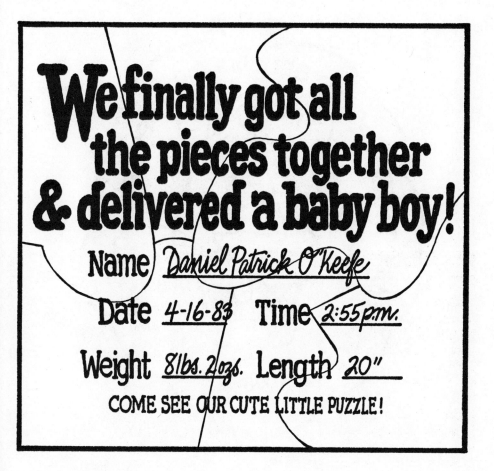

We finally got all
the pieces together
& delivered a baby boy!

Name *Daniel Patrick O'Keefe*

Date *4-16-83* Time *2:55 p.m.*

Weight *8 lbs. 2 ozs.* Length *20"*

COME SEE OUR CUTE LITTLE PUZZLE!

## PUZZLING

What a delightful way to inform friends and relatives about your bundle of joy. Print vital information about the birth on heavy paper or card stock. Cut up the message into pieces similar to a jigsaw puzzle. Place the pieces in an envelope and let the recipient reconstruct it. You can bet friends or relatives won't be puzzled for long!

The Shores are announcing a new baby boy!

MATTHEW JON 3/5/81 2:51am. 7¼ lbs. 21"

NO LION!

## NO LION!

This announcement catches your eye. Cut the lion's head out of gold-colored construction paper. Draw or print details in black ink or marking pen. The mane carries all the information about the new baby. It's the perfect announcement for families who feel like roaring about their new arrival!

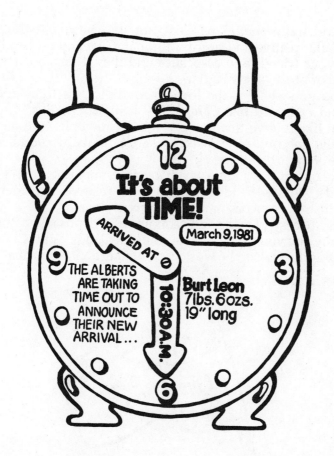

It's about TIME!

March 9, 1981

ARRIVED AT

THE ALBERTS ARE TAKING TIME OUT TO ANNOUNCE THEIR NEW ARRIVAL...

10:30 A.M.

Burt Leon 7 lbs. 6 ozs. 19" long

## TIME HAS COME

This announcement is for the woman who thought her pregnancy would never end! Hands of the clock point to the time of birth. Calendar window gives the date. Other information is carried on the face of the clock. Announce your little one with this timely message.

# Handouts

Cigars are traditionally handed out by new fathers. Why be traditional? Be creative and non-traditional. Give any of the gifts in this chapter to your friends and associates and they'll remember you as the proud—and original—New Father.

You'll find gifts such as the low-cal toothpick, pet rock and leftover pickle. Proud dads will like *Chip Off the Old Block* or *Blowing Your Own Horn*. If you like to give treats to eat, there's an apple, fortune cookie or Sugar Daddy. To counteract sweets, there's the baby toothbrush to be used regularly three times a day!

If you like one of these ideas as a baby announcement, don't limit it to Dad's friends. Modify the idea and send it to relatives and friends. These ideas and illustrations work in many different ways.

Most gifts are easy to make and economical. Friends and associates will remember the day you gave them an unusual Daddy's gift. Choose one of these creative gifts and let the world know you're a Proud Papa!

## LO-CAL TREAT

Many new fathers hand out sugary treats or fattening candies. Here's a low-calorie surprise. Buy a box of toothpicks and attach a message to each one. The message reads: "I didn't want to give you something fattening, so I didn't give you anything at all!" The opposite side of the paper reads: "Our No. 1 Pick" and gives vital information on the birth.

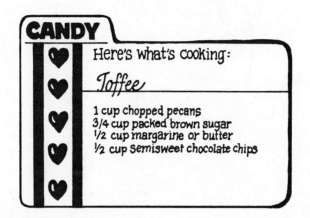

**CANDY**

Here's what's cooking:

*Toffee*

1 cup chopped pecans
3/4 cup packed brown sugar
1/2 cup margarine or butter
1/2 cup semisweet chocolate chips

# RECIPE COLLECTORS

Here's something interesting to give friends—a favorite family recipe. Business executives may want to give a Recipe for Success. Buy some small recipe cards and decorate them with stickers or illustrations. Print the recipe on one side and information about the new arrival on the other. A candy recipe is appropriate to announce your little sweetie.

CASEY JO
12·9·82
6 lbs. 9oz. 18" long

BOTTOM OF ROCK

# PET ROCK-A-BYE

A pet rock makes an inexpensive daddy handout. Collect smooth rocks from a streambed or get them at a gravel pit. Buy acrylic paint and plastic eyes at a craft store. Paint the rock a bright color. Glue on the eyes with all-purpose glue. Paint statistics on the bottom of the rock.

## FLOATING ON AIR

You'll be on Cloud 9 when you deliver this announcement to buddies. Buy a package of balloons at a toy or novelty store. Blow up each balloon and tie a string to temporarily keep it inflated. Use a black marker to write your message on the outside of the balloon. Draw a stork or baby cartoon if you are artistic. Untie the string and deflate the balloon. Your friends get the message when they blow up the balloon!

## HAVE A FORTUNE, COOKIE

What a fortunate idea! Make your own fortune cookies or purchase a bag of cookies from a Chinese specialty shop. If you buy cookies, carefully remove the fortune—tweezers work well. Type or print your message on small strips of paper. Roll the paper up and stuff it into the cookie using a fingernail file or thin knife. Give cookies to fortunate friends.

# I'M A SUGAR DADDY

A *Sugar Daddy* sucker is a sweet way to boast of your new arrival Attach a tag with statistics to the handle of the sucker. Gummed or peel-off labels work well for the tag.

# APPLE OF MY EYE

Fresh fruit catches the attention of friends. An apple is always a welcome treat. Tape a note, label or clever drawing to the apple to brag about your newborn. Your friends will get the message and munch with pleasure!

## NOTHING TO SNEEZE AT

This daddy handout helps with the sniffles. Using permanent markers, draw a stork or other baby symbol on a handerchief. The message might say: "Nothing to sneeze at!" Print pertinent information about the birth. It's a useful and stylish gift to hand out.

## NUTS ABOUT MY BABY

Carefully pry apart a walnut shell and take out the nut. Place the message of the birth inside. Tie the shell halves together with a pink or blue ribbon as appropriate. Your friends and associates will think it's a real nutty gift!

## CHIP OFF THE OLD BLOCK

Here's one for a proud Daddy. Buy plain toy wood blocks or cut blocks from a 2x2 or 2x4 board. Using the wand from a woodburning set, burn your message into the block. Print on as many sides as necessary. Friends will enjoy turning the block over to read your good tidings.

## FOR THE STRAW BOSS

Purchase a package of brightly colored straws. Print your new-baby message on a piece of paper. Roll up the paper and place it in the straw. Your associates will agree it's the last straw!

## PIPE UP

Here's a way to pipe up to your friends. Buy an inexpensive corn-cob pipe. Print your message on a strip of paper. Roll up the paper and place it in the bowl of the pipe. Smokers and non-smokers will get a kick out of this alternative to the cigar.

## BABY KEY FOB

A personalized key ring makes a memorable announcement. Buy key rings and contact paper. Make fobs out of the contact paper. A triangular shape is interesting. Cut the contact paper so it makes a triangular frame. Peel the backing off the contact paper and press a picture of your new baby to the contact-paper frame. Add pertinent data to the back of the picture. Attach fob to the key ring with tape or ribbon.

# NO MORE PICKLES

Wrap in plastic wrap all the pickles your wife no longer wants. Tie each one with a blue or pink ribbon as appropriate. Write a clever message on a strip of paper or large gift tag and attach to the pickle. Watch the reaction of your associates!

# LITTLE TINKER

Purchase a set of Tinkertoys from a toy or department store. Put two wheels and a stick together as shown in the illustration. Write your message on a long, thin piece of paper. Tape one end of the paper to the stick and roll up the message like a scroll.

## FLASH

Flash the news of your baby's arrival. Buy 4-way flash cubes from a camera or department store. Write the message on a strip of paper or label and tape it to the flash cube. Your baby will make news!

## IT'S ABOUT THYME!

Everyone will know the time has come when you hand out these clever herb sachets. Use an attractive square cloth and place thyme spice in the center of the cloth. Fold the cloth into a bag and tie with a colorful ribbon. Tag the sachet with information about your new arrival.

## BRUSH REGULARLY

A small blue or pink toothbrush will announce a new mouth in the family! Write your message on a strip of paper or a self-adhesive label. Attach the message to the toothbrush. Tell your friends or associates to brush three times a day and remember your baby!

## BLOW YOUR HORN

Go ahead, blow your own horn a little. Purchase party noisemakers as shown in the illustration. Unroll the noisemaker and print your message on the paper. Or write the message on a separate piece of paper and tape it to the unrolled noisemaker. Let the noisemaker roll back up. When the recipient blows the horn he'll discover you're a new Daddy. May even start a party!

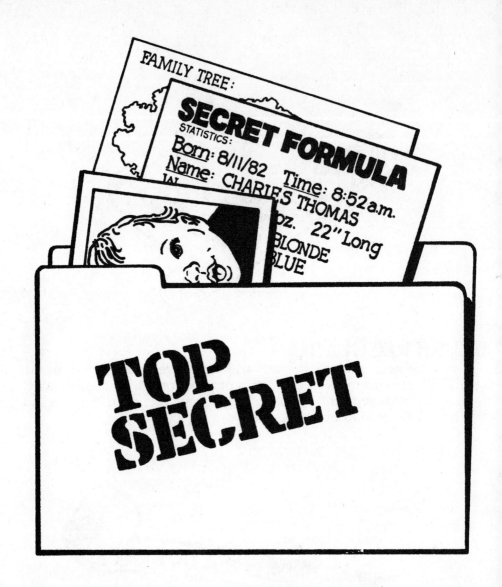

## TOP SECRET

This file is for privileged eyes only. Use a letter-size Manila folder to hold regular-size sheets of paper. Print TOP SECRET on the front of the folder. Print SECRET FORMULA on top of a piece of paper. List the vital statistics of the baby, such as eye color, hair color, weight, length, date of birth, time born, unusual markings, parents, names of brothers and sisters, baby's name and other information. Use other sheets of paper to list relatives, draw a family tree or provide other classified data. This secret will be hard to keep!

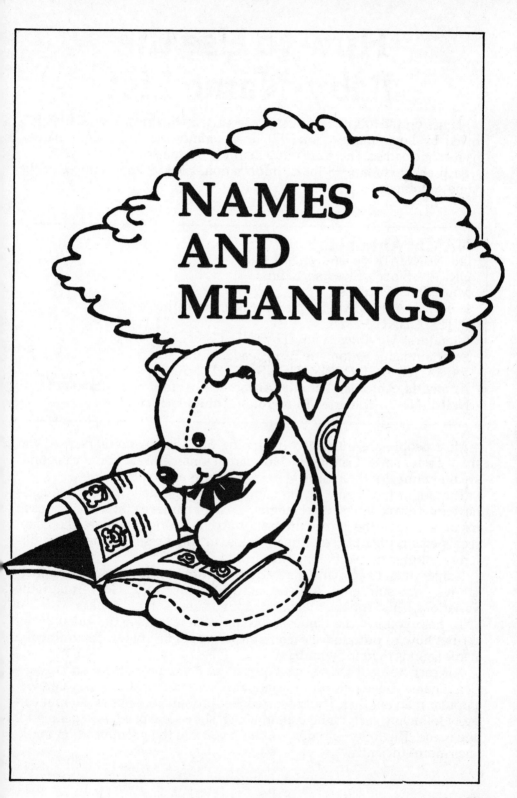

NAMES
AND
MEANINGS

# How to Use the Baby-Name List

Names on the following pages are arranged with girls' names first, followed by boys' names. You will find common names, unique names, even exotic names. There are more than 13,000 names to choose from!

Each entry contains a lot of information. Look at the example of the name Antoinetta.

---

**NAME: Antoinetta**
PRONUNCIATION: (an-twa-NET-tuh)
ORIGIN: Slovak, Swedish, Latin
MEANING: *Priceless*
FORM, IF APPLICABLE: Feminine form of Anthony.
INTERESTING FACTS:
Literature: *My Antonia,* novel by Willa Cather.
Entertainment: Antoinette Perry, leader of the American Theater Wing.
VARIATIONS OR DERIVATIONS OF THE NAME:
**Antonetta, Antonia, Antonie, Antoinette, Antonina, Netta, Netti, Nettie, Netty, Toinette, Toni, Tonia, Tonie, Tony, Tonye**

---

Most people are interested in finding out about famous people who share their name. Listings include famous namesakes. Some categories are Literature, Mythological, Historical, Sports and Biblical.

The origin of a name is sometimes difficult to determine. Languages have intermixed and several languages claim names as their own. In each instance, I give the most commonly accepted origin. Where the claim seems equal, I list two or three origins. In some cases, names from different cultures have different meanings.

Names often have many derivations or variations. Although Antoinetta may not suit you, Toinette may fit your child. Go through the variations. This is one of the most helpful features of this book.

To help you say the names, a pronunciation guide is included. It describes how to pronounce each name, so you'll be able to determine if a name sounds right for your baby.

For each name listed in this book, at least one pronunciation is given. Some names have two pronunciations. One pronunciation may be more popular than another. The most frequent pronunciation is given immediately following each name listing, which shows the principal spelling for the name. The following tips will help you use the pronunciation markings more efficiently.

- Words are separated into syllables by dashes. Example: MAR-tin.
- The syllable that receives the most stress appears in capital letters. Example: HEL-un.
- The symbols for vowel sounds may be new to you. Long vowels, those that are pronounced like the names of the letters, are marked with a line over the vowel. Example: The *a* in Jane is marked JĀN. Short vowels have no additional markings. Example: The *a* in Janet is indicated by JAN-it. There are separate pronunciations for long and short vowel sounds. Some vowels are influenced by other sounds around them and are not long or short. They are listed under *Other Vowel Sounds* in the table below.

# VOWEL SOUNDS

## Long Vowels

| Letter | Written Phonetically | As Sounds In The Word | Is Spelled Phonetically |
|--------|----------------------|-----------------------|-------------------------|
| A | ā | ate | āt |
| E | ē | eat | ēt |
| I | ī | hike | hīk |
| O | ō | oak | ōk |
| U | ū | use | ūz |
| OO | ōō | ooze | ōōz |

## Short Vowels

| Letter | Written Phonetically | As Sounds In The Word | Is Spelled Phonetically |
|--------|----------------------|-----------------------|-------------------------|
| A | a | at | at |
| E | e | edge | ej |
| I | i | it | it |
| O | o | ox | oks |
| U | u | up | up |
| OO | oo | book | book |

## Other Vowel Sounds

| Letters | Written Phonetically | As Sounds In The Word | Is Spelled Phonetically |
|---------|----------------------|-----------------------|-------------------------|
| AIR | air | fair | fair |
| AR | ar | car | kar |
| AW | aw | all | awl |
| ER | er | her | her |
| OI | oi | boy | boi |
| OR | or | more | mor |
| OW | ow | cow | kow |
| UH | uh | about | uh-bowt |

# BABY-NAME WORKSHEET

|  | First | Middle | Last |
|--|-------|--------|------|

1. _____
2. _____
3. _____
4. _____
5. _____
6. _____
7. _____
8. _____
9. _____
10. _____

## RANK NAMES IN ORDER OF PREFERENCE:

First:_____

Second:_____

Third:_____

See pages 283-288 for more Baby-Name Worksheets.

# GIRLS' NAMES

**Abby** (A-bē)
Familiar form of Abigail.
Famous: Abigail Van Buren, *Dear Abby* newspaper columnist.
**Abbe, Abbey, Abbie**

**Abebi** (uh-BĒ-bē)
Nigerian— *We asked for her and she came*
**Abeni**

**Abigail** (A-bi-gāl)
Hebrew— *Father of joy*
Famous: Abigail Adams, wife of President John Adams.
Biblical: One of King David's wives.
**Abagael, Abagail, Abbi, Abbye, Abigael, Gael, Gail, Gale, Gayel**

**Abra** (AB-ruh)
Hebrew— *Mother of the multitude*
Feminine form of Abraham.
**Abira**

**Acacia** (uh-KĀ-shuh)
Greek— *Thorny*
**Cacia, Cacie, Casey, Casia, Kacia, Kacie**

**Acantha** (uh-KAN-thuh)
Greek— *Sharp-pointed, thorned*
**Acandi, Acandy, Candie, Candy, Cantha, Kacia, Kacie**

**Ada** (Ā-duh) or (A-duh)
Teutonic— *Happy*
Latin— *Of noble birth*
Hebrew— *An ornament*
**Adah, Adan, Adey, Adda, Addi Addie, Addy, Adi, Aida, Eada, Eda, Edey**

**Adabelle** (Ā-duh-bel) or (A-duh-bel)
English— *Joyous and fair*
**Adabel, Adabell, Adabellie, Adahbelle, Bell, Belle**

**Adah** (A-duh)
Hebrew— *Ornament*
Famous: Adah Menken, 19th century American actress.
**Ada, Addia, Addie, Addy**

**Adalia** (uh-DĀL-yuh)
German, Spanish— *Noble one*
**Adal, Adala, Adali, Adalie, Adela, Adele, Adelia, Adelle**

**Adamina** (a-duh-MĒN-uh)
Hebrew— *Daughter of the earth*
**Adameana, Ademine**

**Adamma** (uh-DA-muh)
Nigerian— *Child of beauty*

**Adara** (uh-DAIR-uh)
Greek— *Beauty*
Arabic— *Virgin*

**ADALIA**—*Noble one*

**Adelaide** (A-duh-lād)
German—*Noble and of kind spirit*
Literature: Adelaide Anne Proctor, author.
**Adalia, Adaline, Adela, Adele, Adelia, Adelina, Adelind, Adeline, Adella, Dela, Della**

**Adele** (uh-DEL)
German, French—*Noble*
**Adelaide, Adelia, Adeline, Adelle, Akela, Aline, Del, Della, Delly, Hagayah, Heide**

**Adena** (uh-DĒN-uh)
Hebrew—*Sensuous or voluptuous*
**Adina, Dena, Dina**

**Aditi** (uh-DĒ-tē)
Hindi—*Free and unbounded*
Interesting: In Hindi lore, Aditi is mother of the Gods.

**Adora** (uh-DOR-uh)
French—*Beloved*
**Ador, Adore, Adoree, Dora, Dori, Dorie, Dory**

64

**Adrienne** (Ā-drē-en)
French — *Dark one*
Feminine of Adrian.
**Adrea, Adria, Adrian, Adriana, Adriane, Hadria**

**Afina** (uh-FĒ-nuh)
Rumanian — *Blueberry*
**Afin, Efina**

**Afra** (A-fruh)
Hebrew — *Female deer*

**Agatha** (A-guh-thuh)
Greek — *Good*
Literature: Agatha Christie, writer of detective fiction.
**Ag, Agace, Agata, Agathe, Aggi, Aggie, Aggy, Agueda**

**Agnes** (AG-nes)
Greek — *Pure*
Interesting: St. Agnes, martyred at age 13, is commemorated on January 21.
Entertainment: Agnes Moorehead, actress.
**Ag, Aggee, Aggi, Agna, Agnella, Agnese, Agnesse, Agneta, Agnola, Aigneis, Annis, Ina, Ines, Inessa, Inez, Nessa, Nessi, Nessie, Nessy, Nesta, Nevsa, Neysa, Una, Ynes, Ynez**

**Aida** (Ā-duh) or (ī-Ē-duh)
Italian — *Happy*
Entertainment: The opera *Aida*, by Verdi.
**Ada, Aila, Aili, Iraida, Zaida, Zenaida, Zoraida**

**Aileen** (ā-LĒN)
Irish — *Light*
Entertainment: Eileen Farrell, Metropolitan Opera star.
**Ailene, Alaine, Alane, Alanna, Alayne, Allan, Allen, Allene, Allina, Allyn, Eileen, Helen, Ileane, Ilene, Lana, Lanna**

**Airlia** (AIR-lē-uh)
Greek — *Ethereal*

**Ailsa** (ĀL-suh)
Teutonic — *Girl of cheer*

**Alanna** (a-LAN-uh)
Gaelic — *Comely, fair*
Feminine form of Alan.
**Alaine, Alane, Alayne, Allyn**

**Alarice** (al-uh-RĒS)
Teutonic — *Ruler of all*

**Alberta** (al-BERT-uh)
Old English — *Noble or brilliant*
Feminine form of Albert.
**Albetine, Albertine, Ali, Alli, Allie, Ally, Alverta, Auberta, Auline, Bert, Berta, Berte, Berti, Bertie, Berty, Elberta, Elbertina, Elbertine**

**Alda** (AL-duh)
German — *Battle, war*
**Aldith, Alta, Auda, Edith**

**Aldea** (al-DĒ-uh)
Teutonic — *Rich*

**Aldora** (al-DOR-uh)
Greek — *Winged gift*

**Alethea** (a-LĒ-thē-uh)
Greek — *Truth*
**Aletha, Alethia, Alithea, Alithia, Alsta, Althea**

**Aletta** (a-LET-uh)
Spanish — *Winged bird-like*
**Aleta, Alleta, Alletta, Leeta**

## Alexandra (al-eks-AN-druh)

Russian, Greek—*Helper or defender of mankind*
Feminine form of Alexander.
Interesting: Alexandria, important city in Egypt.
Famous: Alexandra, Danish princess and queen of England.
**Alejandra, Alejandrian, Alessandra, Alex, Alexa, Alexandrina, Alexia, Alexina, Alexine, Alexis, Ali, Alix, Alla, Alli, Allie, Allix, Ally, Alya, Cesya, Elena, Lesya, Lexi, Lexie, Lexine, Lexy, Olesya, Sacha, Sande, Sandi, Sandie, Sandra, Sandy, Sandye, Sascha, Sasha, Sashenka, Shura, Shurochka, Sondra, Zandra**

## Alfreda (al-FRĒ-duh)

Teutonic—*Wise or diplomatic counselor*
Feminine form of Alfred.
**Alfi, Alfy, Allie, Elfreda, Elfrida, Elfrieda, Elva, Freda, Freddie, Freddy, Frieda**

## Alice (AL-is)

Greek—*Truth*
Old English—*Noble*
Literature: *Alice in Wonderland*, by Lewis Carroll; 1922 Pulitzer Prize given to Booth Tarkington for *Alice Adams*.
Entertainment: Alicia Alonso and Alicia Markova, ballet dancers; Ali MacGraw, actress.
**Adelaide, Adelice, Ailis, Aleece, Ali, Alicea, Alicia, Alika, Alikee, Alis, Alisa, Alisha, Alison, Alissa, Alix, Alla, Alleece, Alli, Allie, Allison, Allson, Allsun, Allyce, Allys, Alys, Alysia, Alyss, Alyssa, Elissa, Ilysa, Ilyssa, Lissa, Lyssa**

## Alida (uh-LĒ-duh)

Greek—*From the city of fine vestments*
**Aleda, Alyda, Leda, Lida**

## Alina (a-LĒ-nuh)

Polish, Russian—*Bright, beautiful*
**Adeline, Aleen, Alene, Allene, Alta, Alya, Lina**

## Alita (a-LĒ-tuh)

Spanish—*Noble*
**Adela, Adelina, Adelita, Dela, Lela**

## Aliza (uh-LĒ-zuh) or (uh-LĪ-zuh)

Hebrew—*Joyous*

## Alleen (al-LĒN)

Dutch—*Alone*

## Allegra (uh-LĀ-gruh)

Italian—*Lively, joyful, merry*
Entertainment: Allegra Kent, of the New York City Center Ballet.

## Alma (AL-muh)

Latin—*Soul*
Arabic—*Learned*
Interesting: *Alma Mater* means nourishing mother.
Entertainment: Alma Gluck, opera star.

## Almira (al-MĪ-ruh)

Hindi—*Clothes basket*
Arabic—*Exalted*
Feminine form of Elmer.
**Almeria, Almire, Elmira, Mira, Myra**

## Alodie (a-LŌ-dē)

Anglo-Saxon—*Wealthy, prosperous*
**Alodi, Alody**

## Aloysia (a-LOI-shuh)

Teutonic—*Famous in war*

## Alta (AL-tuh)

Latin—*High*
German—*Old*

## Althea (al-THĒ-uh)

Greek—*Wholesome or healing*
**Altheda, Althee, Altheta, Thea**

## Alva (AL-vuh)

Spanish, Latin—*White or fair*
Famous: Thomas Alva Edison, inventor of the light bulb.

AMABEL—*Loveable*

**Alvina** (al-VĒN-uh)
Old English—*Noble friend*

**Alvita** (al-VĒT-uh)
Latin—*Animated*
Feminine form of Alvin.
**Alivinia, Alverta, Alvinia,
Vina, Vinne, Vinnie, Vinny**

**Alyssa** (a-LIS-uh)
Greek—*Sane, logical*
**Alissa, Ilyssa**

**Amabel** (AM-uh-bel)
Latin—*Loveable*
**Amabelle, Belle**

**Amalia** (uh-MĀL-ē-uh)
Polish, Hungarian—*Industrious*
**Amelia, Emil, Emili, Emily**

**Amanda** (uh-MAN-duh)
Latin—*Beloved*
Entertainment: Amanda Blake
  played Kitty on TV series,
  *Gunsmoke.*
**Amandi, Amandie, Amandy,
Manda, Mandi, Mandie,
Mandy**

**Amara** (uh-MAR-uh)
Greek— *Of eternal beauty*
**Amaratha, Amarga, Amargo, Mara**

**Amber** (AM-ber)
French— *Amber*
Arabic— *Jewel*
Literature: *Forever Amber,* by Kathleen Winsor.

**Amdis** (AM-dis)
Latin— *Love of God or immortal*

**Amelia** (uh-MĒ-lē-yuh)
Teutonic— *Hard-working*
Famous: Amelia Bloomer, supporter of the American women suffrage movement; Amelia Earhart, pilot.
**Amalea, Amalia, Amelie, Amelina, Ameline, Amelita, Amy, Emmas**

**Amity** (AM-i-tē)
French, Latin— *Friendship*
**Amitie, Mitti, Mittie, Mitty**

**Amy** (Ā-mē)
French, Latin— *Beloved*
Literature: Amy Laurence Lowell, Pulitzer Prize-winner in poetry.
**Aimee, Amata, Ame, Ami, Amie, Amye, Esma, Essme**

**Anclin** (AN-slin)
French, Latin— *Hand maiden*

**Andrea** (AN-drē-uh) or (an-DRĀ-uh)
Latin, Italian— *Womanly*
Feminine form of Andrew.
**Aindrea, Andee, Andi, Andie, Andre, Andreana, Andree, Andrel, Andria, Andriana, Andromeda, Andy**

**Anestassia** (an-uh-STĀ-shuh)
Russian, Greek— *Resurrection*
**Ana, Anastassia, Anestasie, Anstice, Asia, Nastie, Nessa, Stace, Stacey, Stacie, Stacy, Stasa, Stasya, Tasenka, Tasia, Tasya**

**Angela** (AN-jel-uh)
Greek— *Heavenly messenger*
Entertainment: Angie Dickinson, Angela Cartwright, actresses.
**Ange, Angel, Angele, Angelica, Angelika, Angelina, Angelique, Angelita, Angie, Angline, Angy, Gelya**

**Anita** (uh-NĒ-tuh)
Spanish, Hebrew— *Grace*
Entertainment: Anita Bryant, actress and former Miss America; Anita Ekberg, actress.
**Anitra, Ann**

**Ann** (AN)
Hebrew— *Full of grace, mercy and prayer*
Biblical: Anne was the mother of the Virgin Mary.
Famous: Anne Hathaway, wife of William Shakespeare.
Literature: *Anna Karenina,* by Leo Tolstoy; *Anna Christie,* Pulitzer Prize-winning play by Eugene O'Neill; Ann Landers, columnist.
Entertainment: Anna Pavlova, ballet dancer; Ann-Margret, Anne Bancroft, actresses; Anne Murray, pop singer.
**Ana, Anabel, Anabella, Anabelle, Analiese, Analise, Anet, Anett, Anetta, Anette, Ania, Anica, Anita, Anitra, Anna, Annabel, Annabella, Annabla, Annable, Annaboelle, Annalice, Annaliese, Annalise, Annamariam, Annamarie, Anne, Annebella, Annelise, Annemarie, Annetta, Annette, Anni, Annice, Annie, Annis, Annora, Anny, Anuska, Anya, Hanna, Hannah, Hanni, Hannie, Hanny, Nan, Nana, Nance, Nancee, Nancey, Nanci, Nancie, Nancy, Nanete, Nanette, Nanice, Nanine, Nanni, Nannie, Nanny, Nanon, Nette, Nettie, Netty, Nina, Ninette, Ninon, Nita**

**Anselma** (an-SEL-muh)
Teutonic— *Divine protectress*

**Anthea** (an-THĒ-uh)
Greek— *Like a flower*
**Anthe, Anthia, Thea, Thia**

**Antoinetta** (an-twa-NET-tuh)
Slovak, Swedish, Latin— *Priceless*
Feminine form of Anthony.
Literature: *My Antonia*, novel by
  Willa Cather.
Entertainment: Antoinette Perry,
  leader of the American Theater
  Wing.
**Antonetta, Antonia, Antonie,
Antoinette, Antonina, Netta,
Netti, Nettie, Netty,
Toinette, Toni, Tonia, Tonie,
Tony, Tonye**

**April** (Ā-pril)
Latin— *Opening*
**Aprilette, Averil, Averyl, Aviel**

**Arabela** (air-uh-BEL-uh)
Latin, Spanish— *Beautiful altar*
Entertainment: *Arabella,* opera by
  Richard Strauss.
**Ara, Arabele, Arabella, Arabelle,
Arabellie, Arabelly, Bel, Bell,
Bella, Belle, Bellie**

**Ardelia** (ar-DĒL-ē-yuh)
Latin— *Fervent or zealous*
**Arda, Ardeen, Ardelis, Ardella,
Ardelle, Ardene, Ardent, Ardin,
Ardine, Ardis, Ardra**

**Ardith** (AR-dith)
Hebrew— *Flowering field*
**Alda, Aldith, Ardeth, Ardyth,
Aridatha, Datha, Edith**

**Arella** (a-REL-uh)
Hebrew— *Angel messenger*
**Arela**

**Aretha** (uh-RĒ-thuh)
Greek— *Best*
Celtic— *High*
Entertainment: Aretha Franklin,
  pop singer.
**Retha**

**Aretina** (ar-e-TĒN-uh)
Greek— *Virtuous*

**Ariadne** (ar-ē-AD-nē)
Greek— *Holy one*
Famous: Ariadne, daughter of
  King Minos of Crete.
Entertainment: Opera *Ariadne auf
  Naxos,* by Richard Strauss.
**Ariana, Ariane, Arianie**

**Ariel** (AR-ē-el)
Hebrew— *Lioness of God*
Literature: Prospero's spirit
  servant in Shakespeare's *The
  Tempest.*
**Aeriele, Ariela, Ariella, Arielle**

**Arlene** (ar-LĒN) or (AR-lēn)
Celtic— *A pledge*
Feminine form of Arlen.
Entertainment: TV and radio star
  Arlene Francis.
**Aileen, Aline, Arlana, Arleen,
Arlen, Arlena, Arlette, Arleyne,
Arlie, Arliene, Arlina, Arline,
Arluene, Arly, Arlyne, Lena,
Lenna, Lina**

**Ashley** (ASH-lē)
Old English— *From the ash-tree
  meadow*
**Ash, Ashla, Ashlan, Ashlen**

**Astra** (AS-truh)
Greek— *Like a star*
Entertainment: Singer Astrid
  Gilberto.
**Astrea, Astred, Astrid**

**Atara** (uh-TAR-uh)
Hebrew— *A crown*
**Atera, Ateret**

**Athalia** (uh-THĀL-ē-yuh)
Hebrew— *The Lord is mighty*
Biblical: Queen of Judah.
**Atalie**

**Athena** (uh-THĒ-nuh)
Greek— *Wise*
Mythological: Goddess of wisdom.
**Athen, Athene, Athenia**

**Atlanta** (at-LAN-tuh)
Greek—*Unswaying*
**Atlante**

**Audrey** (AW-drē)
Old English—*Noble strength*
Entertainment: Audrey Hepburn, Audrey Meadows, actresses.
**Audey, Audi, Audie, Audra, Audre, Audrie, Audry**

**Augusta** (AW-gus-tuh) or (aw-GUST-uh)
Latin—*Majestic, sacred*
Feminine form of August.
Literature: Lady Augusta Gregory, playwright, co-founder of the Irish National Theater Society.
**Auguste, Augustina, Augustine, Austin, Austina, Gus, Gussi, Gussie, Gussy, Gusta, Gusti, Gustie, Gusty, Tina**

**Auria** (OR-ē-uh)
Latin—*The aureate or golden*

**Aurilia** (aw-RĒ-lē-yuh)
Latin—*Golden*
**Aura, Aurea, Aurel, Aurelea, Aurelia, Aurelie, Auria, Aurie, Aurora, Aurore, Ora, Oralee, Oralia, Oralie, Orel, Orelee, Orelia, Orelie, Rora, Rori, Rorie, Rory**

**Aurora** (uh-ROR-uh)
Latin—*Dawn*
**Aurore, Ora, Rori, Rorie, Rory, Rota**

**Autumn** (AW-tum)
Latin—*Autumn*

**Ava** (Ā-vuh)
German—*A bird*
Hollywood: Ava Gardner, actress.
**Avi, Avie, Avis**

**Azelia** (uh-ZĒL-yuh)
Hebrew—*Whom the Lord reserved*
**Azelea, Azel, Azela**

**Babette** (bab-ET)
Greek—*Stranger*
**Babe, Babs**

**Bambi** (BAM-bē)
Italian—*Child*
Entertainment: *Bambi*, a Walt Disney film based on storybook animals.

**Barakah** (ba-RAWK-uh)
Arabic—*White one*

**Barbara** (BAR-ber-uh)
Greek—*Stranger or foreign*
Literature: Barbara Cartland, gothic romance writer; *Major Barbara*, by George Bernard Shaw.
Entertainment: Barbara Stanwick, Barbra Streisand, Barbi Benton, actresses.
**Babby, Babette, Babs, Barbette, Barbi, Barbra, Barby, Bobbi, Bobbie, Bonnie**

**Barbo** (bar-BŌ)
Swedish—*Stranger*
See Barbara.

**Bathilda** (ba-TIL-duh)
Teutonic—*Commanding battle-maid*
**Bathilde**

**Bathsheba** (bath-SHĒ-buh)
Hebrew—*Daughter of the oath*
Biblical: Mother of Solomon.
**Batsheva, Sheba**

**Beata** (bē-AT-uh)
Latin—*Blessed or divine*
**Bea, Bee**

**Beatrice** (BĒ-uh-tris)
Latin—*Bringer of joy*
Literature: Beatrix Potter, author
of *Peter Rabbit.*
Entertainment: Beatrice Arthur,
actress who plays *Maude.*
**Bea, Beatrisa, Beatrix,
Bebe, Bee, Beitris, Betrix,
Trix, Trixi, Trixie, Trixy**

**Becky** (BEK-ē)
Hebrew—*The ensnarer*
See Rebecca.

**Bela** (BEL-uh)
Czech—*White*
**Bel, Belia, Bell**

**Belicia** (buh-LĒ-sē-uh) or
(buh-LĒ-shuh)
Spanish—*Dedicated to God*
**Belia, Belikia, Belisia, Belita**

**Belinda** (buh-LIN-duh)
Italian—*Wise and immortal*
Spanish—*Pretty*
**Bel, Belle, Lindie, Linds, Lindy**

**Bella** (BEL-uh)
Latin—*Beautiful*
Famous: Bella Abzug, New York
Congresswoman.
**Bee, Bela, Belinda, Bell,
Belle, Bellie, Belva, Belvia,
Bill, Billi, Billy**

**Bena** (BĒN-uh)
Hebrew—*Wise*
Feminine form of Ben.
**Benay, Benie, Bennie**

**Benedetta** (ben-uh-DET-uh)
Italian—*The blessed*
Feminine form of Benedict.

**Benita** (buh-NĒ-tuh)
Latin, Spanish—*Blessed*
Feminine form of Benedict.
**Bendite, Benedetta, Benedicta,
Benedikta, Beneta, Benne,
Benni, Bennie, Benny, Benoite,
Bernetta, Bernette, Bernita,
Binni, Binnie, Binny**

**Berenice** (bair-uh-NĒS)
Greek—*Bringer of victory*
**Benadette, Bernadette, Bernadina,
Bernardina, Bernardine, Bernelle,
Berneta, Bernetta, Bernette,
Berni, Bernie, Bernice, Berny,
Bunni, Bunnie, Bunny, Nisie,
Nizie, Veronica, Veronika,
Veronique**

**Bernadette** (bern-uh-DET)
See Berenice.
Feminine form of Bernard.
Entertainment: Bernadette Peters,
actress.

**Bertha** (BER-thuh)
German—*Shining*
Feminine form of Albert.
**Berdie, Berta, Berte, Berthe,
Berti, Bertie, Bertina,
Bertine, Berty, Bird**

**Beryl** (BERL)
Greek—*Jewel, precious*
**Berri, Berrie, Berry, Beryle**

**Bessie** (BES-ē)
Hebrew—*Consecrated to God*
**Bess, Besse, Bessy**

**Beta** (BĀ-tuh)
Czech—*Dedicated to God*
**Alzbeta, Bethany, Betica,
Elizabeta, Elizabeth, Liza**

**Beth** (BETH)
Hebrew—*House of God*
**Bethany, Elizabeth**

**Bethany** (BETH-uh-nē)
Arabic—*House of poverty*
Biblical: Village near Jerusalem.
**Beth, Elizabeth**

**BIRDIE**—*Sweet little bird*

**Bethesda** (buh-THES-duh)
Hebrew—*House of mercy*
Interesting: Bethesda, name of a
pool in Jerusalem, the waters of
which became healing when
stirred by an angel.

**Betsy** (BET-sē)
See Elizabeth.
Famous: Betsy Ross, maker of the
first American flag.
**Bette, Betty**

**Bette** (BET-ē) or (BET)
See Elizabeth.
Famous: Betty Ford, wife of
President Gerald Ford.
Entertainment: Bette Davis, Betty
Hutton, Betty Grable, Bette
Midler, actresses.
**Bettina, Bettine, Betty**

**Beulah** (BŪ-luh)
Hebrew—*She who will be married*
Biblical: Another name for Israel.
**Beula**

**Beverly** (BEV-er-lē)
Anglo-Saxon — *Beaver meadow*
Entertainment: Beverly Sills, opera
   singer; Beverly Bayne,
   silent-movie star.
**Bev, Beverle, Beverlee, Beverley,
Beverlie, Bevvy, Buffy**

**Bianca** (bē-ON-kuh)
Italian, Teutonic — *White*
Famous: Bianca Jagger, former
   wife of Rolling Stones' Mick
   Jagger.
**Beanca, Beanka, Biancha,
Bianka, Blanca, Blanche**

**Bibi** (BĒ-bē)
Arabic — *Lacy*

**Billie** (BIL-ē)
Old English — *Strong willed*
Feminine form of Bill.
Music: Billie Halliday, blues singer.
**Billi, Billy, Wilhelmina,
Willie, Willy**

**Bina** (BĒ-nuh)
See Sabina.

**Birdie** (BUR-dē)
Teutonic — *Sweet little bird*
**Bird, Birdella**

**Birget** (BUR-jet)
Norwegian — *Protecting*
**Bergette, Bergitte, Birgitta**

**Blanche** (BLANCH)
French — *Fair, white*
**Bell, Bellanca, Bianca, Blanca,
Blanch, Blanka, Blinni, Blinnie,
Blinny, Branca**

**Blanda** (BLAN-duh)
Latin — *Affable or seductive*
**Blandina**

**Blenda** (BLEN-duh)
Teutonic — *Dazzling*

**Bliss** (BLIS)
Old English — *Bliss or joy*
**Blisse, Blissie**

**Blossom** (BLAW-sum)
Old English — *Flowerlike*
**Blom, Bluma**

**Blythe** (BLĪTH)
Old English — *Joyous*

**Bo** (BŌ)
Chinese — *Precious*
Entertainment: Bo Derek, actress.

**Bobbi** (BO-bē)
See Roberta.
**Bobbie, Bobby**

**Bobett** (bo-BET)
See Barbara.
Feminine form of Bob or Robert.

**Bobina** (bo-BĒN-uh)
Czech — *Brilliant, famous*
**Berta, Roba**

**Bona** (BŌ-nuh)
Hebrew — *Builder*
Spanish — *Bald*

**Bonita** (bō-NĒ-tuh)
Spanish — *Pretty*

**Bonnibel** (BON-ē-bel)
Latin — *Good and beautiful*
**Bonnibelle, Bonniebelle,
Bonniebellie**

**Bonnie** (BON-ē)
French, Latin — *Sweet and good*
Famous: Bonnie and Clyde,
   bankrobbers.
Entertainment: Bonnie Raitt, rock
   singer and actress.

**Brandy** (BRAN-dē)
Dutch — *Brandy drink*
**Brandi, Brandie**

**Brenda** (BREN-duh)
German — *A sword blade*
Entertainment: Brenda Lee, pop
   singer; Brenda Lewis,
   Metropolitan Opera singer.
**Brandon, Bren, Brendan**

**BRUNHILDA**—*Armored woman warrior*

**Brenna** (BREN-uh)
Celtic— *Raven maid*

**Bretta** (BRET-uh)
Irish— *From Britain*
**Bret, Brit, Brita, Brite, Brittany**

**Bridget** (BRI-jet)
Irish— *Resolute strength*
Biblical: Patron saint of Ireland.
Entertainment: Brigit Nilsson,
    Metropolitan Opera soprano;
    Brigit Bardot, actress.
**Beret, Berget, Biddie, Biddy,
Birgitta, Bitgitta, Bride, Bridie,
Brietta, Brigid, Brigida, Brigit,
Brigitta, Brigitte, Brita**

**Brier** (BRI-er)
French— *Heather*

**Brina** (BRE-nuh)
Slavic, Celtic— *Protector*
Feminine form of Brian.
**Breanne, Briana, Bryna**

**Brittany** (BRI-tuh-ne)
Latin— *From England*
**Brit, Britni, Britt, Britta**

**Brooke** (BROOK)
Old English— *From the brook*
Entertainment: Brooke Shields,
    model and actress.

**Brunhilda** (BROON-hil-duh)
German— *Armored woman warrior*
**Brunhilde, Brynhild, Brynhilda,
Hilda, Hildi**

**Calandra** (kuh-LAN-druh)
Greek— *The lark*
**Cal, Calandia, Calendre, Calley,
Calli, Callie, Cally**

**Calantha** (kuh-LAN-thuh)
Greek— *Beautiful blossom*
**Cal, Calanthe, Calli, Callie,
Cally**

**Calida** (kuh-LE-duh)
Greek— *Most beautiful*
**Calesta, Calista, Calla, Calli,
Callie, Cally, Calysta, Kalla,
Kalli, Kallista, Kally**

**Calla** (KAL-uh)
Greek— *Beautiful*
**Cal, Calli, Callie, Cally**

**Caltha** (KAL-thuh)
Latin— *Yellow flower*

**Calypso** (kuh-LIP-so)
Greek— *Concealer*
Mythological: Sea nymph who
    kept Odysseus captive.

**Cam** (KAM)
Vietnamese— *Orange fruit or to be
    sweet*

**Camille** (kuh-MĒL)
Latin—*Self-sacrificing*
**Cam, Camala, Camel, Camila,
Camile, Camilla, Cammi,
Cammie, Cammy, Milli,
Millie, Milly**

**Candace** (KAN-dis)
Greek, Latin—*Glittering*
Historical: Names and titles of
queens of ancient Ethiopia.
Literature: Candace Stevenson,
winner of Poetry Society of
America Award.
Entertainment: Candace Bergen,
actress.
**Candi, Candice, Candida, Candie,
Candis, Candy, Kandace, Kandy**

**Candra** (KAN-druh)
Latin—*Moon*

**Capri** (kuh-PRĒ)
Zodiac—*The goat*
**Capra, Capre, Capria, Kapre,
Kapri**

**Cara** (KAR-uh)
Irish—*Friend*
Latin—*Dear*
**Carina, Carine, Carrie, Carry,
Kara, Karina, Karine, Karrie,
Karry**

**Caresse** (kuh-RES)
French—*Beloved*
**Car, Caresa, Caressa, Carissa,
Charissa, Karesa, Karissa**

**Cari** (KAIR-ē)
Turkish—*Flowing like water*
Literature: *Sister Carrie*, novel by
Theodore Dreiser.
**Carrie, Kairee**

**Carilla** (kuh-RIL-uh)
Feminine form of Charles.

**Carina** (kuh-RĒ-nuh)
Latin—*Keel*
See Karen.
**Caren, Carin, Carine, Caryn,
Karen**

**Carissa** (kuh-RIS-uh)
Greek—*Loving*
**Carrie, Charissa**

**Carita** (kuh-RĒ-tuh)
Latin—*Charity*
See Charity.
**Carie, Caritta, Karita**

**Carla** (KAR-luh)
Teutonic—*One who is strong*
Feminine form of Charles.
Entertainment: Carly Simon, pop
singer.
**Carly, Karla, Karly**

**Carlotta** (kar-LOT-uh)
Spanish, Portuguese, French—
*Petite or feminine*
Interesting: Name was introduced
to France and England by the
wife of Louis XI.
**Carla, Carleen, Carlene, Carletta,
Carlie, Carlina, Carline, Carlita,
Carlota, Carly, Karla, Karletta,
Karlina, Karlita, Karlotta**

**Carmel** (kar-MEL) or (KAR-muhl)
Hebrew—*God's vineyard*
Biblical: Mt. Carmel in Palestine.
**Carma, Carmela, Carmen,
Carmill, Karma, Karmen**

**Carmen** (KAR-min)
Latin—*Song*
Hebrew—*Vine-dresser*
Entertainment: Opera *Carmen*, by
George Bizet.
**Carma, Carmencita, Carmine,
Carmita, Charmine, Karmen**

**Carna** (KAR-nuh)
Hebrew—*Horn*
**Carmita, Carniela, Carniella,
Carnis, Carnit, Karmen, Karnis**

## Carol (KAIR-uhl)

French — *Song of joy*
Feminine form of Carl or Charles.
Famous: Caroline Kennedy, daughter of President John F. Kennedy; Princess Caroline of Monaco.
Entertainment: Carol King, singer and songwriter; Carol Channing, actress; Carrie Fisher, actress who plays Princess Leia in *Star Wars*.

**Carey, Cari, Carla, Carleen, Carlen, Carlene, Carley, Carlin, Carlina, Carline, Carlita, Carlota, Carlotta, Carly, Carlyn, Carlynn, Carlynne, Caro, Carola, Carole, Carolin, Carolina, Caroline, Carolyn, Carolynn, Carolynne, Carri, Carrie, Carroll, Carry, Cary, Caryl, Chariene, Charla, Charleen, Charlena, Charlotta, Charmain, Charmaine, Charmian, Charmion, Charyl, Cheryl, Cheryln, Karel, Kari, Karla, Karleen, Karlen, Karlene, Karlotta, Karlotte, Karole, Karolina, Karoly, Lola, Loleta, Lolita, Lotta, Lotte, Lotti, Lottie, Sharleen, Sharlene, Sharline, Sharyl, Sherrie, Sherry, Sherye, Sheryl**

## Caron (KAIR-uhn)

French — *Pure*

## Casey (KĀ-sē)

Gaelic — *Brave*
**Casie, Kacie, Kasey**

## Cassandra (kuh-SAN-druh)

Greek — *Entangling men*
Mythological: A prophetess of ancient Greece.
Entertainment: Cass Elliott, pop singer with the Mamas and Papas.
**Cass, Cassandre, Cassie, Sandra**

## Catalina (kat-uh-LĒN-uh)

Greek — *Pure*
**Caterina**

## Catherine (KATH-ren)

Greek — *Pure*
Literature: Catherine Barkley, heroine of Hemingway's novel, *A Farewell to Arms;* Catherine Earnshaw, heroine of Emily Bronte's novel, *Wuthering Heights.*
Entertainment: Catherine Deneuve, Cathy Lee Crosby, actresses; Gymnast Cathy Rigby; Catherine Crosby, wife of Bing Crosby.

**Caitlin, Caitrin, Caren, Carin, Caron, Caryn, Cass, Cassy, Catarina, Cate, Caterina, Catha, Catharina, Catharine, Cathe, Cathee, Catherina, Cathi, Cathie, Cathleen, Cathlene, Cathrine, Cathryn, Cathy, Cathyleen, Cati, Catie, Catlaina, Catriona, Caty, Caye, Ekaterina, Kate, Katherine, Kathie, Kathleen, Kathlin, Katleen, Katlin, Katrina, Katrine, Katty, Kit, Kitty, Trina, Trine, Trinette**

## Cecilia (suh-SĒ-lē-yuh)

Latin — *Blind*
Famous: St. Cecilia, patroness of music.
Entertainment: Cicily Tyson and Sissy Spacek, actresses.
**Cecelia, Cecil, Cecile, Ceciley, Cecily, Ceil, Celia, Cicily, Cis, Cissy, Sisely, Sissy**

## Celeste (suh-LEST)

Latin — *Heavenly*
Entertainment: Celeste Holm, actress.
**Cele, Celesta, Celestia, Celestina, Celestine, Celia, Celie, Celina, Celinda, Celinka, Celka**

**Celina** (se-LĒN-uh)
Polish, Latin—*Heavenly*
**Cela, Celek, Celestyn,
Celestyna, Celinka, Celka, Cesia,
Inka, Inok**

**Chaitra** (SHĀ-truh)
Hindi for Aries zodiac sign.

**Chanda** (CHAN-duh)
Sanskrit—*The great goddess*
Mythological: Name assumed by
Devi, the greatest goddess.

**Chandra** (CHAN-druh)
Sanskrit—*Outshines the stars*

**Charity** (CHAIR-i-tē)
Latin—*Benevolent, charitable, loving*
**Charita, Charry, Cherry**

**Charlotte** (SHAR-lot)
French—*Little and womanly*
Feminine form of Charles.
Literature: Novelist Charlotte
Bronte.
**Carla, Carleen, Carlene, Carline,
Carlota, Carlotta, Carly, Charla,
Charleen, Charlene, Charline,
Charlotta, Charmain, Charmaine,
Charmian, Charmion, Charo,
Charyl, Karla, Karleen, Karlene,
Karlotta, Karlotte, Lola,
Loleta, Lolita, Lotta, Lotte,
Lotti, Lottie, Sharleen,
Sharlene, Sharline, Sharyl,
Sherrie, Sherry, Sherye,
Sheryl**

**Charmaine** (shar-MĀN)
Latin—*Little song*
**Charmain, Charmian, Charmion**

**Chastity** (CHAS-tuh-tē)
Latin—*Purity*
Famous: Chastity Bono, daughter
of Sonny and Cher Bono.

**Cherie** (SHAIR-ē) or (shuh-RĒ)
French—*Dear one*
Famous: Cher
Literature: Cherry Ames, heroine
of novels for young girls.
**Cher, Chere, Cherey, Cheri,
Cherry, Sherrel, Sherrell, Sheryl**

**Cheryl** (SHAIR-el)
See Charlotte.
Entertainment: Cherylynn La
Tiere, pop singer; Cheryl Tiegs,
actress and model; Cheryl
Crawford, actress.
**Cherylynn, Sheryl**

**Chloe** (KLŌ) or (KLŌ-ē)
Greek—*Young grass*
Mythological: Greek goddess of
agriculture.
**Cleopatra**

**Chloris** (KLOR-is)
Greek—*Pale*
Mythological: Goddess of flowers
Entertainment: Cloris Leachman,
actress.
**Chloe, Chlor, Clor, Cloris, Kloris**

**Christa** (KRIS-tuh)
Greek—*The anointed*
**Chris, Chrissy, Christabel,
Christabelle, Christal,
Christel, Christiana,
Christiane, Crystal**

**Christina** (kris-TĒN-uh)
Greek—*The anointed*
Feminine form of Christian.
Famous: Christine Brinkley,
model; Christina Onassis,
daughter of Aristotle Onassis.
Entertainment: Tina Louise,
actress; Tina Turner, pop singer.
Sports: Chris Evert Lloyd, tennis
champion.
**Chris, Chrissi, Chrissie,
Chrissy, Christa, Christal,
Christiana, Christie, Christine,
Chrystal, Crystal, Kristianna,
Kristina, Kristine, Tenna, Tina**

**Cinderella** (sin-duh-REL-uh)
French — *Little one of the ashes*
Literature: Famous fairy tale.
**Cinda, Cindee, Cindia,
Cindie, Cindy, Ella**

**Cindy** (SIN-dē)
See Cynthia.
Entertainment: Cindy Garvey, talk
show hostess; Cindy Williams,
star of *Laverne and Shirley.*

**Cipriana** (si-prē-AN-uh)
Spanish — *From the island of Cyprus*
**Kupris, Sipiana**

**Clara** (KLAIR-uh)
Latin — *Bright or illustrious*
Famous: Claire Boothe Luce,
author, playwright and former
congresswoman.
**Clair, Claire, Clarabelle, Clare,
Claresta, Clareta, Claretta,
Clarette, Clarey, Clari,
Claribel, Clarice, Clarinada,
Clarine, Clarissa, Clarita,
Clarrette, Clary, Cliarra,
Klair, Klaire, Klara, Klare,
Klarika, Klarrisa**

**Clareta** (KLAR-et-uh)
Spanish — *Brilliant*
**Clarette, Clarita**

**Clarice** (kluh-RĒS)
French — *Making famous*
Literature: *Clarissa Harlowe,* novel
by Samuel Richardson.
**Clarisa, Clarise, Clarissa,
Clarisse**

**Claudia** (KLAW-dē-uh)
Latin — *Lame*
Feminine form of Claude.
Entertainment: Claudia Cardinale,
Claudette Colbert, Claudine
Longet, actresses.
**Claude, Claudetta, Claudette,
Claudie, Claudina, Claudine,**

**Clementine** (KLEM-en-tīn)
Latin — *The merciful*
Feminine form of Clement.
Entertainment: Song *Oh My
Darling, Clementine.*

**Cleo** (KLE-ō)
Greek — *The famous*
**Clea, Cleopatra, Clio**

**Clitilde** (kluh-TILD-uh) or
(kluh-TILD)
Teutonic — *Famous battle-maiden*
**Clothilde, Clotilda**

**Clover** (KLŌ-ver)
Old English — *Clover blossom*
Entertainment: Movie *Daisy Clover.*
**Klover**

**Colette** (kō-LET)
Latin — *Victorious*
**Collette**

**Colleen** (kaw-LĒN) or (KŌ-lēn)
Irish — *Girl*
Entertainment: Colleen Dewhurst,
actress.
**Coleen, Colene, Collie,
Colline, Colly**

**Connie** (KON-ē)
See Constance.
Entertainment: Connie Frances,
singer; Connie Stevens, actress
and singer.

**Constance** (KON-stans)
Latin — *Constancy*
Entertainment: Constance Bennett,
actress.
**Con, Conni, Connie, Conny,
Constancia, Constancy,
Constanta, Constantia,
Constantine, Costanza,
Konstance, Konstanze**

**Consuela** (kon-SWĀ-luh)
Latin, Spanish — *Consolation*
Literature: Consuelo, heroine in
George Sands novel.
**Consolata, Consuelo**

**CORDELIA**—*Sea jewel*

**Cora** (KOR-uh)
Greek—*Maiden*
Famous: Coretta King, wife of
   Martin Luther King.
**Corabel, Corabella, Corabelle,
Corella, Corena, Corene, Coretta,
Corette, Corey, Cori, Corie,
Corilla, Corina, Corine, Corinna,
Corinne, Coriss, Corissa, Correna,
Corrie, Corrine, Corry, Cory,
Kora, Korella, Korie, Korry**

**Coral** (KOR-uhl)
Greek, Latin—*From the sea coral*
Interesting: Coral was worn by
   South Sea Islanders as a charm to
   ward off evil spirits.
**Caralie, Coralie, Coraline,
Corallie, Koral, Koralie,
Koraline, Korallie**

**Cordelia** (kor-DĒ-lē-uh)
Celtic— *The sea jewel*
Literature: King Lear's faithful
daughter.
**Cordelie, Cordey, Cordi,
Cordie, Cordula, Cordy, Coretta,
Corinna, Corinne, Delia, Kella,
Kordella, Kordellia, Kordula**

**Corliss** (KOR-les)
Old English— *Cheerful or
good-hearted*

**Cornelia** (kor-NĒ-lē-uh)
Latin— *Yellowish or horn colored*
Feminine form of Cornelius.
**Corinna, Cornela, Cornelie,
Cornelle, Cornie, Corny,
Nelia, Nelie, Nell, Nellie**

**Cosima** (ko-SĒ-muh)
Greek, Italian— *Orderly arrangement*
Feminine form of Cosmo.

**Crystal** (KRIS-tul)
Greek— *Brilliantly clear*
Entertainment: Crystal Gayle,
singer and Loretta Lynn's
youngest sister.
**Chris, Cris, Crys, Krystal,
Stell, Stella**

**Cybil** (SIB-ul)
See Sibyl.
Entertainment: Cybil Shepherd,
actress and model.

**Cynara** (si-NAR-uh)
Greek name derived from island in
Aegean Sea, now called Zinara.

**Cynthia** (SIN-thē-uh)
Greek— *Moon goddess*
Historical: Affectionate name
given to Queen Elizabeth I by
Ben Johnson, Walter Raleigh and
Edmund Spenser.
**Cindy, Cyn, Cynth, Cynthie,
Kynthia**

**Cyra** (SĒR-uh)
Greek— *Lord, ruler*
Feminine form of Cyrano.
**Cira, Cyrilla**

**Cyrene** (suh-RĒN)
Greek— *Unknown*
Mythological: Nymph carried by
Apollo to Libya.
**Cyrena**

**Cyrilla** (suh-RIL-uh)
Latin— *Lordly*
Feminine form of Cyril.
**Ciri, Cirilla**

**Dacey** (DĀ-sē)
American— *Southerner*
**Dacia, Dacie, Dacy, Dasi, Dasie**

**Dagania** (dag-uh-NĒ-uh)
Hebrew— *Ceremonial grain*
**Daganya**

**Dagmar** (DAG-mar)
Danish— *Joy of the Danes*
Famous: Beloved Danish queen.
**Dagare, Mar**

**Dagna** (DAG-nuh)
Teutonic— *Fair as the day*
**Dagny**

**DAMALIS** — *The tamer*

**Daisy** (DĀ-zē)
Anglo-Saxon — *Day's eyes*
**Daisey, Daisi, Daisie**

**Dale** (DĀL)
Old English — *From the valley*
Entertainment: Dale Evans, actress
and wife of Roy Rogers.
**Dael, Daile, Dailie, Dayle**

**Dalila** (duh-LĪ-luh)
Swahili — *Gentle*
**Delilah, Lila**

**Dallas** (DAL-us)
Gaelic — *Wise*
**Dalton**

**Damalis** (duh-MAL-is)
Greek — *The tamer*

**Damara** (duh-MAR-uh)
Greek — *Gentle girl*
**Damon, Damaris, Mara, Mari,
Maris**

**Damita** (duh-MĒ-tuh)
Spanish — *Little noble lady*
**Damite, Damitee, Damitie**

**Dana** (DĀ-nuh)
Celtic— *From Denmark*
Mythological: Dana, mother of the
gods.

**Danica** (duh-NĒ-kuh)
Slavic— *The morning star*

**Daniela** (DAN-yel-uh)
Hebrew— *God is my judge*
Feminine form of Daniel.
**Danella, Danelle, Danett,
Danette, Dani, Danice,
Daniella, Danielle, Danila,
Danit, Danita, Danni, Dannie,
Danny, Dannye, Danya, Danye**

**Danit** (dan-ĒT)
Hebrew— *To judge*
Feminine form of Daniel.
**Dania, Danita, Danya**

**Daphne** (DAF-nē)
Greek— *Laurel tree*
**Daffi, Daffie, Daffy, Daph,
Daphie**

**Dara** (DAR-uh)
Hebrew— *Compassion*
**Darda, Darya**

**Daralis** (duh-RAL-is)
Old English— *Beloved or dear*
**Daralice**

**Darby** (DAR-bē)
Gaelic— *Free man*
Old Norse— *From the deer estate*
**Darb, Darbie, Darcee, Darcey,
Darcy, Darsey, Darsie, Dercy**

**Darcie** (DAR-sē)
French, Celtic— *From the stronghold
or dark one*
**Darcee, Darcey, Darcy**

**Darda** (DAR-duh)
Hungarian— *A dart*
Hebrew— *Pearl of wisdom*
**Dardis**

**Daria** (DAR-ē-uh)
Persian— *Queenly*
Feminine form of Darius.
**Dareece, Darees, Dari, Darice,
Darya**

**Darlene** (dar-LĒN)
Anglo-Saxon— *Tenderly beloved*
**Daralice, Daralis, Darelle,
Darla, Darleen, Darline, Darlleen,
Darrelle, Darryl, Daryl**

**Daron** (DAIR-en)
Gaelic— *Great*
Feminine form of Darren.

**Davine** (duh-VĒN)
Hebrew— *The loved*
Feminine form of David.
**Daveta, Davida, Davita, Davina,
Devina, Veda, Vida, Vita, Vitia**

**Dawn** (DAWN)
Anglo-Saxon— *Break of day*

**Deanne** (dē-AN)
See Diana.
Feminine form of Dean.
**Deana, Dena, Deon, Deonne**

**Deborah** (DEB-uh-ruh)
Hebrew— *Bee*
Entertainment: Deborah Harry,
singer known as *Blondie;* Debbie
Boone, singer, daughter of Pat
Boone; Deborah Kerr, Debbie
Reynolds, actresses.
**Deb, Debbee, Debbie, Debby,
Debora, Debra**

**Dee** (DĒ)
Welsh— *Black, dark*
**Dede, Deirdre, Delia, Diana**

**Deedee** (DĒ-dē)
Hebrew— *Beloved*
Entertainment: Dee Dee Lewis,
pop singer.
**Dee Dee, Didi, Jedidiah**

**Dehlia** (DĀ-lē-yuh)
Norwegian— *From the valley*

**Dela** (DĒ-luh)
Spanish—*Hope*
**Della**

**Delia** (DĒ-lē-yuh)
Greek—*Visible from Delos*
Mythological: Name for the moon
goddess.
**Adelaide, Dede, Dee, Deedee,
Dehlia, Delinad, Della, Didi**

**Delilah** (duh-LĪ-luh)
Hebrew—*The temptress*
Biblical: Companion of Samson.
**Dalila, Delila, Lila, Lilah**

**Della** (DEL-uh)
Teutonic—*Of nobility*
Entertainment: Della Reese, pop
singer.
**Del, Dela**

**Delora** (duh-LOR-uh)
Latin—*From the seashore*
**Delores, Deloris**

**Delphine** (del-FĒN)
Greek—*Calmness*
Interesting: Possibly derived from
dolphin.
Mythological: Delphine means
calm sea in Greek mythology.
**Delfeena, Delfine, Delphina,
Delphinia**

**Demetria** (duh-MĒ-trē-uh)
Greek—*From fertile land*
Mythological: Goddess of fertility
and harvests.
**Demeter, Demetra, Demitria,
Demy, Dimitria**

**Deminica** (duh-MIN-i-kuh)
French, Latin—*Born on the Lord's
day*
Feminine form of Dominic.
**Domeniga, Dominga, Domini,
Dominic, Dominica, Dominique**

**Dena** (DĒ-nuh)
Hebrew—*Vindicated*
Feminine form of Dean.
**Deana, Deena, Dinah**

**Denise** (duh-NĒS)
Greek—*Wine goddess*
**Denice, Denni, Dennie, Denny,
Denys, Denyse, Dinnie, Dinny**

**Derora** (duh-ROR-uh)
Hebrew—*Flowing brook*
**Derorice, Derorit**

**Desdemona**
(DEZ-duh-mōn-uh)
Greek—*Girl of sadness*
**Demona, Desdamona, Mona**

**Desiree** (dez-i-RĀ)
French, Latin—*So long hoped for*
**Desire**

**Deva** (DĒ-vuh)
Sanskrit—*Divine*
Interesting: Hindi goddess of the
moon.

**Devi** (dē-VĒ)
Sakti—*Goddess*
Interesting: Hindi goddess of
power and destruction.

**Devora** (de-VOR-uh)
Russian—*A bee*
**Debora, Deborah**

**Diana** (dī-AN-uh)
Latin—*Divine*
Mythological: Roman goddess of
the hunt, moon and fertility.
Biblical: Temple of Diana at
Ephesus was one of the Seven
Wonders of the ancient world.
Famous: Diana, Princess of Wales
Literature: Dian Thomas, author
and TV personality.
Entertainment: Diana Ross, pop
singer; Diahann Caroll, Diane
Keaton, actresses.
**Deana, Deane, Deanna,
Deanne, Dede, Dee, Dena,
Denna, Denne, Di, Diahann,
Dian, Diandra, Diane,
Dianna, Dianne, Didi, Dyan,
Dyana, Dyane, Dyann, Dyanna,
Dyanne**

## Dianthe (dī-AN-thuh)
Greek— *Divine flower*
**Diantha**

## Dinah (DĪ-nuh)
Hebrew— *Vindicated*
Biblical: Daughter of Leah and Jacob, known for her beauty.
Entertainment: Dinah Shore, singer; Dina Merrill, actress.
**Dena, Diane, Dina**

## Dionne (DĒ-on)
Greek— *Divine queen*
Feminine form of Dion.
Mythological: Mother of Aphrodite.
Entertainment: Dionne Warwicke, pop singer.
**Diona, Dione, Dionis**

## Disa (DĒ-suh)
Norwegian— *Active spirit*
Greek— *Double*
**Lisa**

## Dixie (DIKS-ē)
American— *Girl of the south*
Interesting: Term for the American South.
Famous: Dixie Lee Ray, former member of the Atomic Energy Commission and governor of Washington state.

## Docilla (dō-SIL-uh)
Latin— *Teachable*
**Docila, Dosilla**

## Dodi (DŌ-dē)
Hebrew— *Beloved*
**Dode, Dodie, Dody, Dora, Doris**

## Dolly (DOL-ē)
Greek— *Divine gift*
Famous: Dolley Madison, wife of President James Madison.
Entertainment: Dolly Parton, country-western singer; musical *Hello Dolly*.
**Doll, Dolle, Dolley, Dollie, Dorothy**

## Dolores (duh-LOR-is)
Spanish— *Lady of sorrows*
Biblical: Santa Maria de los Dolores, *Mary of the Sorrows*.
Famous: Delores Hope, wife of Bob Hope.
Entertainment: Dolores Del Rio, actress.
**Delora, Deloree, Delores, Deloris, Deloritas, Dolorcitas, Dolorita, Dori, Dorrie, Dorry, Lola, Lolita**

## Donna (DON-uh)
Latin, Italian— *Lady*
Entertainment: Donna Fargo, country-western singer; Donna Reed, actress.
Sports: Swimmer Donna DeVerona.
**Dana, Danella, Dode, Dodi, Dodie, Dody, Donia, Donni, Donnie, Donny, Dora, Doralia, Doralin, Doraline, Doralisa, Doralyn, Doralynn, Doralynne, Dore, Doreen, Dorelia, Dorella, Dorelle, Dorena, Dorene, Doretta, Dorette, Dorey, Dori, Doria, Dorice, Dorie, Doris, Dorlisa, Dorita, Dorothy, Dory**

## Doreen (dor-ĒN) or (DOR-ēn)
Gaelic— *Sullen*
French— *Golden*
**Dora, Doreena, Dorene, Dorine**

## Doris (DOR-is)
Greek— *Bountiful*
Mythological: Wife of Nereus.
Entertainment: Doris Day, actress.
**Dora, Dorian**

**DRISANA** — *Daughter of the sun*

**Dorothy** (DOR-uh-thē)
Greek — *Gift of God*
Literature: Dorothy Sayers, detective fiction; Dorothy in the *Wizard of Oz.*
Entertainment: Dorothy Gish, actress.
Sports: Dorothy Hamill, Olympic gold medal figure skater.
**Dasha, Dode, Dody, Doll, Dolley, Dolli, Dollie, Dolly, Dora, Dorathy, Dori, Dorlisa, Doro, Dorolice, Dorotea, Doroteya, Dorothea, Dorothee, Dorthea, Dorthy, Dory, Dosi, Dosya, Dot, Dotti, Dottie**

**Dove** (DUV)
German — *Dark*

**Drina** (DRĒ-nuh)
Spanish — *Helper*
**Drisa, Drise**

**Drisana** (dri-SAN-uh)
Sanskrit — *Daughter of the sun*
**Drisa**

**Drusilla** (droo-SIL-uh)
Greek — *Soft eyes*
**Dru, Druci, Drucie, Drucilla, Drucy, Drus, Drusi, Drusie, Drusus, Drusy**

**Dulcia** (dul-SĒ-uh)
Latin—*Sweet or delightful*
Literature: For his love, Aldonza,
Don Quixote chose the nickname
Dulcinea.
**Delcina, Delcine, Dulce, Dulcea,
Dulci, Dulciana, Dulcie,
Dulcinea, Dulcy, Dulsea**

**Ea** (Ē-uh)
Babylonian—*Goddess of spring*
Literature: Ea is the goddess of
spring in the Sumerian epic,
*Gilgamesh.*

**Eartha** (ER-thuh)
Old English—*Child of the earth*
Entertainment: Eartha Kitt, pop
singer.
**Erda, Ertha, Heatha, Hertha**

**Easter** (Ē-ster)
Old English—*Easter time*
Mythological: Anglo-Saxon
goddess of spring; Greek goddess
of dawn.
Biblical: Name of a child born at
Eastertide.

**Echo** (EK-ō)
Greek—*Repeated voice*
Mythological: Echo was a nymph
who yearned for love which was
unreturned.

**Eda** (Ē-duh)
Anglo-Saxon—*Happy or prosperous*
**Edda, Edie**

**Edana** (e-DAN-uh)
Celtic—*Zealous or fiery*
Feminine form of Edan.

**Edeline** (Ē-duh-lin) or (Ē-duh-līn)
Teutonic—*Noble and of good cheer*
**Adeline**

**Eden** (Ē-din)
Hebrew—*Delight*
Babylonian—*A plain*
Biblical: Earthly paradise where
Adam and Eve lived.
**Edin**

**Edie** (Ē-dē)
Teutonic—*Rich gift*
Entertainment: Edie Gormé,
singer; Edie Adams, actress and
singer.
**Eadie, Eadith, Eda, Ede,
Edina, Edith, Edythe**

**Edina** (e-DĒN-uh)
Anglo-Saxon—*Prospering, happy*
Interesting: Poetic name for the
city of Edinburgh.

**Edith** (Ē-dith)
Teutonic—*Rich gift*
Literature: Edith Wharton, writer.
Entertainment: Wife of Archie
Bunker, in *All in the Family.*
**Eadie, Eadith, Eda, Ede, Edi,
Edil, Edina, Edita, Editha, Edithe,
Edy, Edyth, Edythe, Eyde**

**Edlyn** (ED-lin)
Anglo-Saxon—*Noblewoman*
**Eddie, Edie, Lyn**

**Edna** (ED-nuh)
Hebrew—*Rejuvenation, pleasure*
Literature: Edna St. Vincent
Millay, poetess.
**Eddi, Eddie, Eddy, Edie, Edny**

**Ednee** (ED-nā)
Anglo-Saxon— *Prosperous protector*
Feminine form of Edmond.
**Edmonda, Edmunda**

**Edolie** (ED-ō-lē)
Teutonic— *Noble and of good cheer*
**Dolie**

**Edrea** (ed-RĒ-uh)
Hebrew— *Mighty*
Teutonic— *Prosperous*
**Eddi, Eddie, Eddy, Edra,
Edrena, Edrine, Edris**

**Edwina** (ed-WĒN-uh)
Anglo-Saxon— *Valued friend*
Feminine form of Edwin.
**Eadwina, Eadwine, Edwin,
Edwine, Edwyna, Win,
Wina, Winnie, Winny**

**Effie** (EF-ē)
Greek— *Of fair fame*
**Effy, Eppie, Euphemia,
Euphemie, Phemie**

**Eglantine** (EG-lan-tēn)
French— *Sweet-briar*
Interesting: A flower name.

**Eileen** (ī-LĒN)
Greek— *Light*
Literature: Ruth McKenney's *My
Sister Eileen.*
**Aileen**

**Eirene** (ī-RĒN)
Norwegian— *Peace*
**Eir, Eirenea, Irene**

**Elaine** (ē-LĀN)
Greek— *Light*
Literature: Elaine, in Tennyson's
*Idylls of the King.*
**Alaine, Alayne, Elana, Elane,
Elayne, Laine, Lainey, Lani**

**Elata** (ē-LĀ-tuh)
Latin— *Exalted or triumphant*

**Elberta** (el-BER-tuh)
Teutonic— *Nobly brilliant*
Feminine form of Elbert.
Interesting: Variety of peach.
**Alberta, Berta, Bertia**

**Eldora** (el-DOR-uh)
Spanish— *Golden or gilded*
Feminine form of Eldorado.
**Eldoree, Eldoria**

**Eldrida** (el-DRĒ-duh)
Anglo-Saxon— *Sage counselor*
Feminine form of Eldred.

**Eleanor** (EL-uh-nor)
Greek— *Light*
Famous: Eleanor Roosevelt, wife of
President Franklin D. Roosevelt.
Literature: Elinor Trent, heroine in
*Old Curosity Shop,* by Dickens.
**Eleanora, Eleanore, Elenore,
Eleonore, Elianore, Elinor,
Elinore, Ella, Elladine, Elle,
Ellene, Elli, Elly, Ellyn,
Elna, Elnora, Elnore, Elora,
Elyn, Helen, Leanor, Leanora,
Lena, Lenora, Lenore, Leonore,
Leora, Nell, Nellie, Nelly, Nora**

**Electra** (e-LEK-truh)
Greek— *Bright, shining*
Mythological: One of seven sister
stars of the Pleiades.
**Lectra**

**Eleni** (EL-uh-nē)
Greek— *Light or torch*
**Elena, Elenie, Elenitsa,
Helen, Nitsa**

**Elexa** (e-LEKS-uh)
See Alexandra.
Feminine form of Alfred.
**Elfrida, Elfride, Freda**

**Elga** (EL-guh)
Teutonic— *Holy*
Anglo-Saxon— *Elfin spear*

**Eli** (Ē-lē)
Norwegian— *Light*

**Eliora** (EL-ē-or-uh)
Hebrew — *The Lord is my light*
**Eleora, Leora**

**Elisa** (e-LĪ-zuh) or (e-LĒ-suh)
Spanish — *Dedicated to God*
Entertainment: Eliza Doolittle, in
*My Fair Lady.*
**Belita, Elisheba, Elisia,
Elisis, Elissa, Elissie, Eliza,
Elyse, Ysabel**

**Elita** (e-LĒ-tuh)
French, Latin — *The chosen, selected*

**Elizabeth** (e-LIZ-a-beth)
Hebrew — *Consecrated to God*
Biblical: Mother of John the Baptist.
Famous: Elizabeth Barrett of
Winnpole Street; Queen
Elizabeth of England.
Literature: Elizabeth, heroine of
Jane Austen's *Pride and Prejudice.*
Entertainment: Elizabeth Taylor,
Elizabeth Montgomery, actresses.
**Belita, Belle, Bess, Bessie,
Bessy, Beth, Betsey, Betsy, Betta,
Bette, Betti, Bettina, Bettine,
Betty, Ealasaid, Elis, Elisa,
Elisabet, Elisabeth, Elisabetta,
Elissa, Eliza, Elizabet, Elsa,
Elsbeth, Else, Elsey, Elsi,
Elsie, Elspet, Elspeth, Elsy,
Helsa, Isabel, Isabell, Lib,
Libbey, Libbi, Libbie, Libby,
Lillibeth, Lily, Lisa, Lisabeth,
Lisbeth, Lise, Lisette, Lissa,
Liz, Liza, Lizabeth, Lizbeth,
Lizzie, Lizzy, Lusa, Ysabel,
Ysabell**

**Ella** (EL-uh)
Anglo-Saxon — *Elfin*
Entertainment: Ella Fitzgerald,
singer.

**Ellen** (EL-un)
See Helen.
Literature: Ellen Glosgow, Pulitzer
Prize-winner for *In This Our Life.*
Entertainment: Ellen Burstyn,
Oscar-winning actress.
**Ellene, Ellie, Elly, Ellyn**

**Elma** (EL-muh)
Greek — *Amiable*
Turkish — *Apple*
Feminine form of Elmo.

**Elmina** (el-MĒN-uh)
Teutonic — *Awe-inspiring fame*
Anglo-Saxon — *Tree*
Feminine form of Elmer.

**Elna** (EL-nuh)
Greek — *Light*

**Elnora** (el-NOR-uh)
Greek — *Light*

**Elodie** (EL-ō-dē)
Latin — *White blossom of the water*

**Eloine** (EL-ō-ēn)
Latin — *Worthy to be chosen*
Biblical: St. Elloy, patron of
workers in precious metals.
**Eloi, Elloi, Elloy**

**Eloise** (EL-ō-ēs)
Teutonic — *Famous in battle*
French, German — *Hale and wide*
Literature: *Hints from Heloise,*
popular newspaper column.
**Eloisa, Heloise**

**Elsa** (EL-suh)
Swedish, Spanish, Greek — *Truthful*
Entertainment: Elsa Martinelli,
actress; in Wagner's opera
*Lohengrin,* bride for whom the
wedding march is played.
**Alicia, Alika, Alisa, Aliz,
Alizka, Alizz, Alya, Else, Elsie,
Elsy, Ilsa, Ilse**

**Elspeth** (EL-speth)
Scottish, Hebrew — *Consecrated to
God*
See Elizabeth.

**ELVIRA** — *Befriended by the elves*

**Elva** (EL-vuh)
Anglo-Saxon — *Elfin*
Feminine form of Alvin.
**Elffie, Ellfia, Elvi, Elvie**

**Elverda** (EL-ver-duh)
Latin — *Virginal*

**Elvira** (el-VĪ-ruh) or (EL-vir-uh)
Anglo-Saxon — *Befriended by the elves*
Feminine form of Elvin.
Entertainment: Character in
Mozart's opera *Don Giovanni;*
pop song *Elvira.*
**Elva, Elvera, Elvie, Elvina**

**Elysia** (e-LĒ-shuh)
Latin — *Sweetly blissful*
Mythological: Elysium was a
dwelling place of happy souls.

**Elza** (EL-zuh)
Hebrew — *God is my joy*

**Ema** (E-muh)
Polynesian — *Beloved*
**Emalaine, Emelin, Emelina,
Emiline, Emma**

**Emalia** (e-MĀ-lē-uh)
Polynesian, Latin — *Flirt*

**Emele** (e-MĒL)
Polynesian — *Industrious*
**Emilia, Emilie, Emily**

## Emily (EM-uh-lē)

Gothic— *Industrious*
Latin— *To flatter*
Feminine form of Emil.
Famous: Emily Post, American
 authority on etiquette.
Literature: Emily Bronte, author of
 *Wuthering Heights.*
**Aimil, Amalea, Amalia, Amalie,
Amelia, Amelie, Ameline,
Amelita, Amy, Eimile, Em,
Emalia, Emelda, Emelia,
Emelina, Emeline, Emelita,
Emelyne, Emera, Emilia, Emilie,
Emiline, Emlyn, Emlynn,
Emlynne, Emmaline, Emmalyn,
Emmalynn, Emmalynne,
Emmelyn, Emmey, Emmi,
Emmie, Emmy, Emmye, Milka**

## Emma (EM-uh)

German— *Universal*
Interesting: Emmy awards are
 given by the National Television
 Academy of Arts and Sciences.
Famous: Script on the Statue of
 Liberty was written by Emma
 Lazarus.
Literature: Heroine of *Madame
 Bovary,* by Flaubert.
**Em, Ema, Emmaline, Emmalyn,
Emmalynn, Emmalynne, Emmi,
Emmie, Emmy, Emmye**

## Emuna (e-MŌŌN-uh)

Hebrew— *Faithful*
**Emunah, Emuni, Emunie**

## Enid (Ē-ned)

Welsh, Latin— *Spotless purity or a
 woodlark*
Literature: Enid, heroine of the
 King Arthur legends in
 Tennyson's *Idylls of the King.*
**En, Enit**

## Erda (ER-duh)

German— *Earth*

## Erica (AIR-i-kuh)

Norwegian— *Ever powerful*
Feminine form of Eric.
Literature: Erica Jong, novelist.
Entertainment: Erica Morini,
 concert violinist.
**Enrica, Enrika, Erichci, Erika,
Erikie, Ricki, Rickie, Ricky, Rikki**

## Erin (AIR-in)

Gaelic— *Peace; Ireland*
**Erina, Erinna, Erlina, Erline**

## Erma (ER-muh)

See Irma.
Literature: Erma Bombeck, author
 and syndicated columnist.
**Ermina, Erminia, Erminie,
Hermione**

## Ernesta (er-NEST-uh)

Teutonic— *Intent in purpose*
Feminine form of Ernest.
**Erna, Ernaline, Ernestine**

## Ertha (ER-thuh)

Old English— *Child of the earth*
**Eartha, Erda, Erth, Herta,
Hertha**

## Esmeralda (ez-muh-RAL-duh)

Spanish, Greek— *The emerald*
**Esma, Esme, Ezmeralda**

## Estelle (e-STEL)

Latin, French— *A star*
Literature: Estella, heroine in
 Dickens' *Great Expectations.*
**Essie, Estel, Estele, Estell,
Estella, Esther, Estrella,
Estrellita, Hetty, Stella**

## Esther (ES-ter)

Persian— *A star*
Biblical: Esther, heroine in the Old
 Testament.
**Essa, Essie, Essy, Esta, Ester,
Estra, Estrella, Etti, Ettie, Etty,
Hester, Hesther, Hetty, Hettie**

**Ethel** (ETH-ul)
Teutonic— *Noble*
Entertainment: Ethel Barrymore,
    Ethel Merman, actresses.
**Ethelburga, Ethelda, Ethelin,
Ethelinda, Etheline, Ethelred,
Ethelyn, Ethyl, Ethyle**

**Etta** (ET-uh)
Teutonic— *Little*
Famous: Etta Place, Butch
    Cassidy's girlfriend.
**Etty, Henrietta**

**Eudocia** (ū-DŌ-shuh)
Greek— *Esteemed or honored*
**Eudosia, Eudoxia**

**Eudora** (ū-DOR-uh)
Greek— *Honored*
**Dora**

**Eugenia** (ū-JĒN-ē-uh)
Greek— *Femine form of Eugene.*
Famous: Empress Eugénie, wife of
    Napoleon III.
**Eugenie, Gena, Gene, Genia**

**Eulalia** (ū-LĀ-lē-uh)
French, Greek— *Fair of speech*
**Eula, Eulalee**

**Eunice** (Ū-nis)
Greek— *Happy victory*
Feminine form of Nicholas.
Biblical: Mother of Timothy.

**Euphenia** (ū-FĒN-ē-uh)
Greek— *Of fair fame*
**Effie, Euphemie, Phemie**

**Eurydice** (ū-RID-uh-sē)
Greek— *Broad separation*
Mythological: Wife of Orpheus.

**Eustacia** (ū-STĀ-shuh)
Latin— *Fruitful or tranquil*
**Eustaci, Stacey, Stacia, Stacie,
Stacy**

**Eva** (Ē-vuh)
Hebrew, Latin— *Life*
Literature: Little Eva, heroine of
    the novel *Uncle Tom's Cabin.*
Entertainment: Eva-Marie Saint,
    Eva Gabor, actresses.
**Evangelina, Eve, Zoe**

**Evadne** (e-VAD-nē)
Greek— *Fortunate*
Mythological: Evadne was a
    water-nymph.

**Evangeline** (ē-VAN-juh-lēn)
Greek— *Bearer of good news*
Literature: Heroine of the poem
    *Evangeline,* by Longfellow.
**Eva, Evangelia, Evangelina,
Evangellia, Eve**

**Evania** (ē-VĀN-ē-uh)
Greek— *Tranquil or untroubled*

**Evanthe** (Ē-vanth)
Greek— *A flower*
**Evadne**

**Eve** (ĒV)
Hebrew— *Life*
Biblical: Eve, the first mother.
Entertainment: Eve Arden, actress.
**Eba, Ebba, Eva, Evaleen,
Evelina, Eveline, Evelyn, Evey,
Evie, Evita, Evonne, Evvie,
Evvy, Evy**

**Ezrela** (EZ-rel-uh)
Hebrew— *God is my help*
**Ezraela, Ezraele, Ezraella, Ezraelle**

**Fabiola** (FĀB-ē-ō-luh) or
 (fab-ē-Ō-luh)
Feminine form of Fabian.
Famous: *Fabiola,* a portrait by Jean
 Jacques Henner; name of the
 Queen of Belgium.
**Fabia, Fabian, Fabrie,
Fabriene, Fabrienne**

**Faith** (FĀTH)
Latin — *Trusting or faithful*
Literature: Novelist Faith Baldwin.
**Fae, Fay, Faye, Fayth, Faythe**

**Falda** (FAL-duh)
Icelandic — *Folded wings*

**Fanchon** (FAN-shōn)
Teutonic — *Free*
Feminine form of Francis.

**Fancy** (FAN-sē)
Latin, Greek — *Fantasy*
See Frances.
Literature: *To Fancy,* by John Keats.
**Fancee, Fanci, Fancie, Fania,
Fanya**

**Fanny** (FAN-ē)
Teutonic — *Free*
Literature: Fanny Burney and
 Fannie Hurst, authors; Fanny
 Browne, Keat's love.
Entertainment: Fanny Brice,
 actress; musical *Fanny,* one of
 Pagnol's trilogy.
**Fan, Fanni, Fannie**

**Fanya** (FAN-yuh)
See Fayina.

**Farica** (fa-RĒ-kuh)
Teutonic — *Peaceful ruler*
**Fara, Farrah, Feriga**

**Farrah** (FAIR-uh)
English — *Beautiful*
Entertainment: Farrah Fawcett,
 actress.
**Farand, Farra, Farrand, Fayre**

**Fatima** (fa-TĒM-uh) or
 (FA-ti-muh)
Arabic — *Unknown*
Famous: Fatimah, daughter of
 Muhammad.
**Fatimah, Fatma**

**Faustina** (faw-STĒN-uh)
Latin — *Very lucky*
**Fausta, Faustine**

**Fawn** (FAWN)
French, Latin — *A young deer*
**Doe, Dorcas, Faunia, Fawnia,
Hinda, Sivia, Tabitha**

**Fay** (FĀ)
French — *Fairy*
Entertainment: Fay Bainter, Faye
 Emerson, Fay Wray, Faye
 Dunaway, actresses.
**Fae, Faina, Fanechka, Fanya,
Faye, Fayette, Fayina**

**Fayina** (fā-ĒN-uh)
Russian, Ukranian — *Free one*
**Faina, Fanechka, Fanya**

**Fayola** (fā-Ō-luh)
Nigerian — *Good luck*

**Fayre** (FAIR)
Old English — *Comely*

**Fedora** (fē-DOR-uh)
Greek — *Divine gift*
Feminine form of Theodore.
**Fedore, Fedoree, Fedoria, Fedorie**

**Felda** (FEL-duh)
Teutonic — *A field*

**Felicia** (fuh-LĒ-shuh)
Polish, Latin — *Happy*
Feminine form of Felix.
Entertainment: Felicia Farr, actress.
**Fela, Felice, Felicidad,
Felicie, Felicity, Felise,
Felita, Feliza, Felka**

**Femi** (FEM-ē)
Yoruban — *Love me*

**Fenella** (fi-NEL-uh)
Celtic — *White-shouldered*
**Fenelia, Fenelle, Fenellea**

**Fern** (FERN)
Old English — *Fern or feather*
**Ferne**

**Fernanda** (fer-NAN-duh)
Gothic — *Adventure*
Feminine form of Ferdinand.
**Ferdinanda, Ferdinande, Fern,
Fernande, Fernandine**

**Fidela** (fi-DEL-uh)
Latin — *Faithful woman*
**Fidelia, Fidelity, Fidella,
Fidellia**

**Fifine** (fē-FĒN)
French, Hebrew — *He shall add*
**Fifi, Fifin**

**Fionna** (fē-Ō-nuh)
Celtic — *The white*
**Fenella, Finella, Fiona, Fionnula**

**Flavia** (FLĀ-vē-uh)
Latin — *Blonde or yellow-haired*

**Flora** (FLOR-uh)
Latin — *A flower*
Mythological: Roman goddess of
spring and flowers.
**Fiora, Fiore, Fleur, Fleurette,
Flo, Flor, Flore, Floreen,
Florella, Floria, Florie, Floris,
Florri, Florrie, Florry, Flossie**

**Florence** (FLOR-ens)
Latin — *Blooming*
Famous: Florence Nightingale,
nurse and philanthropist.
Entertainment: Florence
Henderson, actress.
**Flo, Flor, Flora, Florance,
Flore, Florencia, Florentia,
Florenza, Flori, Floria,
Floridia, Florie, Florinada,
Florine, Floris, Florri,
Florrie, Florry, Floss,
Flossi, Flossie, Flossy, Flouna**

**Fonda** (FON-duh)
Spanish, Latin — *The profound*

**Fortuna** (for-CHOO-nuh)
Latin — *The fortunate*
Mythological: Roman goddess of
good luck.
**Fortune**

**Frances** (FRAN-ses)
Teutonic — *Free*
Feminine form of Francis.
**Fanny, Fereng, Ferike, Fran,
France, Francesca, Franci,
Francille, Francine, Francis,
Franciska, Francoise, Franke,
Frankie, Frannie, Franny**

**Freda** (FRĒ-duh)
Teutonic — *Peaceful*
Feminine form of Frederick.
**Frayda, Fredella, Freida,
Freidia, Frida**

**FLORENCE**—*Blooming*

**Frederica** (fred-er-Ē-kuh)
Teutonic—*Peaceful ruler*
Feminine form of Frederick.
**Farica, Fred, Freddie, Freddy,
Frederic, Fredericka,
Frederique, Fredrika, Frici,
Frida, Frieda, Friederika,
Rica, Ricki, Rickie, Ricky,
Rikki**

**Freya** (FRĀ-uh)
Norwegian—*Noble woman*
Literature: *Freya of the Severn Isles*,
   by Joseph Conrad.
**Fray, Fraya, Frayia, Frayie**

**Fritzi** (FRITZ-ē)
Teutonic—*Peaceful ruler*
Feminine form of Fritz.
**Fritz, Fritzie**

**Frodine** (FRŌ-dēn)
Teutonic— *Wise friend*
**Frodinne**

**Froma** (FRŌ-muh)
German— *Pious*
**Fromma, Frume, Frumie**

**Fulvia** (FUL-vē-uh)
Latin— *The blonde*

**Gabrielle** (GĀ-brē-el) or
(GĀ-bre-el-uh)
Hebrew— *God is my strength*
Feminine form of Gabriel.
Literature: Gabriela Mistral,
Chilean poet, winner of the
Noble Prize for Literature.
**Gabey, Gabi, Gabie, Gabriel,
Gabriela, Gabriell, Gabriella,
Gabriellia, Gabrila, Gaby, Gavra**

**Gada** (GĀ-duh)
Hebrew— *Lucky*

**Gafna** (GAF-nuh)
Hebrew— *Vine*

**Gail** (GĀL)
Old English— *Gay, lively*
See Abigail.
**Gael, Gale, Gayla, Gayle,
Gayleen, Gaylene**

**Gala** (GĀ-luh)
Scandinavian— *Singer*

**Galatea** (gal-a-TĒ-uh)
Greek— *Milk white*
Mythological: Galatea was an
ivory statue brought to life by
Aphrodite.

**Gali** (GĀ-lē)
Hebrew— *A fountain*
**Gal, Galice, Galit**

**Galina** (gā-LĒN-uh)
Russian— *Light*
See Helen.
Entertainment: Galina Ulanova,
ballet dancer; Galina
Visnevskaya, opera singer.
**Galinka, Galya, Galye, Jelena,
Jelene, Lena, Yalena**

**Galya** (GĀL-yuh)
Hebrew— *God has redeemed*

**Garda** (GAR-duh)
Teutonic— *The protected*

**Garland** (GAR-land)
French— *Garland*

**Garnet** (GAR-net)
Teutonic— *Radiant red jewel*
**Ganit, Garnette**

**Gauri** (GOW-rē)
Hindi— *Yellow*

**Gavrila** (ga-VRIL-uh)
Hebrew— *Heroine*

**Gay·** (GĀ)
English— *Lighthearted*
**Gae, Gaye**

**Gazit** (GĀZ-it)
Hebrew— *Hewn stone*

**GABRIELLE**—*God is my strength*

**Gemini** (JEM-i-nē) or (JEM-i-nī)
Greek—*Twin*
**Gemina**

**Gemma** (JEM-uh)
Latin, Italian—*Jewel*

**Gene** (JĒN)
See Eugenia.
**Gena, Gina**

**Geneva** (ja-NĒV-uh)
French—*The juniper tree*
**Gena, Genevra, Ginevra, Janeva**

**Genevieve** (JEN-uh-vēv)
Celtic—*White or pure*
Biblical: St. Genevieve is the patron
    saint of Paris.
Literature: Genevieve Taggard,
    American poet and critic.
Entertainment: Genevieve Bujold,
    actress.
**Gena, Geneva, Genevera,
Genevra, Gennie, Gina,
Ginny, Janeva, Jennie,
Jenny**

**Georgia** (JOR-juh)
Greek— *Husbandman*
Feminine form of George.
Entertainment: Song *Sweet Georgia
  Brown.*
**George, Georgeanna, Georgeanne,
Georagena, Georgetta, Georgette,
Georgi, Georgiana, Georgianna,
Georgianne, Georgie, Georgina,
Georgine, Giorgia**

**Geraldine** (JER-al-dēn)
Teutonic— *Ruler with a spear*
Feminine form of Gerald.
Entertainment: Geraldine Chaplin,
  actress and daughter of Charlie
  Chaplin; Geraldine Farrar,
  singer; Geraldine, character of
  comedian Flip Wilson.
**Geralda, Gerhardine, Geri,
Gerianna, Gerianne, Gerri,
Gerrie, Gerrilee, Gerry,
Gerrylee, Giralda, Jeraldine,
Jeralee, Jere, Jeri, Jerrie,
Jerrilee, Jerry, Jerrylee**

**Gerda** (GER-duh)
Scandinavian— *Protection*
**Garda, Gerdi**

**Germaine** (jer-MĀN)
French— *A German*
Celtic— *The shouter*
Literature: Germaine Greer,
  author.
**Germain, Germana**

**Gertrude** (GER-trōōd)
Teutonic— *Spear-maiden*
Literature: Gertrude Stein, author.
Entertainment: Gertrude
  Lawrence, actress.
**Gerda, Gert, Gerta, Gerti,
Gertie, Gertrud, Gertruda,
Gertrudis, Gerty, Trude,
Trudi, Trudie, Trudy**

**Gilada** (gil-Ā-duh)
Hebrew— *My joy is eternal*
Entertainment: Daughter of
  Rigoletto in Verdi's opera,
  *Rigoletto.*

**Gilberte** (GIL-bert) or
  (JIL-ber-tuh)
Teutonic— *Hostage*
Feminine form of Gilbert.
**Berta, Berte, Berti, Bertie,
Berty, Gigi, Gilberta, Gilbertina,
Gilbertine, Gill, Gilli, Gillie,
Gilly**

**Gilda** (GIL-duh)
Celtic— *God's servant*
Entertainment: Gilda Gray, Gilda
  Radner, actresses.
**Gilli**

**Gillian** (GIL-ē-un) or (JIL-ē-un)
Latin— *Youthful*
**Gill, Gillia, Jilana, Jile,
Jillis, Jilly, Julia, Juliana**

**Gimra** (JIM-ruh)
Hebrew— *Ripened*

**Gina** (JĒN-uh)
Japanese— *Silvery*
Entertainment: Gina Lollobrigida,
  actress.

**Ginger** (JIN-jer)
Latin— *Ginger*
Entertainment: Ginger Rogers,
  actress and dancer.
**Ginny, Jinger, Virginia**

**Giselle** (juh-ZEL)
Teutonic— *A promise*
Entertainment: Giselle McKenzie,
  singer.
**Gisela, Gisele, Gisella, Gizela**

**Gittel** (GIT-el)
Hebrew— *Maiden of the winepress*
**Gitel, Gitle, Gittle**

**Gizi** (JĒ-zē)
Hungarian— *Pledge*
**Giselle, Gizela, Gizike, Gizus**

## Gladys (GLAD-is)
Latin — *Frail*
Celtic — *Princess*
Feminine form of Claude.
Entertainment: Gladys Swarthout,
  actress; Gladys Knight and the
  Pips, rock group.
**Glad, Gladdie, Gladine,
Gladis, Glady, Gladyce**

## Glenna (GLEN-nuh)
Gaelic — *From the valley*
Feminine form of Glen.
Entertainment: Glynis Johns,
  Glenda Jackson, actresses.
**Glen, Glenda, Glenine, Glenn,
Glennie, Glennis, Glyn, Glynis,
Glynnis**

## Gloria (GLOR-ē-uh)
Latin — *The glorious*
Entertainment: Gloria Swanson,
  actress.
**Glori, Gloriana, Gloriane,
Glorianna, Glory**

## Goldie (GOL-dē)
Teutonic — *The golden-haired one*
Famous: Golda Meir, Prime
  Minister of Israel.
Entertainment: Goldie Hawn,
  actress.
**Golda, Goldi, Goldy**

## Grace (GRĀS)
Latin — *The graceful*
Mythological: The three graces of
  mythology are beauty, joy and
  grace.
Famous: Princess Grace of
  Monaco, the former Grace Kelly.
Entertainment: Grace Slick, rock
  singer; Gracie Burns, actress and
  wife of George Burns.
**Gracia, Gracie, Gracye, Grata,
Gratia, Gratiana, Gray, Grayce,
Grazia**

## Grania (GRAN-yuh)
Celtic — *Love*
Interesting: Gaelic folklore heroine.

## Gratiana (grat-ē-AN-uh)
Latin — *Divine favor*
**Grania, Grata, Gratia**

## Greer (GRĒR)
Greek — *Watchful*
Feminine form of Gregory.
Entertainment: Greer Garson,
  actress.

## Greta (GRET-uh)
Slavic — *A pearl*
Entertainment: Greta Garbo,
  actress.
**Gretchen, Grete, Gretel, Gretta**

## Griselda (gri-ZEL-duh)
Teutonic — *The heroine*
**Griseldis, Grishilda, Grishilde,
Grissel, Grizel, Grizelda,
Selda, Zelda**

## Guinevere (GWEN-a-vēr)
Welsh — *Fair lady*
Literature: Wife of King Arthur in
  the Round Table legend.
Famous: Oona Chaplin, wife of
  Charlie Chaplin.
**Gaynor, Gen, Genevieve,
Genna, Genni, Gennie,
Gennifer, Genny, Ginevra,
Guenevere, Guenna, Guinna,
Gwen, Gwendolen, Gwendolin,
Gwendolyn, Gweneth, Gwenith,
Gwenn, Gwenora, Gwenore,
Gwyn, Gwynne, Jan, Janifer,
Jen, Jenifer, Jennee,
Jenni, Jennie, Jennifer, Jenny,
Ona, Oona, Una, Winifred,
Winni, Winnie, Winny**

## Gussie (GUS-ē)
See Augusta.

## Gwendolyn (GWEN-dol-en)
Welsh — *White-browed*
Literature: Wife of Merlin in King
  Arthur legend.
**Guendolen, Guenna, Gwen,
Gwendolen, Gwenni, Gwennie,
Gwenny, Gwyn, Gwyneth,
Wanda, Wendie, Wendy,
Wynne**

**Gypsy** (JIP-se)
Old English— *Wander*
**Gipsy**

**Habibah** (ha-BE-buh)
Arabic— *Beloved*
Feminine form of Habib.
**Haviva**

**Hadassah** (huh-DOS-uh)
Hebrew— *Myrtle*
**Esther**

**Hadiya** (ha-DE-yuh) or
(HA-de-yuh)
Swahili— *Gift*

**Hagar** (HA-gar)
Hebrew— *One who flees*
Biblical: Mother of Ishmael.
**Haggar, Hagit**

**Haidee** (HA-de)
Greek— *Respectful*
Entertainment: Haidee Wright,
actress.

**Haila** (HA-luh)
German— *Healthy, strong*
Entertainment: Haila Stoddard,
actress.

**Haldis** (HAL-dis)
Teutonic— *Stone spirit*

**Hali** (HA-le)
Greek— *Sea*
Feminine form of Henry.
Entertainment: Hayley Mills,
actress.
**Halette, Halimeda, Hallie,
Hally, Hayley**

**Hallie** (HAL-e)
Greek— *Thinking of the sea*
**Hanrieta, Harriet**

**Halona** (ha-LO-nuh)
American Indian— *Of happy fortune*

**Hama** (HA-muh)
Japanese— *Shore*
**Hamako**

**Hana** (HA-nuh)
Japanese— *Flower*
**Hanae, Hanako, Hauna, Haunah**

**Haniya** (ha-NE-yuh) or
(HA-ne-yuh)
Hebrew— *Resting place*
**Hania, Hanice, Hanit**

**Hannah** (HAN-nuh)
Hebrew— *Grace, mercy or prayer*
Biblical: Mother of the prophet
Samuel.
**Hana, Hanna, Hanni, Hannie,
Hanny**

**Hannele** (ha-NEL)
German, Hebrew— *Merciful*
**Hanna, Hannah, Hanne, Hanni**

**Happy** (HA-pe)
English— *Happy child*

**Hara** (HAR-uh)
Sanskrit— *Seizer*
Mythological: Another name for
the god Shiva.

**Harmony** (HAR-mo-ne)
Latin— *Harmony*
**Harmonia, Harmonic**

## Harriet (HAR-ē-et)
French — *Ruler of the home*
Feminine form of Henry.
Literature: Harriet Beecher Stowe, author of *Uncle Tom's Cabin*.
**Harri, Harrie, Harrietta, Harriette, Harriot, Harriott, Hatti, Hattie, Hatty**

## Hasina (ha-SĒ-nuh)
Swahili — *Good*
Hebrew — *Strong*

## Hattie (HA-tē)
Teutonic — *Mistress of the home*
**Harriet, Hatti, Hatty, Henrietta**

## Hazel (HĀ-zel)
Old English — *Authority or commander*

## Heather (HETH-er)
Anglo-Saxon — *A flower*
Entertainment: Heather Angel, actress.
**Heath**

## Hebe (HĒ-bē)
Greek — *Youth*
Mythological: Cupbearer of the Gods.

## Hedda (HED-uh)
Teutonic — *War*
Literature: Hedda Gabler, heroine of one of Ibsen's plays.
Entertainment: Hedda Hopper, Hollywood columnist; Hedy Lamar, actress.
**Heda, Heddi, Heddie, Heddy, Hedvige, Hedwig, Hedwiga, Hedy**

## Hedia (HE-dē-yuh)
Hebrew — *The voice of God*
**Hedya**

## Hedva (HED-vuh)
Hebrew — *Joy*

## Hedwig (HED-wig)
German — *Strife*
**Edvig, Edwig, Hedda, Hedi, Hedvig, Hedy**

## Heidi (HĪ-dē)
German — *Battle-maiden*
Literature: *Heidi*, children's classic by Johanna Spuri.
**Heidie, Hilda**

## Helen (HEL-un)
Greek — *Light*
Famous: Helen of Troy.
Literature: Helen Keller, author.
Entertainment: Helen Hayes, actress; Helen Reddy, singer.
**Aila, Aileen, Ailene, Aleen, Eileen, Elaine, Elana, Elane, Elayne, Eleanor, Eleanore, Eleen, Elena, Elene, Eleni, Elenitsa, Elenore, Eleonora, Eleonore, Elianora, Elinor, Elinore, Ella, Elladine, Elle, Ellen, Ellene, Ellette, Elli, Ellie, Estonian, Galina, Helena, Helene, Helenka, Hellene, Helli, Ileana, Ileane, Ilene, Ilona, Ilonka, Jelena, Lana, Leanor, Leanore, Leen, Lena, Lenka, Lenora, Lenore, Leonora, Leonore, Leora, Lina, Lora, Nell, Nelli, Nellie, Nelly, Nora, Norah**

## Helga (HEL-guh)
Teutonic — *Holy*
**Olga**

## Helma (HEL-muh)
German — *Helmet*
Feminine form of William.
**Helmine, Mina, Minchen, Mine, Minna**

## Heloise (HEL-ō-ēs)
French — *Famous in battle*
Literature: *Hints from Heloise* newspaper column.

## Helsa (HEL-suh)
Hebrew — *Given to God*

**HESTER**—*A star*

**Henrietta** (hen-rē-ET-uh)
French—*Mistress of the home*
Feminine form of Henry.
Famous: Henrietta Szold,
  American Zionist leader.
Literature: Henriette, a heroine in
  Moliere's *Les Femmes Savantes.*
**Enrichetta, Enriqueta, Etta,
Etti, Ettie, Etty, Hatti, Hattie,
Hatty, Hendrika, Henka, Henrie,
Henrieta, Henriette, Henryetta,
Hetti, Hettie, Hetty, Yetta,
Yettie, Yetty**

**Hephzibah** (HEP-si-buh)
Hebrew—*My delight is in her*
Biblical: Wife of King Hezekiah.
Literature: Heroine of
  Hawthorne's *House of Seven
  Gables.*
**Hephziba, Hepsiba, Hepsibah,
Hepsibetha, Hepzibeth**

**Hera** (HAIR-uh)
Greek—*Queen of the Gods*

**Hermione** (her-MĪ-ō-nē)
Greek— *Of the earth*
Feminine form of Herman.
Mythological: Daughter of Helen
of Troy.
Literature: Queen in Shakespeare's
*The Winter's Tale.*
Entertainment: Hermione
Gingold, actress.
**Erma, Harmione, Hermia,
Hermina, Hermine, Herminia,
Hermionia**

**Hermosa** (her-MŌ-suh)
Spanish— *Beautiful*

**Hertha** (HERTH-uh)
Teutonic— *Mother earth*
Mythological: Earth goddess;
goddess of fertility and peace.
Entertainment: Eartha Kitt, singer.
**Eartha, Erda, Erta**

**Hesper** (HES-per)
Greek— *The evening star*

**Hester** (HES-ter)
Greek— *A star*
Literature: Hester Prynne, heroine
of Hawthorne's *The Scarlet Letter.*
**Hestia, Hettie, Hey**

**Hestia** (HES-tē-uh)
Persian— *A star*
Mythological: Goddess of the
home.

**Hetty** (HET-ē)
Persian— *A star*
**Esther, Hester**

**Hilary** (HIL-uh-rē)
Greek— *Cheerful or merry*
**Hillary**

**Hilda** (HIL-duh)
Teutonic— *Woman warrior*
Literature: Hilda Doolittle, poet.
**Hilde, Hildy**

**Hildegarde** (HIL-duh-gard)
Teutonic— *Fortress*
**Hilda, Hildagard, Hildagarde,
Hilde, Hildegaard**

**Hinda** (HIN-duh)
Anglo-Saxon— *Female deer*
**Hynda**

**Hoa** (HŌ-uh)
Vietnamese— *Flower*

**Holly** (HAWL-ē)
Old English— *Holly tree*
Literature: *Hollie Hobby,* heroine of
children's books and greeting
cards.
**Holley, Holli, Hollie**

**Honey** (HUN-ē)
German— *Sweet*
**Honora, Honoria**

**Honora** (on-OR-uh)
Latin— *Honorable*
**Honey, Honor, Honoria,
Honorine, Nora, Norah,
Norri, Norrie, Norry**

**Hope** (HŌP)
Anglo-Saxon— *Optimistic and
cheerful*
Entertainment: Hope Lang, actress.

**Hortense** (HOR-tens)
Latin— *Gardener*
**Hortensie, Ortensia**

**Hoshi** (HŌ-shē)
Japanese— *A star*

**Huberta** (Ū-ber-tuh)
Teutonic— *Bright-minded*
Feminine form of Hubert.

**Huette** (Ū-et)
Teutonic— *Small, intelligent girl*
Feminine form of Hugh.
**Hugette, Huguette**

**Hulda** (HUL-duh)
Austrian— *Gracious*
Hebrew— *Weasel*
**Huldah**

**Huyana** (hī-AN-uh)
Miwok Indian— *Rain falling*

**Hyacinth** (HĪ-uh-sinth)
Greek—*Hyacinth flower*
**Giacinta, Huacintha, Hyacinthe, Hyacinthia, Hyacinthie, Jacenta, Jacinda, Jacinta, Jacintha, Jacinthe, Jacynth**

**Hypatia** (hĪ-PA-tē-uh)
Greek—*Surpassing*

**Ianthe** (Ē-anth)
Greek—*Purple flower*
**Ian**

**Ida** (I-duh)
Old English—*Prosperous*
German—*Hard-working*
Literature: Heroine of *The Princess*, a poem by Tennyson.
Entertainment: Ida Lupino, actress.
**Idalia, Idalina, Idaline, Idelle, Idette**

**Idelia** (ī-duh-LĒ-uh)
Teutonic—*Noble*

**Idona** (Ī-DŌ-nuh)
Teutonic—*Industrious*

**Ignacia** (ig-NĀ-sē-uh)
Latin—*Ardent or fiery*
**Ignatia, Ignatzia**

**Ilana** (i-LA-nuh)
Hebrew—*Big tree*

**Ilene** (ī-LĒN)
See Aileen or Eileen.
**Iline, Illene, Illona**

**Ilka** (IL-kuh)
Slavic—*Hard-worker*
Literature: Ilka Chase.
**Ilke, Milka**

**Ilona** (IL-ō-nuh)
Hungarian—*Beautiful*
**Ica, Ila, Ilka, Ilonka, Ilu, Iluska, Lenci**

**Imala** (IM-al-uh) or (i-MĀ-luh)
North American
Indian—*Disciplinarian*

**Imogene** (IM-ō-jēn)
Latin—*An image*
Literature: Heroine in *Cymbeline*, by Shakespeare.
Entertainment: Imogene Coca, comedienne.
**Emogene, Imogen, Imojean**

**Ina** (Ī-nuh)
See Katherine.
Famous: Ina Coolbrith, stateswoman and poetess.
Entertainment: Ina Claire, comedienne.

**Ines** (ī-NEZ)
Greek—*Chaste*
Literature: Mother of Don Juan in Byron's poem.
**Inesita, Inez, Ynes, Ynez**

**Ingrid** (ING-rid)
Swedish—*Hero's daughter*
Entertainment: Inga Swenson, Inger Stevens, Ingrid Bergman, actresses; Inge Borkh, singer.
**Inga, Inge, Inger**

**Iona** (ī-Ō-nuh)
Greek—*A violet*
Literature: Heroine of *The Last Days of Pompeii*, by Sir Edward Bulwer-Lytton.

**IRIS** — *The rainbow*

## Iphigenia (if-uh-juh-NĒ-uh)
Greek — *Sacrifice*
Mythological: Maiden to be
sacrificed, but rescued by Artemis.

## Irene (ī-RĒN)
Greek — *Peace*
Famous: Scientists Irene and
Frederic Joliot Curie, winners of
Noble Prize in medicine.
Entertainment: Irene Dunn,
actress.

## Iris (Ī-ris)
Greek — *The rainbow*
Literature: Iris Murdoch, novelist.
**Irisa, Irita**

## Irma (ER-muh)
German — *Power*
**Erma, Erme, Irme,
Irmina, Irmine**

## Isabel (IZ-uh-bel)
Spanish — *Consecrated to God*
Historical: Queen Isabella sent
Christopher Columbus on his
voyage to the new world.
Literature: Poem *Isabella* or *The Pot
of Basil.*
**Belia, Belicia, Belita, Bell,
Bella, Belle, Ibbie, Ibby, Isa,
Isabeau, Isabelita, Isabella,
Isabelle, Iseabal, Issi, Issie,
Issy, Izabel, Ysabel**

## Isadora (iz-uh-DOR-uh)
Greek — *Gift of the moon*
Entertainment: Isadora Duncan,
dancer.
**Dora, Dori, Dory, Isidora,
Issy, Izzy**

## Isis (Ī-sis)
Egyptian — *Supreme goddess*
Interesting: Egyptian goddess of
the beginning of time and
mother of all things.

## Isolda (iz-ŌL-duh)
Celtic — *The fair*
Literature: *Tristan and Isolde,* by
Gottfried Von Strassburg.
**Isolde, Isolt, Yseult**

## Ivana (i-VA-nuh)
Hebrew — *God is gracious gift*
Feminine form of Ivan.
**Ivane**

## Ivilla (i-VIL-uh)
Afro-American — *I will arise again*

## Ivy (Ī-vē)
Greek, German — *Ivy tree*
Literature: Ivy Compton-Burnett,
British novelist.
**Ivie, Ivi**

## Izusa (i-ZOO-zuh)
North American Indian — *White
snow*

## Jacinda (ha-SIN-duh)
Greek — *Beautiful, comely*
**Jacenta, Jacinta, Jacynth**

## Jacoba (JĀ-kō-buh) or
(YAK-uh-buh)
Hebrew — *Supplanter*
Feminine form of Jacob.
**Jacki, Jackie, Jacky,
Jacobina, Jacobine**

## Jacqueline (JAK-wil-in)
Hebrew — *Supplanter*
French — *Little Jacques*
Famous: Jacqueline Kennedy,
former First Lady.
Entertainment: Jaclyn Smith,
Jacqueline Bisset, actresses.
**Jackelyn, Jacki, Jackie, Jacklin,
Jackquelin, Jackqueline, Jacky,
Jaclin, Jaclyn, Jacque,
Jacquelyn, Jacquetta,
Jacquette, Jacquie,
Jaquenetta, Jaquenette, Jaquith**

## Jade (JĀD)
Hebrew — *Wise*
**Jadah, Jadda**

## Jael (JĀ-el)
Hebrew — *Mountain goat*

## Jafit (JAF-it)
Hebrew — *Lovely*

**Jaimie** (JĀ-mē)
French — *I love*
Jaime

**Jambu** (JAM-boo)
Hindi — *Rose apple tree*

**Jamie** (JĀ-mē)
Feminine form of James.
Jamee, Jamesina, Jami, Jayme,
Jaymee

**Jamila** (juh-MEL-uh)
Muslim — *Beautiful*

**Jane** (JĀN)
Hebrew — *God's gracious gift*
Feminine form of John.
Famous: *Jane Eyre,* novel by
    Charlotte Bronte; *Pride and*
    *Prejudice,* by Jane Austen; Jane,
    mate of Tarzan, in novel by
    Edgar Rice Burroughs.
Entertainment: Jane Pauley,
    newscaster; Jane Wyman, Jane
    Fonda, Jane Alexander, actresses;
    Janis Joplin, singer and
    songwriter.
Gene, Gianina, Giovanna, Jan,
Jana, Janeczka, Janel, Janela,
Janella, Janelle, Janet, Janetta,
Janette, Janey, Jania, Janice,
Janie, Janina, Janine, Janis,
Janith, Janka, Janna, Jannel,
Janyte, Jasisa, Jayne, Jean,
Jeanette, Jeannine, Jenda,
Jenica, Jeniece, Jenni, Jennie,
Jenny, Jess, Jessie, Jinny,
Jo-Ann, JoAnn, Joan, Joane,
Joanna, Joanne, Joanta, Joasia,
Joeann, Johanna, Joni, Jonie,
Juana, Juanita, Sheena, Shena,
Sine, Vania, Vanya, Zanela,
Zanna

**Janet** (JAN-it)
See Jane.
Entertainment: Janet Blair, Janet
    Leigh, actresses; Janis Ian, singer.
Janice, Janis, Janot, Jessie

**Jardena** (jar-DE-nuh)
Hebrew — *To flow downward*
Feminine form of Jordan.

**Jasmine** (JAZ-min)
Persian — *Fragrant flower*
Jamina, Jasmin, Jasmina, Jemi,
Jemie, Jemmy, Jessamine,
Jessamyn, Yasmin

**Jay** (JĀ)
Latin — *Jaybird*
Jae, Jaie, Jaye

**Jayne** (JĀN)
Hindi — *Victorious*
Entertainment: Jayne Mansfield,
    actress.

**Jean** (JĒN)
See Jane.
Famous: Jeane Dixon, ESP-user
    and fortuneteller.
Entertainment: Jean Arthur, Jean
    Stapleton, Jeanette Nolan,
    actresses.
Gene, Jeane, Jeanette, Jeanie,
Jeanne, Jeannette, Jeannine,
Joan, Nina, Ninon

**Jemima** (juh-MĪ-muh)
Hebrew — *A dove*
Jamima, Jemie, Jemimah,
Jemmie, Jemmy

**Jennifer** (JEN-i-fer)
Welsh — *White, fair*
Entertainment: Jennifer O'Neill,
    actress.
Genna, Genni, Gennie, Gennifer,
Genny, Jen, Jennee, Jenni, Jennie,
Jenny

**Jenny** (JE-nē)
See Jane.
Entertainment: Jenny Lind, opera
    singer.
Janey, Jen, Jennie, Jinny

**Jensine** (jen-SEN)
Danish, Hebrew — *God is gracious*

**Jerri** (JER-ē)
See Geraldine.
**Jeraldine, Jerrie, Jerry, Jeryl, Jerylin**

**Jessica** (JES-i-kuh)
Hebrew — *Wealthy*
Feminine form of Jesse.
Entertainment: Jessica Savitch, newscaster; Jessica Dragonette, singer; Jessica Tandy, heroine of Tennesee Williams' *A Streetcar Named Desire.*
**Jess, Jessalin, Jessalyn, Jesse, Jessi, Jessie, Jessy**

**Jewel** (JOO-ul)
Latin — *Precious stone*
**Jewell, Jewelle**

**Jill** (JIL)
See Julia.
Famous: Queen Juliana of the Netherlands.
Literature: Nursery rhyme, *Jack and Jill.*
Entertainment: Jill Ireland, Jill St. John, Jill Clayburgh, actresses.
**Jillana, Jillen, Jilleun, Juliana**

**Jinny** (JI-nē)
See Virginia.
**Jenni, Jennie, Jenny, Jin, Jinnie**

**Joan** (JŌN)
Hebrew — *God's gracious joy*
Famous: Joan of Arc.
Literature: *St. Joan,* play by George Bernard Shaw; Jo, heroine of Louisa May Alcott's *Little Women.*
Entertainment: Joanne Woodward, Joan Crawford, actresses; Joan Rivers, comedienne.
**Jo, Joana, Joanna, Joanne, Jodi, Jodie, Jody, Joeann, Johanna**

**Jobina** (jō-BĒ-nuh)
American — *Persecuted*
Feminine form of Job.
**Jobey, Jobi, Jobie, Joby, Jobye, Jobyna**

**Jocelyn** (JOS-len)
Latin — *Merry*
Old English — *Just*
**Jocelin, Joceline, Josselyan, Josselyn, Joyce, Joycelin, Lyn, Lynn**

**Jody** (JŌ-dē)
See Joan.
Entertainment: Jodie Foster, actress; Joni Mitchell, singer.
**Jodee, Jodi, Jodie, Joni, Judith**

**Joella** (jō-EL-uh)
Hebrew — *The Lord is willing*
Feminine form of Joel.
**Joela, Joelle, Joellen, Jola, Jolanka, Jolanta, Joli, Yolanda**

**Jolan** (JŌ-lan)
Greek — *Violet blossom*

**Jolie** (JŌ-lē)
French — *Pretty*
**Jolan, Joli, Joly**

**Joline** (JŌ-lēn)
English — *He will increase*
Feminine form of Joseph.

**Jonine** (jō-NĒN)
Hebrew — *Dove*
**Jonati, Jonina, Jonit, Yonina, Yonit, Yonita**

**Jora** (JOR-uh)
Hebrew — *Autumn rain*
**Jorah**

**Josephine** (JŌ-sa-fēn)
Hebrew — *He shall increase*
Feminine form of Joseph.
Famous: Napoleon's wife, Empress Josephine.
**Fifi, Fifine, Fina, Jo, Joette, Joey, Joline, Josefa, Josefina, Josepha, Josephina, Josi, Josie, Josy**

**Joy** (JOI)
Latin — *Merry*
**Joya**

**JORA** — *Autumn rain*

**Joyce** (JOIS)
Latin — *Rejoicing*
Famous: Dr. Joyce Brothers,
  psychologist.
Literature: Joyce Carol Oates,
  author.
**Jocelyn, Joice, Joyous**

**Juanita** (wa-NĒ-tuh)
See Jane.
Entertainment: Song *Juanita*.

**Judith** (JOO-dith)
Hebrew — *Admired*
Entertainment: Dame Judith
  Anderson, actress.
**Guiditta, Jodi, Jodie, Jody,
Judi, Judie, Juditha, Judy, Judye**

**Judy** (JOO-dē)
See Judith.
Literature: Judy Blume, children's author.
Entertainment: Judy Garland, Judy Holiday, actresses.

**Julia** (JOO-lē-uh)
Latin— *Youthful*
Feminine form of Julius.
Famous: Julia Child, gourmet cook and author.
Literature: Julia Peterkin, author.
Entertainment: Julia Marlowe, actress.
**Giulia, Giulietta, Joletta, Julee, Juli, Juliana, Juliane, Juliann, Julianne, Julie, Julienne, Juliet, Julieta, Julietta, Juliette, Julina, Juline, Julita, Julius**

**Julie** (JOO-lē)
See Julia.
Entertainment: Julie Christie, Julie Harris, Julie Andrews, Julie Newmar, actresses.
**Juliene, Julienne**

**Juliet** (joo-lē-ET)
See Julia.
Literature: Heroine of Shakespeare's *Romeo and Juliet*.
Entertainment: Juliet Prowse, modern dancer.
**Julietta, Juliette, Julita**

**June** (JOON)
Latin— *Youthful*
Entertainment: June Lockhart, actress.
**Junetta, Junette, Junia, Junieta, Junina, Junis**

**Juno** (JOO-nō)
Latin— *Queen of the gods*
Mythological: Goddess of heaven, wife of Jupiter. Also a special guard of women.

**Justine** (just-ĒN)
Latin— *Just*
Feminine form of Justin.
**Giustina, Justina, Justinn, Tina**

**Jyotis** (JĪ-ō-tis)
East Indian— *Sun's light*
**Jiotis**

**Kachina** (ka-CHĒ-nuh)
North American Indian— *Sacred dancer*

**Kagami** (ka-GAM-ē)
Japanese— *Mirror*

**Kaimi** (ka-Ē-mē)
Polynesian— *The seeker*

**Kala** (KAL-uh)
Hindi— *Black or time*

**Kalama** (ka-LAM-uh)
Polynesian— *The flaming torch*

**Kalanit** (ka-LAN-it)
Hebrew— *Flower*

**Kali** (KĀL-ē)
Sanskrit— *Energy*
Hindi— *The black goddess*
Interesting: Hindi mother goddess.

**Kalila** (kuh-LĪ-luh)
Arabic— *Girlfriend or sweetheart*

**Kalinda** (ka-LIN-duh)
Hindi— *The sun*
**Kalindi**

**Kalyca** (ka-LĒ-kuh)
Greek— *Rosebud*
**Kali, Kalica, Kalika, Kaly**

**Kama** (KAM-uh)
Hindi— *Love*
Mythological: This goddess rode a
parrot and shot flower-tipped
love arrows from a bow.

**Kamaria** (ka-MAR-ē-uh)
Swahili— *Like the moon*

**Kameko** (ka-MĒ-kō)
Japanese— *Child of the tortoise*
Mythological: The tortoise
symbolizes longevity.

**Kanani** (ka-NA-nē)
Polynesian— *The beauty*

**Kanene** (ka-NĒN)
African— *A little thing in the eye is
big*

**Kanoa** (ka-NŌ-uh)
Polynesian— *The free one*

**Kanya** (KON-yuh)
Hindi— *Virgin*

**Kapua** (ka-POO-uh)
Polynesian— *Blossom*

**Kapule** (ka-POOL)
Polynesian— *A prayer*

**Kara** (KAIR-uh)
Greek— *Pure*
**Karena, Katharine**

**Karen** (KAIR-en)
Greek, Danish— *Pure*
Famous: Karen Horney,
psychiatrist.
Entertainment: Karen Black,
actress; Karen Carpenter, singer
and songwriter.
**Caren, Carin, Karena, Kari,
Karin, Karna**

**Kasia** (KĀZ-yuh)
Polish, Greek— *Pure*
**Kassia**

**Kate** (KĀT)
Greek— *Pure*
Entertainment: Kate Smith, singer,
Kate Jackson, actress.
**Katee, Kati, Katie**

**Katherine** (KATH-er-in)
Greek— *Pure*
Historical: Queen Catherine the
Great, of Russia.
Entertainment: Katherine
Hepburn, Katherine Cornell,
Katherine Ross, Kitty Carlisle,
actresses; Katerina Valenti,
singer.
**Caisie, Caitlin, Caitrin, Caren,
Carin, Caron, Caryn, Cass,
Cassy, Cataina, Catarina, Cate,
Catee, Caterina, Catha, Catharina,
Catharine, Cathe, Cathee,
Catherina, Catherine, Cathi,
Cathie, Cathleen, Cathlene,
Cathrine, Cathryn, Cathy,
Cathyleen, Cati, Catriona,
Caty, Caye, Ekaterina,
Ekaterine, Karen, Karena,
Kari, Karin, Karna, Kass,
Kassi, Kassia, Kassie, Kata,
Katalin, Katalina, Kate,
Katerina, Katerine, Katey,
Katha, Katharine, Kathe,
Kathi, Kathie, Kathleen,
Kathryn, Kathy, Kathye,
Katie, Katina, Katinka,
Katrinka, Katrinkie, Katti,
Katuscha, Katushka, Katya,
Kay, Kaye, Ketti, Kettie,
Ketty, Kit, Kitti, Kittie, Kitty**

**KAMEKO**—*Child of the tortoise*

**Kathleen** (kath-LĒN)
See Katherine.
Entertainment: Song *I'll Take You Home Again, Kathleen.*

**Kathy** (KATH-ē)
See Katherine.
**Kathleen**

**Kaula** (ka-OO-luh)
Polynesian—*Prophet*

**Kavindra** (ka-VIN-druh)
Hindi—*Mighty poet*

**Kay** (KĀ)
See Katherine.
Literature: Kay Boyle, novelist and short-story writer.

**Kei** (KĒ-uh)
Japanese—*Rapture*
**Keiko**

**Kelly** (KEL-ē)
Gaelic—*Warrior woman*
**Keelia, Keely, Kelley, Kelli, Kellia, Kellie**

**Kelsey** (KEL-sē)
Norwegian— *From the ship island*
**Kelci, Kelcie, Kelcy, Kelda,
Kelsi, Kelsy**

**Kendra** (KEN-druh)
Anglo-Saxon— *The knowing woman*

**Kim** (KIM)
Old English— *Chief, ruler*
Entertainment: Kim Novak, Kim
  Hunter, actresses.

**Kimama** (ki-MAW-muh)
Shoshone Indian— *Butterfly*

**Kimberly** (KIM-ber-lē)
Old English— *From the royal fortress
  meadow*
**Cimberly, Cymbre, Kim,
Kimbra, Kimbre, Kimmie**

**Kira** (KĒR-uh)
Persian— *Sun*

**Kirby** (KIR-bē)
Anglo-Saxon— *From the church town*
**Kirbee, Kirbie**

**Kirima** (ka-RĒ-muh)
Eskimo— *A hill*
**Kirimia**

**Kirsten** (KER-sten)
Scandinavian— *The anointed one*
**Kirsti, Kirstin, Kristie**

**Kisa** (KĒ-suh)
Russian— *Kitty*

**Kitty** (KI-tē)
See Katherine.
Literature: *Kitty Foyle*, novel by
  Christopher Morley.
Entertainment: Miss Kitty, heroine
  of TV series *Gunsmoke*.

**Kiva** (KĒ-vuh)
Russian, Hebrew— *Hope*

**Klarika** (kla-RĒ-kuh)
Hungarian— *Brilliant*
**Klara, Klarissa, Klarysa**

**Kolina** (kō-LĒN-uh)
Swedish, Greek— *Pure*
**Katina, Kola**

**Koma** (KŌ-muh)
Japanese— *Filly*
**Komako**

**Kora** (KOR-uh)
Greek— *Maiden*
**Cora, Corabel, Corabella,
Corabelle, Corella, Corena,
Corene, Coretta, Corette,
Corey, Cori, Corie, Corina,
Corinna, Corinne, Coriss,
Corissa, Corrina, Corrine,
Corry, Kore, Koren, Kori, Korie**

**Kristen** (KRIS-ten)
See Christine.
Entertainment: Kristy McNichols,
  actress.
**Krista, Kristel, Kristi,
Kristian, Kristiana,
Kristin, Kristine, Kristy,
Krysta, Krytyna**

**Kyle** (KĪL)
Gaelic— *Comely*
Entertainment: Kyle MacDonnell,
  actress.

**Lahela** (la-HĒ-luh)
Polynesian, Hebrew—*Ewe*
**Rachel, Rahela**

**Lala** (LĀ-luh)
Slavak—*Tulip*

**Lalage** (la-LAWJ)
Greek—*Free of speech*

**Lalasa** (la-LAW-suh)
Hindi—*Love*

**Lana** (LA-nuh)
Polynesian—*To float*
Entertainment: Lana Turner, actress.
**Lane, Lanna, Lanny, Linette, Linnette**

**Lane** (LĀN)
English—*From the narrow road*
Entertainment: Lanie Kazan, actress.
**Laney, Lanie, Lanni, Lanny**

**Lani** (LA-nē)
Polynesian—*Sky*

**Lara** (LAR-uh)
Latin—*Well-known*
Mythological: Nymph punished for her talkativeness.
Literature: Lara, heroine in the novel *Dr. Zhivago*.
**Laraine, Laura, Lorriane**

**Laraine** (luh-RĀN)
Latin—*Sea-bird*
Entertainment: Lorraine Day, Laraine Newman, actresses.
**Lara, Larina, Larine, Laura, Lorraine**

**Lari** (lar-Ē)
English—*Crowned with laurel*

**Larissa** (lar-RĒ-suh) or (la-RIS-uh)
Russian, Greek—*Cheerful one*
**Lacey, Lara, Larochka, Lissa**

**Lark** (LARK)
English—*Skylark*

**Laura** (LOR-uh)
Latin—*Crown of laurel*
Entertainment: Lauren Bacall, actress.
**Lari, Laure, Laureen, Laurel, Laurella, Lauren, Laurena, Laurene, Lauretta, Laurette, Laurice, Laurie, Lora, Loralie, Loree, Loreen, Lorelie, Loren, Lorena, Lorene, Lorenza, Loretta, Lorette, Lori, Lorie, Lorinda, Lorine, Lorita, Lorna, Lorne, Lorri, Lorrie, Lorry**

**Laurel** (LOR-ul)
Greek—*To gain the laurels*
Interesting: In England, the official court poet is called Poet Laureate.
Entertainment: Laurette Taylor, Lauren Hutton, actresses; Laurel Hurley, Metropolitan Opera singer.
**Laurell, Lauren, Laurette**

**Laverne** (luh-VERN)
French—*Springlike*
Mythological: Goddess of profit or gain.
Literature: Wife of Aeneas in Virgil's *Aeneid*.
Entertainment: Main character in show, *Laverne and Shirley*.
**LaVerne, Laverna, Lavina, Lavinia**

**Leah** (LĒ-uh)
Hebrew — *Weary*
Biblical: Wife of Jacob.
Entertainment: Leigh
  Taylor-Young, actress.
**Lea, Leda, Lee, Leigh,
Lia, Lida**

**Leandra** (lē-AN-druh)
Latin — *Like a lioness*
**Leodora, Leoine, Leoline,
Leona, Leonanie, Leonelle**

**Leanne** (lē-AN)
Combination of the names Lee and
  Ann.
**Liana, Lianne**

**Leda** (LĒ-duh)
Greek — *Lady*
Mythological: Leda and the Swan.
**Alida, Leah, Leta, Lettitia**

**Lee** (LĒ)
Gaelic — *Poetic*
Old English — *From the pasture
  meadow*
Entertainment: Lee Grant, Lee
  Remick, actresses.
**Leann, Leanna, LeeAnn, Leigh**

**Leila** (LĀ-luh)
Arabic — *Black*
Literature: Slave girl in Byron's
  narrative poem, *The Giaour.*
**Deliah, Layla, Leela, Leilah,
Lela, Lelah, Leland, Lelia,
Lilla, Lillian**

**Leilani** (lā-LON-ē)
Polynesian — *Heavenly child*

**Lemuela** (LEM-ūl-uh)
Hebrew — *Dedicated to God*

**Lena** (LĒ-nuh)
Latin — *Temptress*
Hebrew — *Dwelling*
Entertainment: Lena Horne, singer
  and actress.
**Lenette, Lina**

**Lenita** (le-NĒ-tuh)
Latin — *Gentle or mild*
**Leneta, Lenetta**

**Lenore** (le-NOR)
See Helen.
Entertainment: Lenore Ulric,
  actress.
**Lenore, Leonora, Leonore,
Nora, Norah**

**Leona** (lē-Ō-nuh)
Latin — *Lion*
Entertainment: Leonie Rysanek,
  Metropolitan Opera singer.
**Leoine, Leola, Leone,
Leonelle, Leonie**

**Leonora** (lē-uh-NOR-uh)
See Helen.
Literature: Leonora Speyer,
  Pulitzer Prize winner in poetry.
**Leonore, Nora, Norah**

**Leontine** (LĒ-on-tīn)
Latin — *Brave as a lion*
Feminine form of Leo.
Entertainment: Leontyne Price,
  Metropolitan Opera singer.
**Leontyne**

**Leora** (lē-OR-uh)
Greek — *Light*

**Leota** (lē-Ō-tuh)
Teutonic — *Women of the people*
**Leoda**

**Leotie** (lē-Ō-tē)
North American Indian — *Prairie
  flower*

**Leslie** (LEZ-lē)
Scottish, Gaelic — *From the gray fort*
Entertainment: Leslie Caron,
  actress.
**Les, Lesley, Lesli, Lesly,
Lez, Lezlie**

**LEILANI**—*Heavenly child*

**Leticia** (luh-TI-shuh)
Spanish, Latin—*Gladness*
Literature: Heroine of Mary
  Robert Rinehart's *Tish* series.
**Leta, Letitia, Lettie, Letty,
Tish**

**Levana** (le-VAN-nuh)
Latin—*Rising sun*

**Levia** (la-VĒ-uh)
Hebrew—*To join*

**Levina** (la-VĒN-uh)
Latin—*Flash, lightning*

**Lexine** (leks-ĒN)
Greek—*Helper of mankind*
**Lex, Lexie, Lexy**

**Leya** (LĀ-uh)
Spanish—*Loyalty to the law*

**Lian** (LĪ-an)
Chinese—*The graceful willow*

**Libby** (LIB-ē)
Hebrew—*Consecrated to God*
Entertainment: Libby Holman,
actress.
**Lib, Libbey, Libbie**

**Lida** (LĪ-duh)
Slavic—*Beloved of people*
**Lidiya, Lyda, Lydia**

**Lila** (LĪ-luh)
Hindi—*Free will of God*
**Leopoldine**

**Lilian** (LIL-ē-un)
Greek—*A lily*
Interesting: In Egypt, the lily is
considered a symbol of life and
resurrection.
Entertainment: Lillian Gish,
actress; Lillian Hellman,
playwright.
**Lib, Lila, Lilac, Lilas, Lili,
Lilia, Liliane, Lilias, Lilis,
Lilith, Lilli, Lillie, Lilly,
Lily, Lilyan, Luika**

**Lilka** (LIL-kuh)
Polish—*Famous warrior-maiden*
**Liza, Lodoiska, Ludisa,
Ludka, Ludwika, Luisa**

**Lily** (LIL-ē)
Latin—*Lily flower*
Entertainment: Lily Pons,
Metropolitan Opera singer; Lilli
Palmer, Lily Tomlin, actresses.
**Lil, Lili, Lilith, Lilli,
Lillian, Lillie, Lilly**

**Linda** (LIN-duh)
Latin—*Beautiful*
Entertainment: Lynda Carter,
Linda Darnell, Linda Blair,
actresses; Linda Ronstadt, singer.
**Lind, Lindi, Lindie, Lindy,
Lynda, Lynde, Lyndy**

**Lindsay** (LIND-zē)
Old English—*From the linden-tree
island*
Entertainment: Lindsay Wagner,
actress.

**Linette** (lin-ET)
Celtic—*Graceful*
French—*Linnet bird*
**Linet, Linnet, Linnett,
Lynette, Lynnet, Lynnette**

**Linnea** (lin-NĀ-yuh)
Norwegian—*Lime tree*
**Lynnea**

**Lisa** (LĒ-suh)
Hebrew—*Consecrated to God*
Interesting: Tin Lizzie, nickname
for an early motor car.
Entertainment: Liza Minnelli,
singer and actress.
**Leesa, Lise, Lisetta, Lisette,
Liza, Lizetta, Lizette, Lizzie**

**Lissa** (LIS-uh)
English—*Honey*

**Lissilma** (lis-SIL-muh)
North American Indian—*Butterfly*

**Livia** (LIV-ē-uh)
Latin—*The olive*
Historical: Wife of Augustus.
**Levvie, Livius**

**Lois** (LŌ-is)
Greek—*Battle-maiden*
Entertainment: Lois Lane,
character in *Superman* series.

**Lokelani** (lō-kuh-LAN-ē)
Polynesian—*Heavenly rose*

**Lola** (LŌ-luh)
Spanish—*Strong woman*
Literature: *Lolita,* novel by
Vladimir Nabokov.
Entertainment: Lola Falana,
actress.
**Loleta, Lolita, Lolite, Lulita**

**Lolly** (LOL-ē)
See Laura.

**Lolotea** (LŌ-lō-tē-uh)
Zuni Indian—*Gift from God*

**Lomasi** (lō-MAS-ē)
North American Indian—*Pretty
flower*

117

**Lona** (LŌ-nuh)
English—*Single or alone*
Entertainment: Loni Anderson,
actress.
**Lonee, Loni, Lonni, Lonnie**

**Lora** (LOR-uh)
See Laura.
**Laura, Lorella, Lorelle, Lori**

**Lorelei** (LOR-uh-li)
German—*Alluring*
Interesting: In German folklore,
Lorelei was a siren of the Rhine.
Literature: Lorelei, heroine of
Anita Loos's novel *Gentlemen
Prefer Blondes.*
**Lorilee, Lura, Lurette, Lurleen,
Lurlene, Lurline**

**Lorelle** (LOR-el)
Latin, Teutonic—*Little*

**Lorena** (lor-Ē-nuh)
Latin—*The laurel*
Feminine form of Lawrence.
**Laura, Lurena**

**Loretta** (lor-ET-uh)
See Laura.
Entertainment: Loretta Young,
actress; Loretta Lynn, singer.
**Lori, Lorie, Lorrie**

**Lorna** (LOR-nuh)
Latin—*The laurel*
Literature: *Lorna Doone,* by
Richard D. Blackmore.

**Lorraine** (lor-ĀN)
French, Teutonic—*Famous in battle*
Entertainment: Lorraine Day,
actress.
**Laraine, Lorain, Loraine,
Lori, Lorrayne**

**Lottie** (LOT-ē)
See Charlotte.
Entertainment: Lotte Lehmann,
opera singer.
**Lotta, Lotte, Lotti, Lotty**

**Lotus** (LŌ-tus)
Egyptian, Greek—*Lotus flower*

**Louella** (loo-EL-uh)
See Louise.
**Lou, Louela, Luella**

**Louise** (loo-ĒS)
Teutonic—*Battle-maiden*
Feminine form of Louis.
Literature: Louisa May Alcott,
author of *Little Women.*
Entertainment: Louise Lasser,
actress.
**Alison, Allison, Aloise, Aloisea,
Aloysia, Eloisa, Eloise, Heloise,
Lisette, Lois, Loise, Lola,
Lotita, Lou, Louisa, Louisette,
Loyce, Lu, Ludovika, Luisa,
Luise, Lulita, Lulu**

**Love** (LUV)
English—*Love*

**Luana** (loo-A-nuh)
German, Hebrew—*Graceful woman
warrior*
**Lawana, Lewanna, Louanna,
Louanne, Luane, Luanni, Luwana**

**Luba** (LOO-buh)
Slavic—*Love*
**Lubba**

**Lucasta** (loo-CAS-tuh)
Latin—*Light, chaste*
Literature: Name invented by
Richard Lovelace for Lucy
Sacheverell.
**Lucastia, Lukasta, Lukastia**

**Lucerne** (loo-SERN)
Latin—*Life*

**Lucia** (LOO-chē-uh) or
(loo-SĒ-uh)
Latin—*Light*
Entertainment: Donizetti's opera
*Lucia di Lammermoor,* by Sir
Walter Scott.
**Lucie, Lucine, Lucius**

**Lucille** (loo-SĒL)
See Lucy.
Entertainment: Lucille Ball, actress.
**Lucilla, Lucillia**

**Lucinda** (loo-SIN-duh)
See Lucy:
**Cindy, Lucindia, Lucky**

**Lucretia** (loo-KRĒ-shuh)
Latin—*Rich rewards*
Interesting: In Roman legend,
Lucretia was known for wifely
virtues.
Entertainment: Lucrezia Bori,
opera singer.
**Lucrece, Lucrezia, Lukretia**

**Lucy** (LOO-sē)
Latin—*Light bringer*
Feminine form of Luke.
Literature: Lucie Manette, heroine
of Dickens' *A Tale of Two Cities.*
Entertainment: Luci Arnaz, actress.
**Lu, Luce, Luci, Lucia, Luciana,
Lucie, Lucienne, Lucilla, Lucille,
Lucina, Lucinda, Lucine, Lucita,
Lucius, Luz**

**Ludmilla** (lood-MIL-uh)
Old Slavic—*Dear to the people*
**Ludie, Ludovika, Mila**

**Luella** (loo-EL-uh)
Old English—*Elf*
Entertainment: Louella Parsons,
Hollywood columnist.
**Loella, Lou, Louella, Lu,
Luelle, Lula, Lulu**

**Lukina** (loo-KĒ-nuh)
Ukrainian—*Graceful and bright*
**Luciana, Lukyna**

**Lulani** (loo-LA-nē)
Polynesian—*Highest point in heaven*
**Luanna, Luannie**

**Lulu** (LOO-loo)
North American Indian—*Rabbit*
**Luella, Lulie**

**Luna** (LOO-nuh)
Latin—*Of the moonlight*
Mythological: Roman goddess of
the moon.
**Lunetta, Lunette, Lunneta,
Lunnete**

**Lurleen** (lur-LĒN)
See Lorelei.
Famous: Lurleen Wallace,
governor of Alabama.
**Lura, Lurette, Lurlene, Lurline**

**Lydia** (LID-ē-uh)
Latin—*A woman of Lydia*
**Lidia, Lydie**

**Lynn** (LIN)
Anglo-Saxon—*A cascade*
Entertainment: Lynn Redgrave,
actress.
**Lyn, Lynette, Lynna, Lynne,
Lynnet**

**Lyris** (LIR-is)
Greek—*Lyrical*
**Liris**

**Mabel** (MĀ-bul)
Latin—*Loveable*
Literature: Mable Hoffman,
cookbook author.
Entertainment: Mabel Normand,
actress in silent movies;
Maybelle Carter, singer and
mother of June Carter.
**Amabel, Mab, Mabelle, Mable,
Mae, Maible, Maybelle**

**Macha** (MA-cha)
North American Indian— *The aurora*

**Machi** (MA-chē)
Japanese— *Ten thousand*

**Madeline** (MAD-uh-lin)
Hebrew— *Woman from Magdala*
Literature: Heroine of *Eve of St. Agnes,* by John Keats.
Entertainment: Madeline Kahn, actress.
Dalenna, Lena, Lenna, Lina, Linn, Lynn, Lynne, Madalena, Madalyn, Maddalena, Maddi, Maddie, Maddy, Made, Madel, Madelaine, Madeleine, Madelena, Madelene, Madelina, Madella, Madelle, Madelon, Madge, Madid, Madlen, Madlin, Mady, Magda, Magdala, Magdalena, Magdalene, Maidel, Maighdlin, Mala, Malena, Malina, Marleah, Marleen, Marlena, Marlene, Marline, Maud, Maude

**Madge** (MADJ)
Greek— *A pearl*

**Madra** (MAW-druh)
Italian— *Mother*

**Mae** (MĀ)
See May.
Entertainment: Mae West, actress.

**Magda** (MAG-duh)
Hebrew— *A high tower*
Literature: Heroine in *The Sunken Bell,* a play by Hauptmann.
Madalena, Magdala, Magdalena, Magdalina, Magdaline, Magdelene

**Magena** (muh-JĒN-uh)
North American Indian— *The coming moon*

**Maggie** (MAG-ē)
Greek— *A pearl*
Literature: Maggie Wylie, heroine of Barrie's *What Every Woman Knows;* Maggie Tulliver, heroine of *Mill on the Floss,* by George Eliot.
Mag, Maggee, Maggy

**Mahala** (muh-HĀ-luh)
North American Indian— *Woman*
Mahalia, Mahela, Mahila

**Mahalia** (muh-HĀL-yuh)
Hebrew— *Affection*
Entertainment: Mahalia Jackson, singer of spirituals.
Mahala

**Mahesa** (muh-HĒ-suh)
Hindi— *Great Lord*

**Mahina** (muh-HĒ-nuh)
Polynesian— *Moon*

**Mahira** (muh-HIR-uh)
Hebrew— *Quick*
Mehira

**Maia** (MĪ-yuh)
Greek— *Nurse or mother*
Mythological: Daughter of Atlas and Pleione; Goddess of springtime.

**Maida** (MĀ-duh)
Anglo-Saxon— *A maiden*
Maddie, Maddy, Mady, Magda, Maidel, Maidie, Mayda

**Maisie** (MĀ-sē)
Greek— *A pearl*

**Malka** (MAL-kuh)
Hebrew— *Queen*

**Malva** (MAL-vuh)
Greek— *Soft*
Famous: Malvina Hoffman, sculptor and author.
Malve, Malvina

**MADRA**—*Mother*

**Mamie** (MĀ-mē)
See Mary.
Famous: Mamie Eisenhower, wife
of President Dwight Eisenhower.

**Mana** (MAN-uh)
Polynesian—*Supernatural power*

**Manda** (MAN-duh)
Spanish—*Battle-maiden*
**Armanda**

**Mandisa** (man-DĒ-suh)
South African—*Sweet*

**Mandy** (MAN-dē)
English—*Worthy of love*
**Mandi, Mandie**

**Mangena** (man-JĒN-uh)
Hebrew—*Song*
**Mangina**

**Manidatta** (man-i-DAT-uh)
East Indian—*Pearl given*
Interesting: The pearl is believed to
ward off evil.

**Mansi** (MAN-sē)
Hopi Indian—*Plucked flower*
**Mancy, Mansy**

**Manuela** (man-WEL-uh)
Hebrew—*God with us*
Feminine form of Manuel.

## Mapela (ma-PĀ-luh)
Polynesian— *Loveable*
**Mabel**

## Mara (MAR-uh)
Hebrew— *Bigger*
**Damara, Mamie, Manechka, Manette, Manya, Maralina, Maraline, Marcsa, Maretta, Marette, Mari, Maria, Marica, Marie, Marija, Marika, Marilla, Marilyn, Maring, Mariquilla, Mariquita, Marishka, Mariska, Marita, Maritsa, Mariya, Marja, Marla, Marusya, Marya, Masha, Mashenka, May, Mica, Mickam, Mimi, Miriam, Mollie, Mura, Muriel**

## Marcella (mar-SEL-uh)
Latin— *Warlike*
Feminine form of Mark.
**Marcela, Marcelle, Marcellina, Marcelline, Marcile, Marcille, Marcy, Marquita**

## Marcia (MAR-shuh) or (MAR-sē-uh)
Latin— *Warlike*
Feminine form of Mark.
Entertainment: Marsha Mason, actress.
**Marcelia, Marcie, Marcile, Marcille, Marcy, Marquita, Marsha**

## Margaret (MAR-gret)
Greek— *A pearl*
Famous: Margaret Thatcher, Prime Minister of Great Britain; Margaret Mead, anthropologist.
Literature: Margaret Mitchell, author of *Gone With The Wind*.
Entertainment: Margaret Leighton, Maggie Smith, actresses.
**Greta, Gretal, Gretchen, Gretel, Grethel, Gretta, Madge, Mag, Maggi, Maggie, Maggym, Maiga, Maisie, Margalo, Margareta, Margarete, Margaretha, Margarethe, Margaretta, Margarette, Margarita, Marge, Margery, Marget, Margette, Margie, Margit, Margo, Margot, Marguerita, Marguerite, Margy, Marji, Marjie, Marjorie, Marjory, Marketa, Meg, Megan, Meggi, Meggie, Meggy, Meghan, Meta, Peg, Pegeen, Peggi, Peggie, Peggy, Rita**

## Margery (MAR-jer-ē)
See Margaret.
Famous: Margaux Hemingway, model, actress and granddaughter of Ernest Hemingway.
Entertainment: Marjorie Mane, actress who played the character Ma Kettle.
**Margaux, Marge, Margi, Margie, Margy, Marje, Marjie, Marjorie, Marjy**

## Margo (MAR-gō)
See Margaret.
Entertainment: Dame Margot Fonteyn, ballet dancer; Margot Kidder, actress.
**Margot, Margott**

**MARIS**—*Of the sea*

**Maria** (ma-RĒ-uh)
See Mary.
Entertainment: Marie Osmond, singer and performer; Maria Tallchief, ballet dancer; Maria, heroine in *Sound of Music*.
**Marie**

**Marian** (MAIR-ē-un)
See Mary.
Literature: Marianne Moore, American poetess; Maid Marian, sweetheart of Robin Hood.
**Mariam, Mariana, Marianna, Marianne, Marion, Maryann, Maryanne**

**Mariana** (mair-ē-AN-uh)
See Mary.
Literature: Wife of Angelo in Shakespeare's *Measure for Measure*.

**Marilyn** (MAIR-uh-lin)
See Mary.
Entertainment: Marilyn Miller, star of the Ziegfeld Follies, Marilyn Monroe, actress.
**Marilee, Marilin, Marylee, Marylin, Merrile, Merrili**

**Marina** (muh-RĒ-nuh)
Latin—*From the sea*
**Marna, Marne, Marni, Marnie**

## Maris (MAR-is)
Latin—*Of the sea*
Entertainment: Marissa Berenson, actress and model.
**Marisa, Marissa, Marris, Marys, Meris**

## Marjorie (MAR-jor-ē)
See Margery.
Literature: Marjorie Kinnan Rawlings, Pulitzer Prize winner; *Marjorie Morningstar,* novel by Herman Wouk.

## Marlene (mar-LĒN)
See Marilyn.
Entertainment: Marlene Dietrich, who popularized *Lili Marlene.*
**Marla, Marleen, Marlena, Marlyn, Marna**

## Marnie (MAR-nē)
See Marian.
**Marna, Marne, Marni**

## Marta (MAR-tuh)
Swedish, Russian—*Mistress*

## Martha (MAR-thuh)
Arabic—*A lady*
Biblical: Sister of Mary Magdalen and Lazarus.
Famous: Martha Washington, wife of President George Washington.
Entertainment: Martha Graham, pioneer of modern dance; Martha Rae, comedienne.

## Mary (MAIR-ē)
Hebrew—*Bitter*
Biblical: Mother of Christ.
Entertainment: Mary, of the singing group Peter, Paul and Mary; Mary Pickford, Marlo Thomas, Mary Tyler Moore, actresses.
**Mair, Maire, Mairlee, Malia, Mame, Mami, Mamie, Manon, Manya, Mara, Marabel, Maren, Maria, Mariam, Marian, Marianna, Marianne, Marice, Maridel, Marie, Mariel, Marietta, Marilee, Marilin, Marilyn, Marin, Marion, Mariquilla, Mariska, Marita, Maritsa, Marja, Marje, Marla, Marlo, Marnia, Marya, Maryann, Maryanne, Maryellen, Marylin, Marylou, Marysa, Masha, Maura, Maure, Maureen, Maurene, Maurine, Maurise, Maurizia, Mavra, Meridel, Meriel, Merrili, Mimi, Minette, Minnie, Minny, Miriam, Mitzi, Mitzie, Moira, Moll, Mollie, Molly, Muire, Murial, Muriel, Murielle, Muriellie, Murita, Polly**

## Matilda (muh-TIL-duh)
Teutonic—*Powerful in battle*
Famous: Wife of William the Conqueror.
Entertainment: Australian song, *Waltzing Matilda.*
**Maitilde, Matelda, Mathilda, Mathilde, Matii, Matilde, Mattie, Matty, Maud, Maude, Tilda, Tilly**

## Matrika (muh-TRĒ-kuh)
Hindi—*Mother*
**Matrica**

## Maude (MAWD)

See Matilda.

Literature: *Maud,* by Tennyson; Maud Gonne, heroine in *When You Are Old,* by William Butler Yeats.

Entertainment: Character in TV program, *Maude;* Maude Adams, actress.

**Maudie**

## Maureen (mor-ĒN)

French — *Dark-skinned*

Celtic — *Great*

Entertainment: Maureen O'Hara, Maureen Stapleton, actresses.

**Maura, Maurene, Maurine, Maurise, Maurita, Maurizia, Moira, Mora, Moreen, Morena, Morene, Moria**

## Mavis (MĀ-vis)

French — *Strong thrush*

## Maxine (maks-ĒN)

Latin — *Greatest*

Feminine form of Max.

Entertainment: Maxine Elliott, actress.

**Max, Maxi, Maxie, Maxime**

## May (MĀ)

Latin — *Great one*

**Mae, Maia, Maye**

## Mead (MĒD)

Greek — *Honey-wine*

**Meade, Meadie**

## Meda (MĒ-duh)

North American Indian — *Priestess*

**Meeda**

## Medea (me-DĒ-uh)

Greek — *Part goddess; sorceress*

## Mega (MĀ-guh)

Spanish — *Gentle*

## Megan (MĀ-gan)

Anglo-Saxon — *Great*

Literature: Heroine in *The Apple Tree,* by Galsworthy.

**Meg, Meggi, Meggie, Meggy, Meghan**

## Mehetabel (muh-HET-uh-bel)

Hebrew — *One of God's favored*

**Mehitable, Metabel**

## Mel (MEL)

Portuguese — *Honey*

## Melanie (MEL-uh-nē)

Greek — *Dark-clothed*

Entertainment: Melanie, pop singer.

**Malan, Mel, Mela, Melan, Melania, Melany, Melina, Melli, Mellie, Melloney, Melly, Milena**

## Melantha (me-LAN-thuh)

Greek — *Dark flower*

## Melba (MEL-buh)

Greek — *Soft*

Latin — *Mallow flower*

Feminine form of Melvin.

Entertainment: Melba Moore, singer.

**Malva, Melva**

## Melcia (MEL-sē-uh)

Polish — *Ambitious*

**Amalie**

## Meli (MEL-ē)

Greek — *Honey*

**Mere**

## Melina (muh-LĒ-nuh)

Latin — *Canary-yellow color*

Entertainment: Melina Mercouri, actress.

**Malina, Melanie**

## Melinda (muh-LIN-duh)

Greek — *Dark, gentle*

**Linda, Lindy, Lynda, Malina, Malinda, Malinde, Mandy, Melinde**

**Melisenda** (mel-i-SEN-duh)
Spanish, German—*Honest*
**Millicent**

**Melissa** (muh-LIS-uh)
Greek—*Honey bee*
Mythological: Nymph who taught
man to use honey.
Entertainment: Melissa Hayden,
ballet dancer; Melissa
Manchester, pop singer.
**Lisa, Lissa, Malissa, Mel,
Melesa, Melessa, Melicent,
Melisa, Melisande, Melise,
Melisenda, Melisent, Melisse,
Melita, Melitta, Melleta,
Mellicent, Mellie, Melly,
Melosa, Melose, Mili,
Milicent, Milissent,
Millicent, Millie,
Millisent, Milly,
Misha, Missie, Missy**

**Melody** (MEL-ō-dē)
Greek—*Song*
**Lodie, Melodee, Melodie**

**Melvina** (mel-VĒN-uh)
Celtic—*Chieftainess*
Feminine form of Melvin.
**Malvina, Melba, Melva**

**Mercedes** (MER-se-dēs) or
(mer-SĀ-dēs)
Spanish—*Merciful*
Biblical: Maria de Mercedes (Mary
of Mercies).
Literature: Sweetheart of Edmond
Dante's *Count of Monte Cristo.*
Entertainment: Mercedes
McCambridge, actress.
**Merci, Mercy**

**Mercy** (MER-sē)
English—*Compassion, mercy*

**Meredith** (MAIR-uh-dith)
Old Welsh—*Guardian from the sea*
Entertainment: Meredith Baxter
Birney, actress.
**Meridith, Merridie, Merry**

**Meris** (MAR-is)
Latin—*Of the sea*
**Mari, Maris**

**Merle** (MERL)
Latin—*Blackbird*
Entertainment: Merle Oberon,
actress.
**Merl, Merla, Merlina,
Merline, Merola, Meryl,
Myrle, Myrlene**

**Merrie** (MAIR-ē)
Anglo-Saxon—*Pleasant*
**Marrille, Meri, Merilee,
Merrielle, Merrili, Merry**

**Merritt** (MAIR-it)
Anglo-Saxon—*Of merit*

**Meta** (ME-tuh)
German—*A pearl*
**Greta, Meda, Mehetabel
Mettabel**

**Mia** (MĒ-uh)
Latin—*Mine*
Entertainment: Mia Farrow,
actress.

**Michaela** (mi-KĀ-luh)
Hebrew—*Who is like the Lord*
Feminine form of Michael.
**Mia, Micaela, Michaelina,
Michaeline, Michel, Michelina,
Micheline, Michelle, Micki,
Mickie, Micky, Midge, Miguela,
Miguelita, Mikaela, Miquela,
Miquelie**

**Michelle** (mi-SHEL)
See Michaela.
Entertainment: Michelle Morgan,
Michelle Lee, actresses; *Michelle,*
song by the Beatles.

**Michi** (MĒ-chē)
Japanese—*The righteous*

**Micka** (MI-kuh)
Slavic—*Bitter*
**Mara, Mica**

**Migdala** (mig-DAW-luh)
Hebrew — *Fortress*
**Migdela, Migdele, Migdelia**

**Migina** (mi-JĒ-nuh)
Omaha Indian — *Moon returning*
**Mihuca, Mitexi**

**Mignon** (MIN-yon)
French — *Dainty, delicate*
Literature: Mignon Eberhart, author of detective fiction.
Entertainment: Heroine of the opera *Mignon,* by Ambroise Thomas.
**Mignonette, Mignonettie**

**Mildred** (MIL-dred)
German — *Mild power*
**Madge, Midge, Mil, Milli, Millie, Milly**

**Millicent** (MIL-i-sent)
Teutonic — *Industrious*
**Lissa, Mel, Melicent, Melisande, Melisenda, Mellisent, Melly, Milicent, Milissent, Milli, Millie, Millisent, Milly, Milzie, Missie, Missy**

**Milly** (MIL-ē)
See Mildred.
Entertainment: Movie, *Thoroughly Modern Milly.*
**Millie**

**Mimi** (MĒ-mē)
Teutonic — *Unwavering protector*
Entertainment: Mimi, heroine of Puccini's opera *La Boheme.*
**Mimee**

**Mina** (MĪN-uh)
See Wilhelmina.
**Minette, Minnie, Myna**

**Minal** (min-AL)
North American Indian — *Fruit*

**Minda** (MIN-duh)
Indian — *Knowledge*

**Mindy** (MIN-dē)
English — *Love*
**Minna**

**Minerva** (mi-NER-vuh)
Greek — *Wisdom*
Mythological: Roman goddess of wisdom.

**Minette** (mi-NET)
French, German — *Unwavering protector*
**Guilette, Guillaumette, Guillelmine, Mimi, Wilhelmine**

**Minna** (MIN-uh)
German — *Memory*
**Mina, Minda, Mindy, Minetta, Minette, Minne, Minnie, Minny**

**Miquela** (mi-KĀ-luh)
Zuni Indian — *Who is like God*
**Micaela, Miquel**

**Mira** (MIR-uh)
Latin — *Wonderful*
**Mireille, Mirella, Mirelle, Miri, Miriam, Mirilla, Myra, Myrilla**

**Mirabel** (MIR-uh-bel)
Latin — *Of extraordinary beauty*
**Mira, Mirabella, Mirabelle**

**Miranda** (mir-AN-duh)
Latin — *Admirable*
Literature: Heroine of *The Tempest,* by Shakespeare.
**Mira, Miran, Myra, Randa, Randie, Randy**

**Miriam** (MIR-ē-um)
Hebrew — *Bitter*
Literature: Hero's first love in *Sons and Lovers,* by D.H. Lawrence.
**Mimi, Mirjan, Mitzi, Mitzie**

**Mirth** (MIRTH)
Anglo-Saxon — *Joy, pleasure*

**Missie** (MIS-sē)
English — *Young girl*
**Missy**

**MYRA**—*Quiet song*

**Moanna** (mō-AW-nuh)
Polynesian—*Ocean*

**Modesty** (MOD-est-ē)
Latin—*Modest*
**Modesta, Modestia, Modestine**

**Moina** (mō-Ē-nuh)
Celtic—*Gentle and soft*
**Moyna**

**Moira** (MOI-ruh)
Gaelic—*Great*
Entertainment: Moira Shearer, actress.
**Maura, Maureen**

**Molly** (MOL-ē)
See Mary.
Historical: Molly Pitcher,
   Revolutionary War heroine.
**Mollee, Molli, Mollie**

**Mona** (MŌ-nuh)
Teutonic, Latin— *Single or solitary*
Famous: *Mona Lisa,* painting by
   Leonardo da Vinci.
**Moina, Monia, Moyna**

**Monica** (MON-i-kuh)
Latin— *Adviser*
Biblical: Mother of St.
   Augustine.
**Mona, Monique**

**Morasha** (mor-A-shuh)
Hebrew— *Inheritance*

**Morgana** (mor-GA-nuh)
Welsh— *Edge of the sea*
Feminine form of Morgan.
Literature: Morgan LeFay, sister of
   King Arthur.
**Morgan, Morgania**

**Moriah** (mo-RĪ-uh)
Hebrew— *God is my teacher*
**Morice, Moriel, Morit**

**Morla** (MOR-luh)
Hebrew— *Chosen by the Lord*
**Morlia**

**Morna** (MOR-nuh)
Gaelic— *Beloved*
**Myrna**

**Moselle** (mō-ZEL)
Hebrew— *Child rescued from the
   water*
**Mosellie, Mozelle, Mozellie**

**Moya** (MOI-uh)
Celtic— *The great*
**Moira**

**Mura** (MŪR-uh)
Japanese— *Village*

**Muriel** (MŪR-ē-el)
Arabic— *Myrrh*
Gaelic— *Sea bright*
Literature: Muriel Sparks, author.
**Meriel, Murial, Murielle**

**Musa** (MOO-suh)
Latin— *A muse*
**Musetta, Musette**

**Myra** (MĪ-ruh)
French— *Quiet song*
Literature: Myra Kelly, author;
   *Myra Breckenridge,* novel by Gore
   Vidal.
Entertainment: Dame Myra Hess,
   pianist; Myrna Loy, actress.
**Merna, Mira, Miranda, Mirna,
Moina, Morna, Moyna, Myrna**

**Myrtle** (MIR-tel)
Greek— *Myrtle*
**Myrta, Myrtia, Myrtice, Myrtie**

**Nada** (NĀ-duh)
Slavic— *Hope*

**Nadine** (nā-DĒN)
French, Slavic— *Hope*
Feminine form of Nathan.
Sports: Nadia Comaneci, gymnast.
**Dusya, Nada, Nadenka, Nadia,
Nadiya, Nady, Nadya, Nadyusha,
Nadzia, Nathka**

**NATA**—*Rope dancer*

**Nagida** (na-GĒ-duh)
Hebrew— *Wealth*

**Nan** (NAN)
See Ann.
Entertainment: Nanette Fabray, actress.
**Nana, Nance, Nancee, Nanci, Nancie, Nancy, Nanelia, Nanelle, Nanette, Nanice, Nanine, Nanna, Nannie, Nanny, Nanon, Nette, Nettie, Netty, Ninon**

**Nancy** (NAN-sē)
See Ann.
Famous: Nancy Reagan, wife of President Ronald Reagan.
Literature: Nancy Drew, stories for girls.
Entertainment: Nancy Sinatra, pop singer; Nancy Walker, actress.
**Nance, Nancee, Nancey, Nanci, Nancie, Nanice, Nannie, Nanny**

**Nani** (NA-nē)
Polynesian— *Beautiful*

**Naomi** (nā-Ō-mē)
Hebrew — *Pleasant*
Biblical: Mother-in-law of Ruth.
Literature: Naomi Mitchison,
  English author.
**Naoma, Noami, Noemi, Nomi**

**Nara** (NAIR-uh)
North American Indian,
  Japanese — *Oak*

**Nari** (NAR-ē)
Japanese — *Thunderpeal*
**Nariko**

**Narilla** (na-RIL-uh)
English — *Obscure*
**Narilia, Narilie, Narrila,
Narrilia, Narrilla**

**Nashira** (na-SHIR-uh)
Zodiac — *Star*

**Nasnan** (NAZ-nan)
Carrier Indian — *Surrounded by a
  song*

**Nasya** (NĀZ-yuh)
Hebrew — *Miracle of God*
**Nasia**

**Nata** (NĀ-tuh)
North American Indian — *Speaker*
Hindi — *Rope dancer*
Polish — *Hope*
**Natia**

**Natalie** (NA-tuh-lē)
Latin — *Christmas-born*
Entertainment: Natalie Wood,
  actress; Natalie Cole, singer.
**Nat, Nata, Natala, Natalina,
Nataline, Natasha, Nathalia,
Nathalie, Natividad, Natty,
Netti, Nettie, Netty, Noel**

**Natane** (na-TAW-nē)
Arapaho Indian — *Daughter*

**Natasha** (na-TA-shuh)
Slavic — *Born on Christmas*
**Natalie, Natascha, Nathalia,
Natica**

**Navit** (nuh-VĒT)
Hebrew — *Pleasant*
**Naava, Nava**

**Neala** (NĒ-luh)
Celtic — *Chieftainess*
Feminine form of Neal.

**Neci** (NĀ-sē)
Hungarian, Latin — *Intense and fiery*

**Neda** (NĒ-duh)
Slavic — *Sunday's child*
Feminine form of Edward.
**Nedda, Nedi, Nedra**

**Nediva** (ne-DĒ-vuh)
Hebrew — *Noble and generous*

**Nelda** (NEL-duh)
Old English — *Of the elder tree*

**Nelia** (NĒL-ē-yuh)
Spanish — *Yellow*
**Melia**

**Nell** (NEL)
See Allen.
Entertainment: Nell Gwyn,
  actress; songs *Nelly Bly* and *Nelly
  Was A Lady.*
**Nella, Nellie, Nellis, Nelly,
Nelma**

**Neona** (nē-Ō-nuh)
Greek — *New moon*

**Nerine** (na-RĒN)
Greek — *Sea nymph*

**Nerissa** (ner-IS-uh)
Greek — *Of the sea*
Literature: Confidante of Portia in
  *Merchant of Venice,* by
  Shakespeare.
**Nerita**

**Nessa** (NES-uh)
Greek — *Pure*
**Agnes, Nessia, Nesta,
Netty, Neysa**

**Netia** (NĒ-shuh) or (ne-TĒ-uh)
Hebrew—*Plant*
**Neta, Netta**

**Netis** (NE-tis)
North American Indian—*Trusted friend*

**Neva** (NĒ-vuh)
Spanish—*Snowy*
**Nevada**

**Niabi** (ne-AW-bē)
North American Indian—*A fawn*

**Nicole** (ni-KŌL)
Greek—*Victory of the people*
Feminine form of Nicholas.
Literature: Heroine of *Aucassin and Nicolette,* by F. W. Bourdillon.
**Nicolette, Nicoli, Nicolina, Nicoline, Nika, Niki, Nikki**

**Nika** (NĒK-uh)
Greek—*Victory*
Russian—*Belonging to God*
**Domka, Mika**

**Niki** (NI-kē)
Greek—*Victorious army*
**Nikoleta, Nikolia**

**Nina** (NĒ-nuh)
North American Indian—*Mighty*
Spanish—*Little girl*
**Nanon, Ninetta, Ninette, Ninnetta, Ninnette, Ninon**

**Nishi** (NĒ-shē)
Japanese—*West*

**Nissa** (NIS-uh)
Scandinavian—*Friendly elf*

**Nita** (NĒ-tuh)
Choctaw Indian—*Bear*

**Nitara** (ni-TAR-uh)
Hindi—*Deeply rooted*

**Nitsa** (NĒT-suh)
Greek—*Light*

**Nizana** (ni-ZA-nuh)
Hebrew—*Bud*
**Nitana, Nizan**

**Noel** (nō-EL)
Latin, French—*Christmas-born*
**Noella, Noelle, Noellyn, Noelyn, Novelia**

**Nola** (NŌ-luh)
Latin—*A small bell*

**Noleta** (nō-LĒ-tuh)
Latin—*The unwilling*

**Nona** (NŌ-nuh)
Latin—*Ninth*
Interesting: Name sometimes given to the ninth child.

**Nora** (NOR-uh)
Latin—*Honor*
Greek—*Light*
Literature: Nora Helmer, heroine of *A Doll's House,* by Ibsen.
**Norah, Norina, Norine**

**Norma** (NOR-muh)
Latin—*Ruler or pattern*
Entertainment: *Norma,* opera by Bellini; Norma Talmadge, Norma Shearer, actresses.
**Noreen, Normia**

**Noura** (NŌŌR-uh)
Arabic—*Light*

**Nova** (NŌ-vuh)
Hopi Indian—*Chasing*

**Nurit** (NŪR-et)
Hebrew—*Little yellow flower*
**Nurice, Nurita**

**Nusa** (NŌŌ-suh)
Hungarian, Hebrew—*Graceful*
**Anci, Aniko, Annuska, Nina, Ninacska**

**Oba** (Ō-buh)
Yoruban— *River goddess*

**Octavia** (ok-TĀ-vē-uh)
Latin— *The eighth*
Feminine form of Octavius.
**Ottavia, Tavi, Tavia**

**Odelet** (Ō-de-let)
French, Greek— *Little song*
**Odel, Odele, Odelette,
Odellett, Odellette**

**Odelia** (ō-DĒ-lē-uh)
Teutonic— *Wealthy or prosperous*
Hebrew— *I will praise God*
Feminine form of Odell.
**Odelinda, Odella, Odetta,
Odette, Odilia, Otha, Othelia,
Othilia, Ottilie, Uta**

**Odera** (ō-DAIR-uh)
Hebrew— *Plough*

**Ogin** (Ō-jin)
North American Indian— *Wild rose*

**Ola** (Ō-luh)
Norwegian— *Descendant or
reminder of his ancestor*

**Olathe** (Ō-lath)
North American Indian— *Beautiful*

**Olayinka** (ō-LĀ-in-kuh)
Yoruban— *Honors surround me*

**Olethea** (ō-LĒ-thē-uh)
Latin— *Truth*
**Alethea**

**Olga** (ŌL-guh)
Teutonic, Russian— *Holy*
**Elga, Helga, Oldnka, Olechka,
Olia, Olive, Olivia, Olva**

**Oliana** (ō-LĒ-an-uh)
Polynesian— *Oleander*

**Olisa** (ō-LĒ-suh)
African— *God*

**Olivia** (ō-LIV-ē-uh)
Latin— *Olive tree*
Interesting: The olive tree is a
symbol of peace.
Literature: Countess in *Twelfth
Night,* by Shakespeare.
Entertainment: Olivia de
Havilland, actress; Olivia
Newton-John, pop singer.
**Liva, Livi, Livia, Livvi,
Livvie, Livvy, Nola, Nolana,
Nolita, Noll, Nollie, Olga,
Olia, Olive, Olivette, Olli,
Ollie, Olly, Olva**

**Olympia** (ō-LIM-pē-uh)
Greek— *Heavenly*
Entertainment: Olympia, heroine
in *Tales of Hoffman,* by Offenbach.
**Olimpia, Olympe, Olympie**

**Oma** (Ō-muh)
Arabic— *Commander*
Feminine form of Omar.

**Omena** (ō-MĒN-uh)
Finnish— *Apple*

**Ona** (Ō-nuh)
Hebrew— *Graceful*
**Ane, Anikke, Annze, Onele,
Onute, Oona, Una**

**Ondine** (ON-dēn)
Latin— *Of water*
**Undine**

**Onella** (ō-NEL-uh)
Hungarian, English— *Light*

**Opal** (Ō-pel)
Sanskrit—*Precious stone*
**Opalina, Opaline**

**Ophelia** (ō-FĒL-ē-uh)
Greek—*Serpent*
Literature: Heroine in
    Shakespeare's *Hamlet*.
**Ofelia, Ofilia, Ophelie, Phelia**

**Oralie** (OR-uh-lē)
Latin—*Golden*
**Aurelia, Ora, Oralia,
Orel, Oriana, Orlene**

**Oribel** (OR-i-bel)
Latin—*Golden beauty*
**Orlena, Orlene**

**Orino** (or-Ē-nō)
Japanese—*Weaver's field*
**Ori**

**Oriole** (OR-ē-ōl)
Latin—*Fair-haired*
**Oriel**

**Orlantha** (or-LAN-thuh)
Teutonic—*Fame of the land*

**Orlenda** (or-LEN-duh)
English, Russian—*Female eagle*
**Orlitza**

**Ornice** (OR-nēs)
Hebrew—*Cedar tree*
**Oenit, Orna**

**Ortrude** (OR-trōōd)
Teutonic—*Serpent-maid*
**Ortrud**

**Orva** (OR-vuh)
French—*Of golden worth*

**Ottilie** (Ō-til-ē)
Teutonic—*Fortunate battle-maid*
German—*Fatherland*
**Odette, Odille, Ottilia, Ottillia,
Uta**

**Page** (PĀJ)
French—*Useful assistant*
Anglo-Saxon—*Child*
Interesting: Name was sometimes
    used in knighthood.
**Paige**

**Paka** (PA-kuh)
Swahili—*Pussycat*

**Palila** (puh-LĒ-luh)
Polynesian—*Bird*

**Paloma** (puh-LŌ-muh)
Spanish—*Dove*

**Pamela** (PAM-el-uh)
Greek—*All honey*
Literature: Heroine in *Arcadia*, by
    Sir Phillip Sidney; Samuel
    Richardson's novel, *Pamela, or
    Virtue Rewarded*.
Entertainment: Pamela Brown,
    Pamela Tiffin, actresses.
**Pam, Pamelina, Pamella,
Pammi, Pammie, Pammy**

**Pandita** (pan-DĒ-tuh)
Hindi—*Scholar*

**Pandora** (pan-DOR-uh)
Greek — *Talented, gifted*
Mythological: Pandora was the
first woman. She opened a sealed
box containing all the gifts of the
gods to mankind including the
ills of the world.
**Doria**

**Pansy** (PAN-sē)
Greek — *Fragrant*
**Pansie**

**Panthea** (PAN-thē-uh)
Greek — *Of all the gods*

**Patia** (PAT-ē-uh)
Spanish — *Leaf*

**Patience** (PĀ-shens)
French — *Enduring expectation*
Entertainment: Heroine of Gilbert
and Sullivan's opera, *Patience.*

**Patricia** (puh-TRI-shuh)
Latin — *Of the nobility*
Feminine form of Patrick.
Famous: Patricia Nixon, wife of
President Richard Nixon.
Entertainment: Patty Duke-Astin,
actress; Patsy Cline,
country-western singer; Patti
Page, pop singer; Patrice Munsel,
opera singer.
**Pat, Patrica, Patrice,
Patrizia, Patsy, Patti,
Patty, Tricia, Trish**

**Paula** (PAWL-uh)
Latin — *Small*
Feminine form of Paul.
Literature: Heroine of *The Second
Mrs. Tanqueray,* by Pinero; *Perils
of Pauline,* by Style and Wilcox.
Entertainment: Paulette Goddard,
Paula Prentiss, actresses.
**Paole, Paolina, Paule,
Pauletta, Paulette, Pauli,
Paulie, Paulina, Pauline,
Paulita, Pauly, Pavla, Polly**

**Pavla** (PAV-luh)
Latin — *Little*
**Pavlina**

**Pazia** (PĀ-zyuh)
Hebrew — *Golden*
**Paz, Paza, Pazice, Pazit**

**Peace** (PĒS)
English — *The peaceful*

**Pearl** (PERL)
Latin, French — *Pearl*
Literature: Pearl Buck, Pulitzer
Prize winner.
Entertainment: Pearl Bailey,
singer; Pearl Primus, dancer.
**Pearla, Pearle, Pearlie,
Pearline, Perl, Perla,
Perle, Perry**

**Peg** (PEG)
Greek — *Pearl*
**Margaret, Meg, Peggi,
Peggie, Peggy**

**Pegeen** (pe-GĒN)
Celtic — *Pearl*

**Pelagie** (pe-LAW-gē)
Greek — *Pertaining to the sea*
**Pelagrie**

**Penelope** (pe-NEL-ō-pē)
Greek — *Weaver*
Literature: Faithful wife in
Homer's *Odyssey.*
**Pela, Pelcia, Pen,
Penelopa, Pennie, Penny**

**Penthea** (pen-THĒ-uh)
Greek— *The fifth*

**Peony** (PĒ-ō-nē)
Greek— *Flower*
**Peonie**

**Pepita** (pe-PĒ-tuh)
Spanish— *She shall add*
**Pepi, Peta**

**Perdita** (per-DĒ-tuh)
Latin— *Lost*
Literature: Perdita in *The Winter's Tale*, by Shakespeare.

**Perry** (PAIR-ē)
French— *Pear tree*

**Persis** (PER-sis)
Greek— *Woman from Persia*
Literature: Wife of Silas Lapham in *The Rise of Silas Lapham*, by William Dean Howells.

**Petra** (PĒ-truh) or (PE-truh)
Latin— *Rock*
Feminine form of Peter.
**Perrine, Pet, Peta, Petrina, Petronella, Petronia, Petronilla, Petronille, Pette, Pier, Pierette, Pierrette**

**Petula** (pe-TOO-luh)
Latin— *Searcher*
Entertainment: Petula Clark, singer.
**Pet, Petulah**

**Petunia** (pe-TOON-yuh)
American Indian— *From the petunia flower*

**Phedra** (FĀ-druh)
Greek— *Bright*
**Phaedra, Phaidra**

**Phenice** (fa-NĒS)
Hebrew— *From a palm tree*
**Phenica, Phenicia**

**Philana** (fil-AN-uh)
Greek— *Lover of mankind*
Feminine form of Philander.
**Philina, Philine, Phillane**

**Philippa** (FIL-ip-uh)
Greek— *Lover of horses*
Feminine form of Philip.
Literature: Pippi Longstocking, character in children's stories.
**Felipa, Filippa, Phil, Philipa, Philippe, Philippine, Phillida, Phillie, Philly, Pippa, Pippi, Pippy**

**Philomena** (fil-ō-MĒN-uh)
Greek— *Loving friend*
**Mena**

**Phoebe** (FĒ-bē)
Greek— *Shining or brilliant*
Mythological: Goddess of the moon.
**Phebe**

**Phyllis** (FIL-is)
Greek— *Green bough*
Entertainment: Phyllis George, actress and former Miss America.
**Filide, Filippa, Phil, Philippine, Philis, Phillie, Phillis, Philly, Phyl, Phylis, Pippa, Pippy**

**Pia** (PĒ-uh)
Italian— *Devout*

**Pierrette** (PĒR-et)
French— *Steady*

**Pilar** (PĒ-lar)
Spanish— *Pillar*

**Pinga** (PEN-guh)
Hindi— *Dark*

**Piper** (PĪ-per)
Old English— *Player of the pipe*
Entertainment· Piper Laurie, actress.

**Placidia** (pla-SI-dē-uh)
Latin— *The serene*
**Placida**

**Polii** (PŌ-lē)
Polynesian— *Younger sister*

**PHILIPPA**—*Lover of horses*

**Polly** (POL-ē)
Hebrew—*Bitter*
Literature: Pollyanna, character in
  children's stories.
Entertainment: Polly Bergen,
  actress.
**Pol, Poll, Pollie,
Pollyanna, Pollyannie**

**Pomona** (po-MŌ-nuh)
Latin—*Fertile*

**Poppy** (POP-ē)
Latin—*Poppy flower*

**Portia** (POR-shuh)
Latin — *Offering*
Literature: Heroine in *Merchant of Venice* and wife of Brutus in *Julius Caesar,* both by Shakespeare.

**Prane** (PRĀN)
Lithuanian, Latin — *Free one*
**Pranele, Pranute**

**Prima** (PRĒ-muh)
Latin — *The first born*

**Primalia** (prē-MĀ-lē-uh)
Latin — *The first*

**Primavera** (prē-ma-VAIR-uh)
Latin — *Spring's beginning*

**Primrose** (PRIM-roz)
Latin — *First rose*

**Priscilla** (pri-SIL-uh)
Latin — *Of ancient time*
Biblical: Priscilla was helper to Apostle Paul.
Literature: Heroine in *The Courtship of Miles Standish,* by Henry Wadsworth Longfellow.
**Cilla, Pris, Prisca, Priscell, Priscellia, Prisilla, Prissie, Prissy, Sil**

**Prudence** (PROO-dens)
Latin — *Prudent*
**Pru, Prud, Pruddie, Prudi, Prudy, Prue**

**Prunella** (proo-NEL-uh)
French, Latin — *Plum color*

**Psyche** (SĪ-kē)
Greek — *The soul*
Mythological: Mortal loved by Cupid.

**Queenie** (KWĒ-nē)
See Regina.
**Queena, Queenie, Queeny**

**Quenby** (KWEN-bē)
Scandinavian — *Womanly*

**Quenie** (KWĒ-nē)
Old English — *Queen*
**Quenna**

**Querida** (ker-RĒ-duh)
Spanish — *Beloved*

**Quinta** (KWIN-tuh)
Latin — *Fifth*
**Quentin, Quintilla, Quintina**

**Quirita** (ker-RĒ-tuh)
Latin — *Citizen*
**Quartilla**

**Rabi** (RĀ-bē)
Arabic— *Breeze*
**Rabiah**

**Rachel** (RĀ-chel)
Hebrew— *Ewe*
Biblical: Wife of Jacob and mother
of Joseph.
Entertainment: Raquel Welch,
actress.
**Rachele, Rachelle, Rae, Rahel,
Rakel, Raquel, Raquela, Ray,
Raya, Rochell, Rochelle,
Shell, Shelley, Shelly, Tey**

**Radmilla** (rad-MIL-uh)
Slavic— *Worker for the people.*

**Raizel** (RĀ-zel)
Hebrew— *Rose*
**Rayzel, Razil**

**Ramla** (RAM-luh)
Swahili— *Fortuneteller*

**Ramona** (ruh-MŌ-nuh)
Spanish— *Mighty or wise*
Feminine form of Raymond.
**Rama, Romona, Romonda**

**Rana** (RĀ-nuh)
Sanskrit— *Royal*
Mythological: Goddess of the sea.
**Rani, Rania, Rayna**

**Ranita** (ra-NĒ-tuh)
Hebrew— *Song*
**Ranice, Ranit**

**Raphaela** (ra-fī-EL-uh)
Hebrew— *Blessed healer*
Feminine form of Raphael.
**Rafaela, Rafaelia**

**Rawnie** (RAW-nē)
English— *Lady*

**Razilee** (RA-zi-lē)
Hebrew— *My secret*
**Razili**

**Rebba** (RĒ-buh)
Hebrew— *Fourth-born*
**Reba, Rebah**

**Rebecca** (re-BEK-uh)
Hebrew— *The captivator*
Biblical: Wife of Isaac.
Literature: Heroine of *Ivanhoe,* by
Sir Walter Scott; Becky Sharp in
*Vanity Fair,* by Thackeray; book
*Rebecca of Sunnybrook Farm.*
**Beba, Becca, Becka, Becki,
Beckie, Becky, Bekki, Rebeca,
Rebeka, Rebekah, Ree, Reeba,
Riba, Rikah, Riva, Rivalee,
Rivi, Rivy**

**Regina** (re-JĒN-uh)
Latin— *Queen*
**Raina, Regan, Reggi, Reggie,
Regine, Reina, Reine, Reyna,
Rina**

**Rei** (RĒ-uh)
Japanese— *Gratitude*
**Reiko**

**Remy** (RĀ-mē)
French— *From Rheims*

**Rena** (RĒ-nuh)
Greek— *Peace*
**Eirene, Eirni, Ereni, Nitsa**

**Renata** (re-NAT-uh)
Latin— *Reborn*
Entertainment: Renata Tebaldi,
opera singer.
**Renae, Renate, Rene, Renee,
Renie, Rennie**

**Reseda** (re-SĒ-duh)
Latin—*Healing*
Interesting: Reseda is also the
Latin word for the flower
mignonette.

**Rhea** (RĒ-uh)
Greek—*Earth or motherly*
Mythological: In Greek
mythology, Rhea is the mother of
Zeus. In Roman mythology,
Rhea is the mother of Romulus
and Remus.

**Rhoda** (RŌ-duh)
Greek—*A garland of roses*
Entertainment: Rhonda Fleming,
actress; character in TV show
*Rhoda*.
**Rhonda, Roda, Rodi, Rodie,
Rodina, Ronda**

**Rica** (RĒ-kuh)
See Frederica.
**Ricca, Ricki, Rickie, Ricky,
Riki, Rikki, Rycca**

**Ricarda** (ri-KAR-duh)
Teutonic—*Powerful ruler*
Feminine form of Richard.
**Erica, Frederica, Ricky, Roderica**

**Rida** (RĒ-duh)
Arabic—*Favor*

**Rihana** (RĒ-an-uh)
Muslim—*Sweet basil*

**Rimona** (ri-MŌ-nuh)
Hebrew—*Pomegranate*
**Mona**

**Risa** (RĒ-suh)
English—*Laughter*

**Rita** (RĒ-tuh)
See Margaret.
Entertainment: Rita Hayworth,
actress; Rita Coolidge, singer.

**Ritsa** (RĒT-suh)
Greek—*Helper and defender*

**Riva** (RĒ-vuh)
French—*Shore*
**Ree, Reeva, Rivalee,
Rivi, Rivy**

**Roanna** (rō-AN-uh)
Latin—*Sweet*
**Roana, Roanne**

**Roberta** (rō-BER-tuh)
Teutonic—*Of shining fame*
Entertainment: Roberta Peters,
opera singer; Roberta Flack, pop
singer.
**Bobbe, Bobbette, Bobbi, Bobbie,
Bobby, Bobbye, Bobina, Bobine,
Bobinette, Robbi, Robbie, Robby,
Robena, Robenia, Robin, Robina,
Robinette, Robinia, Rubert,
Ruperta**

**Robin** (RO-bin)
Old English—*Robin*
**Robbin, Robena, Robenia,
Robina, Robinet, Robinett, Robyn**

**Rochelle** (rō-SHEL)
French—*Little rock*

**Roderica** (rod-RĒ-kuh)
Teutonic—*Famous ruler*
Feminine form of Roderick.
**Rica, Roch, Rochella,
Rochette, Roshelle, Shell,
Shelley, Shelly**

**Rohana** (rō-AN-uh)
Hindi—*Sandalwood*

**Rolanda** (rō-LAN-duh)
Teutonic—*Fame of the land*

**Rolla** (RŌ-luh)
See Rolf.

**Roma** (RŌ-muh)
Latin—*Eternal city*
**Romaine, Romelle, Romilda,
Romina**

**RONA**—*Mighty power*

**Romilda** (rō-MIL-duh)
Teutonic—*Glorious battle-maiden*

**Romola** (rō-MŌ-luh)
Latin—*The Roman*

**Rona** (RŌ-nuh)
Norwegian—*Mighty power*
Entertainment: Rona Barrett,
  Hollywood columnist.
**Rhona, Ronalda**

**Ronli** (RON-lē)
Hebrew—*Joy in mine*
**Rona, Roni, Ronia,
Ronice, Ronit**

**Ronni** (RON-ē)
See Roanna.
**Roanna, Roni, Ronnie,
Ronny, Rowena, Veronica**

**Rosa** (RŌ-suh)
Latin—*A rose*
Famous: Rosalyn Carter, wife of
  President Jimmy Carter.
**Rosabel, Rosabella, Rosabelle,
Rosalyn**

**Rosalba** (rō-SAL-buh)
Latin—*White rose*

**Rosalia** (rō-SĀ-lē-uh)
Italian—*Melody or tune*
**Rosaleen, Rosalie, Rozalia,
Rozalie, Rozele**

**Rosalind** (ROZ-uh-lind)
Spanish, Latin—*Fair rose*
Entertainment: Rosalind Russell, actress.
Ros, Rosalinda, Rosalinde, Rosaline, Rosalyn, Rosalynd, Roselin, Roseline, Roslyn, Roz, Rozalin

**Rosamond** (ROZ-uh-mund)
Teutonic—*Famous guardian*
Ros, Rosamund, Rosamunda, Rosemonde, Roz, Rozamond

**Rosanne** (rō-ZAN)
Latin—*Gracious rose*
Ranna, Roanna, Roanne, Rosanna, Roseann, Roseanne

**Rose** (RŌZ)
Greek—*Rose*
Rasia, Rhada, Rhodie, Rhody, Rois, Rosa, Rosaleen, Rosalia, Rosalie, Rosel, Rosella, Roselle, Rosena, Rosene, Rosetta, Rosette, Rosie, Rosina, Rosita, Rosy, Rozalie, Roze, Rozele, Rozella, Rozina, Zita

**Roselani** (rō-ze-LAN-ē)
English, Polynesian—*Heavenly rose*
Roselane, Roseline

**Rosemary** (RŌZ-mair-ē)
Latin—*Mary's rose*
Entertainment: *Rose Marie*, light opera; Rosemary Clooney, singer; Rose Marie, actress.
Rosemaria, Rosemarie

**Rosetta** (rō-ZE-tuh)
Italian—*Little rose*
Entertainment: Rosina Lhevinne, concert pianist.
Rosett, Rosette, Rosina

**Rowena** (rō-WĒ-nuh)
Celtic—*White mane*
Literature: Heroine of *Ivanhoe*, by Sir Walter Scott.
Ranna, Rena, Ro, Ronni, Ronnie, Ronny, Row, Rowe

**Roxanne** (roks-AN)
Persian—*Dawn*
Historical: Persian wife of Alexander the Great.
Rosana, Rox, Roxana, Roxane, Roxi, Roxie, Roxine, Roxy

**Rozele** (rō-ZEL)
Lithuanian—*Rose*
Roz, Roze, Rozyte

**Rozene** (rō-ZĒN)
North American Indian—*Rose*

**Ruby** (ROO-bē)
Latin—*Precious stone*
Rubetta, Rubi, Rubia, Rubie, Rubina

**Rue** (ROO)
Greek—*Herb of grace*

**Ruth** (ROOTH)
Hebrew—*A friend*
Biblical: Friend of Naomi.
Entertainment: Ruth Buzzy, comedienne.
Ruthann, Ruthanna, Ruthanne, Ruthe, Ruthi, Ruthie

**Sabina** (sa-BĒN-uh)
Latin — *Sabine woman*
Interesting: Poppaea Sabina,
Roman empress.
**Bina, Sabine, Sabrina**

**Sabra** (SĀ-bruh)
Hebrew — *Thorny cactus*
**Zabra**

**Sabrina** (suh-BRĒ-nuh)
Latin — *From the border*
**Brina, Zabrina**

**Sachi** (SA-shē)
Japanese — *Bliss child*
**Sachiko**

**Sada** (SĀ-duh)
Japanese — *The chaste*
**Sadie**

**Sadie** (SĀ-dē)
Hebrew — *Princess*
Entertainment: Sadie Hawkins in
*Li'l Abner* comic strip.
**Sada, Sadye, Saidee,
Sarah, Sydel, Sydelle**

**Sadira** (sa-DĒR-uh)
Arabic — *Ostrich returning to water*

**Sadzi** (SAD-zē)
Indian — *Sun heart*

**Sagara** (sa-GAIR-uh)
Hindi — *Ocean*

**Sakari** (sa-KAR-ē)
Indian — *Sweet*

**Saki** (SA-kē)
Japanese — *Cape*

**Sakti** (SAK-tē)
Hindi — *Energy*
Interesting: Hindi goddess.

**Sakura** (sa-KOOR-uh)
Japanese — *Cherry blossom*
Interesting: Japanese symbol of
wealth and prosperity. In China,
a cherry blossom symbolizes
good education.

**Salama** (suh-LAW-muh)
Arabic — *Safety*

**Salena** (sa-LĒN-uh)
Latin — *Salty*

**Sally** (SAL-ē)
Hebrew — *Princess*
Entertainment: Sally Fields, Sally
Struthers, actresses.
**Sal, Salina, Sallee, Salli,
Sallie**

**Salome** (suh-LŌ-me) or
(SAL-ō-mā)
Hebrew — *Peaceful*
Biblical: Daughter of Herodias and
Herod.
Literature: *Salome*, play by Oscar
Wilde.
Entertainment: Salome Jens,
actress.
**Sam, Samara, Sammy, Samuela**

**Samala** (suh-MĀ-luh)
Hebrew — *Asked of God*
**Samale**

**Samantha** (suh-MAN-thuh)
Arabic — *Listener*
Entertainment: Samantha Eggars,
actress.
**Sam, Sammy**

**SASHA**—*Helper of mankind*

**Samara** (suh-MA-ruh)
Hebrew—*From Samaria*
Interesting: Samaria, a city in
Palestine.
**Sam, Samaria, Sammy**

**Samuela** (sam-ū-EL-uh)
Hebrew—*Name of God*
Feminine form of Samuel.
**Samantha, Samella, Samuella**

**Sandra** (SAN-druh)
Greek—*Helper of mankind*
Entertainment: Sandra Dee,
actress.
**Sandi, Sandie, Sandy, Sandye**

**Sanuye** (SAN-u-ā)
Indian—*Red cloud coming with
sundown*

**Sapphire** (SA-fīr)
Greek—*Sapphire*
Hebrew—*The beautiful*
Biblical: Wife of Ananias.
Literature: *Sapphira and the Slave
Girl,* novel by Willa Cather.
**Sapphira**

**Sappho** (SA-fo)
Greek—*Unknown*
Literature: *Sapho,* novel by Daudet.
**Sapho**

**Sarah** (SAIR-uh)
Hebrew— *Princess*
Biblical: Wife of Abraham, mother of Isaac.
Entertainment: Sarah Bernhardt, Sarah Miles, actresses.
**Sadella, Sadie, Sadye, Sahri, Saidee, Sal, Salaidh, Sallee, Salli, Sallie, Sally, Sara, Sarena, Sarene, Sarette, Sari, Sarine, Sarita, Sayre, Serita, Shara, Sharai, Sharon, Sharona, Sher, Sheree, Sheri, Sherie, Sherri, Sherrie, Sherry, Sherye, Soralie, Sorcha, Sorella, Sydel, Sydelle, Zara, Zarah, Zaria**

**Saril** (suh-RIL)
Turkish— *Sound of running water*

**Sasha** (SA-shuh)
Russian— *Helper of mankind*
**Sacha, Sascha**

**Satinka** (sa-TĒN-kuh)
North American Indian— *Magic dancer*

**Sawa** (SAW-wa)
Japanese— *Marsh*
Indian— *Rock*

**Scarlett** (SKAR-let)
English— *Scarlet red*
Literature: Heroine in *Gone with the Wind,* by Margaret Mitchell.
**Scarlet, Scarllet, Scarllett**

**Secunda** (se-KOON-duh)
Latin— *The second*

**Seda** (SĒ-duh)
Armenian— *Echo through the woods*
**Zelda**

**Seema** (SĒ-muh)
Hebrew— *Treasure*
**Cyma, Seena, Simah**

**Sela** (SĒ-luh)
Hebrew— *A rock*

**Selena** (suh-LĒ-nuh)
Greek— *Moon*
Mythological: Selene, goddess of the moon.
**Celene, Celie, Celina, Celinda, Celine, Sela, Selene, Seleta, Selia, Selie, Selina, Selinda, Seline, Sena**

**Selima** (suh-LĒ-muh)
Hebrew— *Peaceful*
Feminine form of Solomon.

**Selma** (SEL-muh)
Celtic— *Fair*
Teutonic— *Divine helmet*
**Anselma, Zelma**

**Senalda** (se-NAL-duh)
Spanish— *A sign*

**Seraphina** (sair-uh-FĒN-uh)
Hebrew— *Burning ardent*
**Sera, Serafina, Serafine**

**Serena** (suh-RĒN-uh)
Latin— *Tranquil*
**Reena, Rena, Serene**

**Serilda** (suh-RIL-duh)
Teutonic— *Armored warrior-maid*

**Setsu** (SET-soo)
Japanese— *Fidelity*
**Setsuko**

**Shada** (SHAW-duh)
North American Indian— *Pelican*

**Shahar** (sha-HAR)
Muslim— *The moon*

**Shaina** (SHĀ-nuh)
Hebrew— *Beautiful*
**Shaine, Shane, Shanie, Shayna, Shayne**

**Shani** (SHA-nē)
African— *Marvelous*

**Shannon** (SHA-non)
Gaelic— *Small or wise*
**Channa, Shana, Shane, Shauna, Shawna**

**Shappa** (SHAW-puh)
North American Indian — *Red thunder*

**Sharon** (SHĀR-on)
Hebrew — *Level plain*
**Shara, Sharai, Shari, Sharma, Sharmin, Sharona, Sherri, Sherrie, Sherry, Sherye**

**Sheba** (SHĒ-buh)
Hebrew — *From the Sheba*
Biblical: Queen of Sheba.
Interesting: The Southwestern part of Arabia.
**Saba**

**Shehan** (SHĒ-han)
Hebrew — *Request, petition*

**Shela** (SHĒ-luh)
Celtic — *Musical*
Literature: Shelagh Delany, playwright.
Entertainment: Sheila Graham, Hollywood columnist.
**Celia, Selia, Sheela, Sheelagh, Sheelah, Sheila, Sheilah, Shelagh, Shelley, Shelli, Shellie, Shelly**

**Shelley** (SHEL-ē)
Old English — *From the meadow on the ledge*
Entertainment: Shelley Winters, actress.
**Rachel, Shelby, Shell, Shelli, Shellie, Shelly**

**Shera** (SHAIR-uh)
Hebrew — *Song*

**Sherry** (SHAIR-ē)
See Cher.
Entertainment: Sheree North, actress.
**Sheree, Sheri, Sherri, Sherrie, Sherye, Sheryl**

**Shina** (SHĒ-nuh)
Japanese — *Good or virtue*
**Sheena**

**Shiri** (SHIR-ē)
Hebrew — *My song*
**Shira, Shirah**

**Shirley** (SHER-lē)
Old English — *From the white meadow*
Literature: Heroine of *Shirley,* by Charlotte Bronte.
Entertainment: Shirley Temple, Shirley Booth, Shirley MacLaine actresses.
**Sher, Sheree, Sheri, Sherill, Sherline, Sherri, Sherrie, Sherry, Sherye, Sheryl, Shir, Shirl, Shirlee, Shirleen, Shirlene, Shirline**

**Shoshannah** (shō-SHA-nuh)
Hebrew — *Rose*
**Shoshana**

**Shulamith** (SHOO-luh-mith)
Hebrew — *Peace*
**Sula, Sulamith**

**Shumana** (shoo-MAN-uh)
Hopi Indian — *Rattlesnake girl*

**Sibley** (SIB-lē)
Greek — *Prophetess*
Literature: *Sybil,* novel by Benjamin Disraeli.
Entertainment: Dame Sybil Thorndike, actress.
**Sib, Sibbie, Sibby, Sibeal, Sibel, Sibella, Sibelle, Sibilla, Sibylla, Sibylle, Sybil, Sybila, Sybilla, Sybille**

**Sidonia** (si-DŌN-ē-uh)
Hebrew — *To ensnare*
**Sadonia, Sidney, Sidonie, Sydney**

**Sidra** (SID-ruh)
Latin — *Related to the stars*

**Silva** (SIL-vuh)
Latin — *Woodland maid*
**Silvia, Silvie, Sylvia**

**SHUMANA**—*Rattlesnake girl*

**Silver** (SIL-ver)
Anglo-Saxon—*White*

**Simone** (se̅-MŌN)
Hebrew—*Heard by the Lord*
Feminine form of Simon.
Literature: Simone de Beauvoir,
French author.
Entertainment: Simone Signoret,
actress.
**Simona, Simonetta, Simonette,
Simonne**

**Sirena** (si-RĒN-uh)
Greek—*A siren*

**Situla** (si-TŌŌL-uh)
Indian—*Valley quail running uphill*
Latin—*Well bucket*

**Sivia** (SIV-e̅-uh)
Hebrew—*Doe or beautiful woman*
**Sivie**

**Sofi** (SŌ-fē)
Greek— *Wisdom*
**Sofia, Sofya, Sophia, Sophey, Sophi, Sophie, Sophron, Sophy**

**Solana** (sō-LA-nuh)
Spanish— *Sunshine*

**Solite** (SŌ-lēt)
Latin— *Accustomed*

**Sondra** (SAWN-druh)
See Alexandra.

**Sonia** (SŌN-yuh)
See Sophia.
Literature: Heroine of *Crime and Punishment*, by Dostoyevsky.
**Sofia, Sonia, Sonja, Sonni, Sonnie, Sonny, Sonya, Soph, Sophey, Sophi, Sophie, Sophy, Sunny**

**Sophia** (sō-FĒ-uh)
Greek— *Wisdom*
Literature: Heroine of *Tom Jones*, by Henry Fielding.
Entertainment: Sophie Tucker, Sophia Loren, actresses.
**Sofia, Sofie, Sonia, Sonja, Sonni, Sonnie, Sonny, Sonya, Sophie, Sophronia, Sophy, Sunny**

**Spring** (SPRING)
Old English— *Spring time*

**Stacy** (STĀ-sē)
Greek— *One who shall rise again*
**Stace, Stacey, Stacia, Stacie**

**Star** (STAR)
English— *A star*
**Starr**

**Stella** (STEL-uh)
Latin— *Star*
Entertainment: Stella Stevens, Stella Adler, Estelle Parsons, actresses.
**Estelle**

**Stellara** (STEL-ar-uh)
Zodiac— *Child of the stars*

**Stephanie** (STE-fuh-nē)
Greek— *Crowned*
Feminine form of Stephen.
Entertainment: Stephanie Powers, actress; Stevie (Stephanie) Nicks, singer.
**Stefa, Steffi, Steffie, Stepha, Stephani, Stephanna, Stephi, Stephie, Stesha, Stevana, Stevanna, Stevena, Stevie**

**Stesha** (STESH-uh)
Russian— *Crowned one*

**Stina** (STĒ-nuh)
German— *Christian*

**Storm** (STORM)
Old English— *Stormy*
**Stormi, Stormie, Stormy**

**Sue** (SOO)
Hebrew— *A lily*
**Suki, Susan, Susey**

**Sula** (SOO-luh)
Icelandic— *Large sea bird*
**Ursola, Ursula**

**Summer** (SUM-er)
Old English— *Summer*

**Sunny** (SUN-ē)
English— *Cheerful*

**Surata** (sur-AT-uh)
Hindi— *Blessed joy*

## Susan (SOO-zan)
Hebrew—*Lily*
Biblical: Accused adultress, saved by Daniel.
Historical: Susan B. Anthony, fighter for women's rights.
Literature: Susan Glaspell, founder of Provincetown Playhouse.
Entertainment: Susan Hayward, Susan St. James, Suzanne Pleshette, Suzanne Somers, Susie Wong, actresses.
**Sasanna, Sue, Suisan, Sukey, Suki, Susana, Susanetta, Susanette, Susanna, Susannah, Susanne, Susette, Susi, Susie, Susy, Suzanna, Suzanne, Suzette, Suzi, Suzie, Suzy, ZsaZsa**

## Suzu (SOO-zoo)
Japanese—*Little bell*
**Suzue, Suzuki, Suzuko**

## Svetla (SVET-luh)
Czech—*Light*
Famous: Svetlana Stalin, author and daughter of Joseph Stalin.
**Svetlana**

## Swanhilda (swan-HIL-duh)
Teutonic—*Swan-maiden*

## Sydney (SID-ne)
French—*From the city of St. Denis*

## Sylvia (SIL-ve-uh)
Latin—*Forest-maiden*
Literature: Sylvia Porter, author and columnist.
**Silva, Silvan, Silvana, Silvia, Silvie, Sylvana, Sylvanna, Zilva, Zilvia**

## Tabia (TAB-e-uh)
Swahili—*Talents*

## Tabitha (TA-bi-thuh)
Arabic—*A gazelle*
**Tab, Tabbi, Tabbie, Tabby**

## Taci (TA-ke) or (TA-se)
Zuni Indian—*Washtub*

## Tadita (ta-DE-tuh)
Omaha Indian—*To the wind*

## Taffy (TAF-fe)
Welsh—*Beloved*

## Taima (TA-ma)
North American Indian—*Crash of thunder*

## Takara (ta-KAR-uh)
Japanese—*Precious object*

## Talasi (ta-LAW-se)
Hopi Indian—*Corn-tassel flower*

## Talia (TAL-e-uh)
Greek—*Blooming*
Entertainment: Talia Shire, actress.
**Tallie, Tally, Thalia**

## Tallulah (tuh-LOO-luh)
Choctaw Indian—*Leaping water*
English—*Vivacious*
Entertainment: Tallulah Bankhead, actress.
**Tallie, Tallow, Tallula, Tally**

**Tama** (TĀ-muh)
American Indian— *Thunderbolt*
Japanese— *Jewel*

**Tamaki** (ta-MAW-kē)
Japanese— *Armlet*
**Tamako**

**Tamara** (TAM-uh-ruh) or
(ta-MAR-uh)
Hebrew— *Palm tree*
**Tamar, Tamarah, Tamma,
Tammi, Tammie, Tammy**

**Tami** (TA-mē)
Japanese— *People*
**Tamiko**

**Tammy** (TAM-ē)
Hebrew— *Perfection*
Entertainment: Tammy Wynette,
country-western singer.

**Tani** (TAW-nē)
Japanese— *Valley*

**Tansy** (TAN-sē)
Greek— *Immortality*
Latin— *Tenacious*

**Tanya** (TAWN-yuh)
Russian— *Fairy queen*
Literature: Titania, name of fairy
queen in *A Midsummer's Night's
Dream,* by Shakespeare.
Entertainment: Tanya Tucker,
country-western singer.
**Tanechka, Tania, Tankya,
Tatiana, Tatiania, Titania**

**Tara** (TAIR-uh)
Celtic— *Tower or crag*

**Tawnie** (TAW-nē)
English— *Little one*

**Tecla** (TEK-luh)
Greek— *Divine fame*
**Tekla, Telca, Telka, Thecla**

**Tedra** (TED-ruh)
See Theodora.

**Temina** (te-MEN-uh)
Hebrew— *Whole or honest*

**Tempest** (TEM-pest)
French— *Stormy*

**Templa** (TEM-pluh)
Latin— *A temple*

**Teresa** (tuh-RĒ-suh)
Greek— *The harvester*
Entertainment: Teresa Wright,
Terri Garr, actresses; Teresa
Brewer, pop singer.
**Rezi, Riza, Teca, Tera,
Terese, Teresina, Teresita,
Teressa, Terez, Teri, Terike,
Terri, Terrie, Terry, Terrye,
Terza, Treszka**

**Terry** (TAIR-ē)
See Theresa.
Feminine form of Terence.
**Tera, Teri, Terra, Terrie, Terrye**

**Tertia** (TER-shuh)
Latin— *The third*

**Tesia** (TES-shuh)
Polish, Greek— *Loved by God*
**Fila, Hortenspa, Teofila**

**Tess** (TES)
See Teresa.
Literature: *Tess of the D'Urbervilles,*
by Thomas Hardy.
**Tessa, Tessi, Tessie, Tessy**

**Thadine** (THĀ-dēn)
Hebrew— *The praised*
Feminine form of Thaddeus

**Thais** (THĀ-is)
Greek— *The bond*
Interesting: *Thais,* an opera and
novel by Anatole France.

**Thalassa** (tha-LAS-suh)
Greek— *From the sea*

**Thalia** (THĀL-yuh)
Greek— *Joyful or blooming*
Mythological: Thalia, one of the
Three Graces.

**THERESA**—*Reaper*

**Thea** (THĒ-uh)
  Greek—*Goddess*
  Mythological: Thea, supernatural
    being who opposed the
    Olympian Gods.

**Thecla** (THEK-luh)
  Greek—*Of divine fame*
  **Thekla**

**Theda** (THĒ-duh)
  See Theodora.
  Entertainment: Theda Bara,
    silent-movie actress.

**Thelma** (THEL-muh)
Greek— *Nursling*
Literature: *Thelma,* by Marie
  Corelli.
Entertainment: Thelma Ritter,
  comedienne.
**Telma**

**Themis** (THĒ-mis)
Greek— *Order, custom and justice*

**Theodora** (thē-ō-DOR-uh)
Greek— *Divine gift*
Feminine form of Theodore.
**Dora, Fedora, Feodora, Ted,
Tedda, Teddi, Teddie, Teddy,
Tedi, Tedra, Teodora, Theda,
Thekla, Theodosia, Theola**

**Theone** (THĒ-ō-nē)
Greek— *Godly*

**Thera** (THAIR-uh)
Greek— *The unmastered or wild*

**Theresa** (tuh-RĒ-suh)
Greek— *Reaper*
Literature: *Thérèsa Raquin,* novel
  by Emile Zola.
**Tera, Teresa, Terese, Teresita,
Teressa, Teri, Terri, Terrie,
Terry, Terrye, Tess, Tessa,
Tessi, Tessie, Tessy, Theda,
Therese, Tracey, Tracie, Tracy,
Tresa, Trescha, Tressa, Zita**

**Thirza** (THIR-zuh)
Hebrew— *Delight, pleasantness*
**Thyrza, Tirtzah, Tirza**

**Thisbe** (THIZ-bē)
Greek— *Region of doves*
Literature: Pyramus and Thisbe, in
  *A Midsummer Night's Dream,* by
  Shakespeare.

**Thomasine** (TOM-uh-sēn)
Hebrew— *The twin*
Feminine form of Thomas.
Literature: Heroine in *The Return
of the Native,* by Thomas Hardy.
**Tammi, Tammie, Tamzin,
Thomasa, Thomasin, Thomasina,
Toma, Tomasina, Tomasine,
Tommi, Tommie, Tommy**

**Thora** (THOR-uh)
Teutonic— *Thunder*
Mythological: Scandinavian
  goddess and friend of mankind.
**Thordia, Thordis, Tyra**

**Tia** (TĒ-uh)
Greek, Egyptian— *Princess*
Historical: Princess Tia was the
  sister of the pharaoh, King
  Ramses.

**Tiffany** (TI-fuh-nē)
Greek— *Appearance of God*
Interesting: Tiffany's, famous
  jewelry store in New York City.
**Tiff, Tiffi, Tiffie, Tiffy**

**Tilda** (TIL-duh)
See Mathilda.
**Tillie, Tilly**

**Timothea** (tim-ō-THĒ-uh)
Greek— *Honoring God*
Feminine form of Timothy.
**Thea, Tim, Timmi, Timmie,
Timmy**

**Tina** (TĒ-nuh)
Unknown.
Entertainment: Tina Louise,
  actress; Tina Turner, singer.
**Teena, Tine**

**Tirtha** (TIR-thuh)
Hebrew— *Ford*

**Tirza** (TIR-zuh)
Hebrew— *Cypress tree or desirable*

**Tivona** (ti-VON-uh)
Hebrew— *Lover of nature*
**Von**

**Tobey** (TŌ-bē)
German—*Dove*
Hebrew—*Good*
**Tobe, Tobi, Tobias, Tobit,
Toby, Tobye, Tova, Tove,
Tybi, Tybie**

**Toni** (TŌ-nē)
See Antoinette.
Entertainment: Toni Tennille,
    singer.
**Toinette, Tonia, Tonie, Tony**

**Tracy** (TRĀ-sē)
Gaelic—*Battler*
Latin—*Courageous*
Sports: Tracy Austin, tennis
    champion.
**Tracey, Tracie**

**Tricia** (TRI-shuh)
See Patricia.
Famous: Tricia Nixon, daughter of
    President Richard M. Nixon.
**Trisha**

**Trina** (TRĒ-nuh)
See Katherine.
**Trenna**

**Trista** (TRIS-tuh)
Latin—*Woman of sadness*

**Trixie** (TRIKS-ē)
See Beatrice.
**Trix, Trixy**

**Troth** (TROTH)
Anglo-Saxon—*Truth or pledge*

**Trudey** (TROO-dē)
See Gertrude.
**Truda, Trude, Trudel,
Trudi, Trudie**

**Truly** (TROO-lē)
English—*Truly*

**Tuesday** (TOOS-dā)
Old English—*Tuesday*
Entertainment: Tuesday Weld,
    actress.

**Udele** (Ū-del)
Anglo-Saxon—*Prosperous*

**Ula** (Ū-luh)
Celtic—*Sea jewel*
**Eula, Ulla**

**Ulalume** (u-LA-loo-ma)
Latin—*Wailing*

**Ulani** (Ū-la-nē)
Polynesian—*Cheerful*
**Ulane**

**Ullah** (Ū-luh)
Hebrew—*A burden*
**Ulla, Ullia**

**Ulrica** (ool-RĒ-kuh)
Teutonic—*Ruler of all*
Feminine form of Ulric.
**Rica, Ulrika**

**Umeko** (Ū-mē-kō)
Japanese—*Plum-blossom child*
**Umekio**

**Una** (OO-nuh)
Gaelic, English, Latin—*One*
Entertainment: Una Merkel,
    actress.
**Euna**

**Undine** (un-DĒN)
Latin—*Of water*
**Ondine**

**Unity** (Ū-ni-tē)
English—*Unity*
**Unus**

**Upala** (oo-PAL-uh)
Indian—*Opal*

**Urania** (ū-RĀ-nē-uh)
Greek—*Heavenly*
**Uranie**

**Urbana** (ur-BAN-uh)
Latin—*Courteous*
**Urban**

**Uria** (ū-RĒ-uh)
Hebrew—*Light of the Lord*

**Urit** (ŪR-ēt)
Hebrew—*Light*
**Urice**

**Ursula** (ER-suh-luh)
Latin—*Little she-bear*
Entertainment: Ursula Andress,
  actress.
**Orsa, Orsola, Sula, Ulla,
Ulli, Urmi, Ursa, Ursala,
Ursel, Ursulina, Ursuline**

**Uta** (Ū-tuh)
See Ottilie.
Entertainment: Uta Hagen, actress.

**Utina** (ū-TĒN-uh)
North American Indian—*Woman
  of my country*

**Valda** (VAL-duh)
Teutonic—*Battle-heroine*
**Val, Valdis**

**Valeda** (va-LĒ-duh)
Latin—*The strong or healthy*

**Valentina** (val-en-TĒN-uh)
Latin—*Vigorous and strong*
**Val, Vale, Valeda, Valencia,
Valentia, Valentin, Valerie,
Valli, Vally, Valore**

**Valerie** (VAL-er-ē)
Latin—*Strong*
Entertainment: Valerie Harper,
  actress.
**Val, Vale, Valera, Vally**

**Valeska** (va-LES-kuh)
Polish, Russian—*Glorious ruler*
**Vladislav**

**Valonia** (va-LŌN-ē-uh)
Latin—*Of the vale*
Mythological: Latin goddess of
  valleys.
**Vallonia**

**Valora** (va-LOR-uh)
Latin—*The valorous*

**VANESSA** — *Butterfly*

**Vanessa** (va-NĒ-suh)
Greek — *Butterfly*
Entertainment: Vanessa Redgrave,
  Vanessa Brown, actresses;
  *Vanessa,* American opera by
  Samuel Barber.
**Nania, Van, Vanna, Vanni,
Vannie, Vanny**

**Vania** (va-NĒ-uh)
Hebrew — *God's gracious gift*
**Van**

**Vara** (VAIR-uh)
Greek — *The stranger*

**Vashti** (VASH-tē)
Persian — *Beautiful*
**Vashta, Vasti**

**Veda** (VĀ-duh)
Sanskrit— *Wise*
**Vedette, Velda, Veleda**

**Vedia** (VĀ-dē-uh)
Teutonic— *Sacred spirit of the forest*

**Velma** (VEL-muh)
See Wilhelmina.
Entertainment: Vilma Banky,
   silent-movie actress.
**Vilma**

**Velvet** (VEL-vet)
English— *Velvety*
Literature: *National Velvet,* novel
   by Enid Eagnold.

**Venus** (VĒ-nus)
Latin— *Venus*
Mythological: Goddess of beauty.
**Venita, Vin, Vinita, Vinnie,**
**Vinny**

**Vera** (VIR-ruh)
Latin— *True*
Russian— *Faith*
Entertainment: Vera Miles,
   actress; Vera Zorina, ballet
   dancer.
**Veradis, Vere, Verena,**
**Verene, Verina, Verine,**
**Verla, Vernice, Vernita**

**Veradis** (VĒR-uh-dis)
Latin— *Truthful, genuine*

**Verda** (VER-duh)
Latin— *Young and fresh*
**Verdie**

**Verena** (va-RĒ-nuh)
Teutonic— *Defender*
**Vera, Verna**

**Verity** (VAIR-i-tē)
Latin— *Truth*
**Verita**

**Verna** (VER-nuh)
Latin— *Spring-born*

**Veronica** (vuh-RON-i-kuh)
Latin— *True image*
Entertainment: Veronica Lake,
   actress.
**Ranna, Vera, Veronika,**
**Veronike, Veronique, Vonni,**
**Vonnie, Vonny**

**Vesta** (VES-tuh)
Sanskrit, Latin— *Guardian of the*
   *sacred fire*
Mythological: Goddess of hearth
   and home.
**Vest**

**Victoria** (vik-TOR-ē-uh)
Latin— *Victory*
Historical: Name given to the
   queen of England.
Entertainment: Victoria de los
   Angeles, opera singer; Vicki
   Carr, singer; Victoria Principal,
   actress.
**Vick, Vicki, Vickie, Vicky,**
**Victorie, Victorine, Vikki, Vikkii,**
**Vikky, Vitoria, Vittoria**

**Vida** (VĒ-duh)
Hebrew— *Beloved*
**Veda, Vita, Vitia**

**Vidonia** (vi-DON-yuh)
Portuguese— *Vine branch*

**Violet** (VĪ-uh-let)
Latin— *Violet flower*
**Eolande, Iolande, Iolanthe,**
**Vi, Viola, Violante, Viole,**
**Violetta, Violette, Yolanda,**
**Yolande, Yolane, Yolanthe**

**Virginia** (VER-jin-yuh)
Latin— *Virgin maiden*
Historical: Colony of Virginia.
Literature: Virginia Woolf,
   novelist.
Entertainment: Virginia Mayo,
   actress.
**Ginger, Ginni, Ginnie, Ginny,**
**Jimmy, Virg, Virgie,**
**Virgilia, Virginie, Virgy**

**Viridis** (vi-RĒ-dis)
Latin— *Youthful and blooming*

**Vita** (VĒ-tuh)
Latin— *Life*

**Vivian** (VI-vē-un)
Latin— *Full of life*
Literature: Vivian, imprisoned by
    Merlin in King Arthur legend.
Entertainment: Vivien Leigh,
    actress.
**Vevay, Vi, Viv, Vivi, Vivia,
Viviana, Vivianne, Vivie, Vivien,
Vivienne, Vivyan, Vivyanne**

**Voleta** (vō-LĒ-tuh)
French— *The veiled*

**Wakanda** (wa-KAN-duh)
Sioux Indian— *Inner magical power*

**Wallis** (WAL-lis)
Teutonic— *Girl of Wales*
Feminine form of Wallace.
Historical: Wallis Simpson, who
    married the Duke of Windsor
    after he gave up the throne of
    England for her.
**Walli, Wallie, Wally**

**Wanda** (WAN-duh)
Teutonic— *Wander*
Entertainment: Wanda
    Landowska, harpsichordist.
**Vanda, Wandie, Wandis, Wenda,
Wendeline, Wendi, Wendie,
Wendy, Wendye**

**Wendy** (WEN-dē)
See Wanda.
Literature: Wendy, character in
    children's classic, *Peter Pan*.
Entertainment: Wendy Barrie,
    Wendy Hiller, actresses.
**Wendelin, Wendeline, Wendi,
Wendie, Wendye, Windey,
Windy**

**Wenona** (wē-NŌ-nuh)
North American Indian—
    *First-born daughter*
**Wenonah**

**Wesley** (WES-lē)
English— *From the west meadow*
**Wesla**

**Whitney** (WIT-nē)
English— *From the white island*

**Wilhelmina** (wil-hel-MĒ-nuh)
Teutonic— *Determined guardian*
Feminine form of William.
Sports: Billie Jean King, tennis
    champion.
**Billi, Billie, Billy, Guglielma,
Guillema, Guillemette, Min,
Mina, Minna, Minni, Minnie,
Minny, Valma, Velma,
Vilhelmina, Vilma, Wileen,
Wilhelmine, Willa, Willabel,
Willabella, Willabelle,
Willamina, Willetta, Willette,
Willi, Willie, Willy, Wilma,
Wilmet, Wilmette, Wylamina,
Wylma**

**Willette** (wil-LET)
See William.
Literature: Willa Cather, novelist.
**Willa**

**Willow** (WIL-ō)
English— *Freedom*

**Wilma** (WIL-muh)
See Wilhelmina.
Sports: Wilma Rudolph Ward,
   Olympic sprinter.

**Wilona** (wi-LŌ-nuh)
Anglo-Saxon— *The desired*
**Wilone**

**Winema** (wi-NĒ-muh)
Indian— *Chieftainess*

**Winnie** (WIN-nē)
See Gwyneth.
Literature: *Winnie the Pooh,* by
   A.A. Milne.
**Winni, Winny**

**Winnifred** (WI-ni-fred)
Teutonic— *Friend of peace*
Entertainment: Winifred Lenihan,
   actress.
**Freddi, Freddie, Freddy,
Fredi, Ona, Oona, Una,
Winifred, Winnie, Winny**

**Winola** (wi-NŌ-luh)
Teutonic— *Gracious friend*

**Winona** (wi-NŌ-nuh)
Sioux Indian— *First-born daughter*
**Wenona, Wenonah, Winnie,
Winny, Winonah**

**Winter** (WIN-ter)
Old English— *Winter*

**Wisia** (WI-shuh)
Polish— *Victory*
**Wicia, Wikitoria, Wikta,
Wiktorja**

**Wynne** (WIN)
Welsh— *Fair*
**Winne, Winny, Wyanet**

**Xanthe** (ZAN-thē)
Greek— *Golden yellow*
Historical: Wife of Socrates.
**Xantha, Xanthus**

**Xaviera** (za-vē-AIR-uh)
Arabic— *Brilliant*

**Xenia** (ZĒ-nē-uh)
Greek— *Hospitable*
**Xena, Zena, Zenia**

**Ximena** (zi-MĒ-nuh)
Spanish— *Unknown*
Literature: Heroine of *El Cid,* by
   Corneille.
**Ximenes**

**Xylia** (ZĪ-luh) or (ZĪ-lē-uh)
Greek— *Of the wood*
**Xylina**

**Yachi** (YA-chē)
Japanese—*Eight thousand*

**Yachne** (YAWK-nē)
Lithuanian, Hebrew—*Gracious*

**Yamka** (YAM-kuh)
Hopi Indian—*Flower budding*

**Yasmeen** (YAS-mēn)
Arabic—*Jasmine flower*

**Yasu** (YAW-sōō)
Japanese—*The tranquil*
**Yasuko**

**Yepa** (YĒ-puh)
North American Indian—*The snow-maiden*

**Yesmina** (yez-MĒ-nuh)
Hebrew—*Right hand, strength*

**Yetta** (YET-tuh)
Old English—*Giver*

**Yeva** (YĀ-vuh)
Russian, Hebrew—*Life-giving*

**Yolanda** (yō-LAN-duh)
Greek—*Violet flower*
**Eolande, Iolande, Iolnathe, Yolande, Yolane, Yolanthe**

**Yoluta** (yō-LŌŌ-tuh)
North American Indian—*Farewell to the spring flower*

**Yonina** (yō-NĒ-nuh)
Hebrew—*Dove*
**Jona, Jonati, Jonina, Yona, Yonit, Yonita**

**Yoshiko** (yō-SHĒ-kō)
Japanese—*Good*
**Yoshi**

**Yovela** (yō-VĒ-luh)
Hebrew—*Rejoicing*

**Yseult** (Ē-zōōlt)
Celtic—*The fair*

**Yuri** (Ū-rē)
Japanese—*Lily*

**Yvonne** (ē-VON)
French—*Archer*
Entertainment: Yvonne De Carlo
Yvonne Printemps, Yvette
Mimieux, actresses.
**Evonne, Yevette, Yvette**

**Zada** (ZĀ-duh)
Syrian—*Lucky one*

**Zahara** (za-HAR-uh)
Swahili—*Flower*

**Zaltana** (zal-TA-nuh)
North American Indian—*High mountain*

**Zaneta** (za-NĒ-tuh)
Hebrew—*God's gracious gift*

**Zara** (ZAIR-uh)
Hebrew—*Dawn*
**Zarah, Zaria, Zarie**

**Zel** (ZEL)
Turkish—*A bell*

**Zelda** (ZEL-duh)
See Griselda.
Famous: Zelda Fitzgerald, wife of
F. Scott Fitzgerald.
**Selda, Zelde**

**Zenia** (ZE-nē-uh)
Greek—*The hospitable*
**Xenia, Zenecia, Zeni, Zenija,
Zenobia, Zina**

**Zenobia** (ze-NŌ-bē-uh)
Arabic—*Her father's ornament*

**Zerdali** (zer-DĀ-lē)
Turkish—*Wild apricot*

**Zia** (ZĒ-uh)
Latin—*Kind of grain*
**Zea**

**Zina** (ZĒ-nuh)
African—*Name*

**Zipparah** (zi-PAW-ruh)
Hebrew—*Sparrow*
Biblical: Wife of Moses.
**Zifarah, Zifora, Zippora**

**Zita** (ZĒ-tuh)
Greek, Spanish—*Little rose*
**Zitela, Zitella**

**Zizi** (ZĒ-zē)
Hungarian, Hebrew—*Dedicated to
God*
**Beti, Boske, Boski, Bozsi,
Eresike, Erqsbet, Erzsi,
Erzsok, Liszka, Liza, Zsoka**

**Zoe** (ZŌ) or (ZŌ-uh)
Greek—*Life*
Literature: Zoe Akins, author of
the play *The Old Maid.*

**Zoheret** (ZŌ-her-et)
Hebrew—*She shines*

**Zola** (ZŌ-luh)
Italian—*Ball of the earth*

**Zona** (ZŌ-nuh)
Greek, Latin—*Girdle belt*
Literature: Zona Gale, author.

**Zora** (ZOR-uh)
Greek—*Dawn*
**Zorah, Zorana, Zorina, Zorine**

**Zuleika** (ZOO-lē-kuh)
Arabic—*The fair one*

**Zuri** (ZOO-rē)
Swahili—*Beautiful*

# BOYS' NAMES

**Aaron** (AIR-un)
Hebrew — *Light or mountain*
Biblical: First high priest of Israel, brother of Moses.
**Aharon, Ari, Arnie, Arny, Aron, Haroun, Ron, Ronnie, Ronny**

**Abasi** (uh-BĀ-sē)
Swahili — *Stern*
**Abbas**

**Abbotson** (A-but-sun)
Hebrew — *Son*

**Abbott** (A-but)
Arabic — *Father*
**Ab, Abba, Abbe, Abbey, Abbie, Abbot, Abby**

**Abdel** (AB-del)
Arabic — *Servant*
**Abdul, Abdullah**

**Abel** (Ā-bel)
Hebrew — *Breath*
Biblical: Second son of Adam and Eve, slain by Cain.
Literature: Hero of *Green Mansions,* by W. H. Hudson.
**Abe, Abey, Abie**

**Abelard** (A-bel-ard)
Teutonic — *Nobly resolute*
**Ab, Abbey, Abby, Abel**

**Abi** (A-bē)
Turkish — *Elder brother*

**Abijah** (a-BĒ-juh)
Hebrew — *The Lord is my father*
**Abisha**

**Abner** (AB-ner)
Hebrew — *Father of light*
Biblical: Commander of King Saul's army.
Literature: *Li'l Abner,* comic strip by Al Capp.
**Abbner**

**Abraham** (Ā-bruh-ham)
Hebrew — *Father of multitude*
Biblical: First Hebrew patriarch.
Historical: Abraham Lincoln, President.
Entertainment: Civil war song *We Are Coming, Father Abraham.*
**Abe, Abey, Abie, Abrahan, Abram, Abramo, Abran, Avram, Avrom, Bram**

**Abram** (Ā-brum)
Hebrew — *Exalted father*
Famous: James Abram Garfield, President.
**Avram, Avrom, Bram**

**Absalom** (AB-suh-lom)
Hebrew — *Father of peace*
Literature: *Absalom, Absalom,* by William Faulkner.

**Acayib** (a-KĀ-yib)
Turkish — *Wonderful and strange*

**Ace** (ĀS)
Latin — *Unity*
**Acey, Acie, Ase**

**ADLER**—*Eagle*

**Achilles** (a-KIL-ēz)
Unknown
Mythological: Hero of Homer's
*Iliad.*

**Ackerley** (A-ker-lē)
Old English—*From the oak-tree
meadow*
**Ackley**

**Adair** (uh-DAIR)
Celtic—*From the oak-tree ford*

**Adal** (Ā-dal)
German—*Noble*

**Adalbert** (Ā-dal-bert)
German—*Noble bright*
**Adalard, Adelard, Dalbert,
Delvert**

**Adam** (AD-um)
Hebrew—*Man of the red earth*
Biblical: First man created by God.
Literature: Adam Smith, author of
*The Wealth of Nations;* novel
*Adam Bede,* by George Eliot.
**Ad, Adamo, Adams, Adan,
Adao, Addie, Addis, Addy,
Ade, Adem, Adham**

**Adamson** (AD-um-sun)
Hebrew—*Son of Adam*

**Adar** (Ā-dar)
Syrian—*Prince or ruler*

**Addison** (A-di-sun)
Anglo-Saxon—*Adam's descendant*
**Ad, Addie, Addy**

**Adel** (Ā-del)
German—*Noble*
**Adelar, Adelard, Adelbern, Adelhart**

**Adelbert** (Ā-del-bert)
Teutonic—*Nobly bright*
**Adelburt, Bert**

**Adelric** (Ā-del-rik)
Teutonic—*Noble commander*
**Adalric**

**Adigun** (A-di-gun)
Nigerian—*Righteous*

**Adin** (Ā-din)
Hebrew—*Voluptuous or sensual*

**Adir** (Ā-dir)
Hebrew—*Majestic*

**Adlai** (AD-lā)
Hebrew—*Justice of Jehovah*
Famous: Adlai E. Stevenson, U.S.
   Ambassador to the United
   Nations and candidate for
   President.

**Adlar** (AD-lar)
Teutonic—*Noble and brave*

**Adler** (AD-ler)
Teutonic—*Eagle*
**Ad**

**Adley** (AD-lē)
Hebrew—*The just*

**Adolph** (Ā-dolf)
Teutonic—*Noble wolf or noble hero*
Historical: Adolph Hitler, German
   dictator.
**Ad, Adolf, Adolpha, Adolphe,
Adolpho, Adolphus, Dolf, Dolph**

**Adon** (Ā-don)
Hebrew—*Lord*
**Adomis, Adonis, Adonnis**

**Adri** (AD-rē)
Hindi—*Rock*

**Adrian** (Ā-drē-un)
Latin—*Black earth*
Entertainment: Sir Adrian Boult,
   conductor.
**Ade, Adriano, Adrien, Hadrian**

**Adriel** (Ā-drē-el)
Hebrew—*Of God's flock*
**Adrial**

**Agler** (AG-ler)
Greek—*Gleaming*

**Agustin** (aw-GUS-tin)
Spanish—*The exalted one*
**Austin**

**Ahab** (Ā-hab)
Hebrew—*Uncle*
Literature: Captain Ahab,
   character in Herman Melville's
   *Moby Dick.*

**Ahanu** (a-HAW-noo)
North American Indian—*He laughs*

**Aharon** (a-HAR-on)
Hebrew—*Exalted*

**Ahearn** (Ā-hern)
Celtic—*Lord of the horses*
**Ahern**

**Aidan** (Ā-dan)
Celtic—*Fire or warmth of the home*

**Ainsley** (ĀNS-lē)
Old English—*From Ann's meadow*
**Ainslie**

**Ainsworth** (ĀNS-werth)
Old English—*From Ann's estate*

**Airell** (AR-el)
Celtic—*Chief*

**Ajax** (Ā-jaks)
Greek—*Eagle*
Turkish—*Frost on a clear winter
   night*
Literature: Hero in Homer's *Iliad.*

**Ala** (AW-luh)
Arabic—*Glorious*

**Alabi** (AL-uh-bē)
Yoruban— *A boy born after many girls*

**Alan** (AL-an)
Gaelic— *Handsome or cheerful*
Literature: Allen-a-Dale, character in *Ivanhoe*, by Sir Walter Scott.
Entertainment: Alan Ladd, Alan Alda, Allen Stewart Konigsberg (Woody Allen), Alan Arkin, Alan Bates, Al Pacino, actors; Alan Jay Lerner, music composer.
**Ailin, Al, Alain, Alair, Aland, Alano, Alanson, Alayne, Allan, Allayne, Allen, Alley, Alleyn, Allie, Allyn**

**Alaric** (AL-ar-ik)
Teutonic— *Ruler of all*
**Alric, Alrick**

**Alastair** (AL-a-stair)
See Alexander.
Literature: Alistair McLean, novelist.
Entertainment: Alastair Sim, Alistair Cooke, actors.
**Al, Alasdair, Alasteir, Alaster, Alistair, Alister, Alistir, Allister, Allistir**

**Alben** (AL-ben)
Latin— *Fair-blond*
**Al, Alban, Albie, Albin, Alby**

**Albern** (AL-bern)
Teutonic— *Of noble valor*

**Albert** (AL-bert)
German— *Noble, bright*
Historical: Albert Luthuli, Zulu chief, Nobel-Peace-Prize winner.
Famous: Prince Albert, husband of Queen Victoria; Albert Einstein, scientist.
Literature: Albert Camus, French novelist.
Entertainment: Fat Albert, cartoon character created by Bill Cosby.
**Adelbert, Ailbert, Al, Alberto, Albie, Albrecht, Aubert, Bert, Berty, Elbert**

**Albion** (AL-bē-on)
Latin— *White or fair*

**Alcott** (AL-kot)
Old English— *From the old cottage*
**Alcot**

**Alden** (AWL-den)
Anglo-Saxon— *Old friend or protector*
**Al, Aldin, Aldwin, Elden, Eldin**

**Aldis** (AWL-dis)
Old English— *From the old house*
**Al, Aldo, Aldous, Aldus**

**Aldous** (AWL-dus)
German— *Old and wise*
Literature: Aldous Huxley, author of *Brave New World*.

**Aldred** (AWL-dred)
Anglo-Saxon— *Ancient counselor*

**Aldrich** (AWL-drich)
Teutonic— *Sage or noble ruler*
**Al, Aldric, Aldridge, Alric, Eldridge, Rich, Rickie, Ricky**

**Aldwin** (AWL-dwin)
Anglo-Saxon— *Old friend*
**Allwin**

**Alein** (AL-ēn)
Hebrew— *Alone*

**Aleron** (AL-er-on)
French— *Shoulder-badge or knight armor*
**Aleren**

**Aleser** (a-LĀ-ser)
Arabic— *Lion*

**Alexander** (al-eks-AN-der)
Greek— *Helper of mankind*
Famous: Alexander the Great;
  Alexander Graham Bell, inventor
  of the telephone; Sir Alexander
  Fleming, discoverer of penicillin;
  Sandro Botticelli, painter of *The
  Birth of Venus;* Alessandro
  Scarlatti, founder of modern
  opera.
Literature: Alexandre Dumas,
  Aleksandr Solzhenitsyn,
  authors; Alex Haley, author of
  *Roots.*
Entertainment: Alec Guinness,
  Alejandro Rey, actors.
**Al, Alasdair, Alastair,
Alaster, Alec, Alejandro,
Alejo, Alek, Alekos,
Aleksandr, Alessandro, Alex,
Alexandr, Alexandre, Alexandro,
Alexandros, Alexio, Alexis,
Alic, Alick, Alik, Alisander,
Alistair, Alister, Alix,
Allister, Allistir, Lyaksandr,
Sander, Sandra, Sandro, Sandy,
Sanya, Sascha, Sasha, Saunder,
Shura, Shurik**

**Alf** (ALF)
Norwegian— *Elfin*
Entertainment: *Alfie,* movie
  starring Michael Caine.
**Alfie, Alfy, Alv**

**Alfred** (AL-fred)
Old English— *Elf counselor*
Famous: Alfred the Great; Alfred
  Bernhard Nobel, inventor of
  dynamite and founder of the
  Nobel prizes.
Entertainment: Alfred Drake,
  actor; Alfred Hitchcock, film
  director.
**Abery, Al, Alf, Alfie,
Alfredo, Alfy, Fred, Freddie,
Freddy**

**Alger** (AL-jer)
Teutonic— *Noble spear man*
**Al, Algar, Algernon,
Elgar, Elger, Elgernon**

**Ali** (A-lē)
Arabic— *Greatest*

**Alim** (al-IM)
Arabic— *Wise, learned*
**Alem**

**Alison** (AL-i-sun)
Teutonic— *Of holy fame*
**Allison**

**Allan** (AL-un)
See Alan.
**Allen**

**Allard** (AL-ard)
Teutonic— *Nobly resolute*
**Alard**

**Allister** (AL-i-ster)
See Alexander.
**Alaster**

**Almon** (AL-mon)
Hebrew— *Forsaken*

**Almund** (AL-mund)
Anglo-Saxon— *Protector of the
  temple*

**Alon** (AL-on)
Hebrew— *Oak tree*

**Alonzo** (a-LON-zō)
See Alphonse.
Sports: Alonzo Stagg, football
  coach.
**Alfonso, Alonso, Lon**

**Aloysius** (al-ō-WI-shus)
Teutonic— *Famous in war*

**Alpheus** (AL-fē-us)
Greek— *River god*

**Alphonse** (AL-fons)
Teutonic— *Eager for battle*
Literature: Alphonse Daudet,
  author.
**Alf, Alfie, Alfons, Alfonso,
Alford, Alfy, Alphonse, Alonso,
Alonzo, Fons, Fonsie, Fonz,
Fonzie, Lon**

**Alrik** (AWL-rik)
Swedish, Teutonic— *Ruler of all*

**Alroy** (AWL-roi)
Spanish— *The king*

**Alson** (AL-son)
Old English— *Son of all*

**Alston** (AL-ston)
Anglo-Saxon— *From the old manor*

**Alton** (AL-ton)
Old English— *From the old manor*
**Alten**

**Alvar** (AWL-var)
Latin— *White or fair*

**Alvin** (AL-vin)
Teutonic— *Friend of all*
Famous: Thomas Alva Edison,
   inventor of the light bulb.
**Aloin, Aluin, Aluino, Alva,
Alvan, Alvie, Alvy, Alwin,
Alwyn, Elvin**

**Alvis** (AL-vis)
Scandinavian— *All-knowing*

**Amadis** (uh-MA-dis)
Latin— *Love of God*

**Amado** (uh-MA-dō)
Spanish, Latin— *Loving deity*
**Amadeo, Amadis, Amando**

**Amasa** (uh-MA-suh)
Hebrew— *Burden*

**Ambert** (AM-bert)
Teutonic— *Bright*

**Ambrose** (AM-brōz)
Greek— *Belonging to the immortals*
Literature: Ambrose Bierce, author.
**Ambee, Ambie, Ambros,
Ambrosi, Ambrosio, Ambrosius,
Amley, Brose**

**Ameer** (a-MER)
Arabic— *A prince*

**Amiel** (a-MEL)
Hebrew— *Lord of my people*

**Amin** (a-MIN)
Indian— *Faithful*
**Amitan, Amnon**

**Amory** (Ā-mō-rē)
German— *Industrious*
Literature: Amory Blaine, hero of
   *This Side of Paradise,* by F. Scott
   Fitzgerald.
**Almericus, Amalric, Amelric,
Americus, Amerigo, Amery,
Emery, Emmerich, Emmery**

**Amos** (Ā-mos)
Hebrew— *Burden*
Biblical: Prophet of Old Testament.
Entertainment: Amos and Andy,
   comedy team.
**Amoss**

**Amyas** (a-MĒ-as)
Latin— *One who shall love God*

**Anastasius** (an-uh-STĀ-shus)
Greek— *One who shall rise again*
**Anastas, Anastasius, Anastatius,
Anstice**

**Anatole** (AN-uh-tōl)
Greek— *From the east*
Literature: Anatole France, French
   novelist.
**Anatol, Anatolio**

**Anders** (AN-ders)
See Andrew.
**Anderson**

**André** (ON-drā)
Russian, French— *Strong and manly*
Literature: André Maurosi, André
   Malraux, authors; André Gide,
   Nobel Prize winning author.
**Anders, Andi, Andor, Andras,
Andreas, Andres, Andrew,
Andrey, Andris, Andrius, Aniol,
Endre, Evagelos, Jedrek,
Jedrus, Ondra, Ondro**

**ANDRE**—*Strong and manly*

## Andrew (AN-dr$\overline{oo}$)
Greek—*Manly*
Biblical: Apostle of Jesus Christ.
Famous: Andrea del Sarto, painter
of *The Faultless Painter;* Andrew
Young, former Ambassador to
the United Nations.
Entertainment: Andre Segovia,
guitarist; Andy Williams, singer.
**Anders, Andie, Andonis,
Andre, Andrea, Andreas, Andres,
Andrey, Andy, Dre, Dru,
Drud, Drugi**

## Aneurin (a-N$\overline{U}$R-in)
Welsh—*Very golden*
Latin—*Honorable*
Famous: Aneurin Beva, British
labor leader.

## Angell ($\overline{A}$N-jel)
Greek—*Messenger*

## Angelo (AN-juh-l$\overline{o}$)
Greek—*Angel or saintly*
Literature: Angel Clare, hero of
*Tess of the D'Urbervilles,* by
Thomas Hardy.
**Ange, Angel, Angie, Angy**

## Angus ($\overline{A}$NG-us)
Celtic—*Exceptionally strong*
Interesting: In Irish folklore,
Angus Og is the God of laughter,
love, wisdom and understanding.
**Ennis, Gus**

## Ansel (AN-sel)
French—*Adherent of a nobleman*
Famous: Ansel Adams,
photographer.
**Ancell, Ansell**

## Anselm (AN-selm)
Teutonic—*Divine helmet*
**Anse, Ansel, Anselma, Anselme,
Anselmi, Anselmo, Elmo, Selma**

**Anson** (AN-sun)
Old English—*Son of a nobleman*
Teutonic—*Son of John*
Entertainment: Anson Williams,
actor in *Happy Days.*
**Ansun, Hanson**

**Anthony** (AN-thō-nē)
Latin—*Priceless*
Historical: Mark Antony and
Cleopatra.
Famous: *The Temptation of St.
Anthony,* painting by
Hieronymus Bosch.
Entertainment: Anthony Quinn,
Anthony Perkins, Tony Curtis,
actors.
**Antoine, Anton, Antone,
Antoni, Antonin, Antonio,
Antonius, Antony, Toni, Tonie,
Tony**

**Anton** (AN-ton)
Latin—*Unestimable*
**Andonias, Andonis, Antal,
Antavas, Antek, Anthony, Anti,
Antin, Antinko, Antoine,
Antonen, Antonin, Antons,
Antos, Tolek, Tonda, Tonek,
Tonik, Tonis, Tony, Tosya,
Tusya**

**Apang** (a-PANG)
North American
Indian—*First-place winner*

**Apenimon** (uh-PE-ni-mon)
North American Indian—*Trusty*

**Apollo** (uh-PAW-lō)
Greek—*Manly beauty*
Mythological: Greek god of light,
healing and arts.
**Apolo, Polio, Polo**

**Archer** (AR-cher)
Old English—*Bowman*

**Archibald** (AR-chi-bald)
German—*Nobly or genuinely bold*
Literature: Archibald MacLeish,
winner of three Pulitzer Prizes.
**Arch, Archaimbaud,
Archambault, Archer,
Archibaldio, Archibaldo,
Archibold, Archie, Archy**

**Arden** (AR-den)
Latin—*Ardent, fiery*
**Ard, Ardean, Ardie, Ardin, Ardy**

**Ardon** (AR-don)
Hebrew—*Bronze*
**Ardean**

**Arel** (AIR-el)
Hebrew—*Lion of God*

**Aren** (AIR-en)
Norwegian—*Eagle*

**Argus** (AR-gus)
Greek, Danish—*Watchful or vigilant*
**Gus, Guss**

**Argyle** (AR-gīl)
Celtic—*From the land of the Irish*

**Aric** (AIR-ik)
Teutonic—*Ruler*
**Arick**

**Ariel** (AIR-ē-el)
Hebrew—*Lion of God*
Biblical: Chief who followed Ezra.
Ariel was the name given to
Jerusalem by Isaiah.
Literature: *Ariel,* biography by
Andre Maurois.
**Airel**

**Aries** (AIR-ēz)
Zodiac—*Ram*

**Arkin** (AR-kin)
Norwegian—*The eternal King's son*

**Arkwright** (ARK-rīt)
Old English—*Maker of chests*

**Arlen** (AR-len)
Gaelic—*Pledge*
**Arlin**

**ARCHER**—*Bowman*

**Arley** (AR-lē)
Zodiac—*The bowman*

**Arlo** (AR-lō)
See Harlow.
Entertainment: Arlo Guthrie,
folksinger.

**Arman** (AR-man)
Russian, Teutonic—*Army man*
**Armand, Armando, Armin,
Armond, Armund**

**Armon** (AR-mon)
Hebrew—*Castle or place*
**Armoni, Armony**

**Armstrong** (ARM-strong)
Old English—*With a strong arm*

**Arne** (AR-nē)
Norwegian—*Eagle*
**Arney, Arni, Arnie**

**Arnold** (AR-nuld)
German—*Eagle power*
Literature: Arnold Bennet, author
of *The Old Wive's Tale*.
Sports: Arnold Palmer, golfer.
**Arnaldo, Arnaud, Arney, Arni,
Arnie, Arnoldo, Arny**

**Arnon** (AR-non)
Hebrew—*Rushing stream*
Interesting: Name for an energetic
child.
**Arnan**

**Aron** (AIR-on)
Czech, Polish— *Lofty or exalted*
**Aaron**

**Arpiar** (AR-pē-ar)
Armenian— *Sunny, of sunshine*

**Arri** (AR-ē)
Greek— *Seeking the positive results*

**Arrio** (AR-rē-ō)
Spanish— *Warlike*
**Ario**

**Arslan** (ARS-lan)
Turkish— *Lion*

**Artemas** (AR-tuh-mus)
Greek— *Safe and sound*
Biblical: Character in the New
Testament.
**Art, Artemis, Artemus,**
**Artie, Arty**

**Arthur** (AR-ther)
Celtic— *Noble*
Welsh— *Bear hero*
Literature: British king of the
Round Table in *Idylls of the King,*
by Lord Alfred Tennyson; *Morte
d'Arthur,* by Sir Thomas Malory;
Sir Arthur Conan Doyle, creator
of Sherlock Holmes; Arthur
Miller, playwright.
Entertainment: Artur Rubinstein,
pianist; Art Garfunkel, singer.
Sports: Arthur Ashe, tennis
champion.
**Art, Artair, Arte, Arther,**
**Artie, Artur, Arturo, Artus,**
**Arty, Aurthur, Aurthus**

**Arundel** (uh-RUN-del)
Old English— *From the eagle dell*

**Arvad** (AR-vad)
Hebrew— *Wander*
**Arv, Arvid, Arvie**

**Arve** (ARV)
Norwegian— *Heir*
**Arvid**

**Arvel** (AR-vel)
Welsh— *Wept over*

**Arvin** (AR-vin)
German— *People's friend*
**Arv, Arvie, Arvy**

**Asa** (Ā-suh)
Hebrew— *Physician or healer*
**Ase**

**Asadel** (Ā-suh-del)
Arabic— *Most prosperous*

**Ashby** (ASH-bē)
Scandinavian— *From the ash-tree
farm*
**Ashton**

**Asher** (ASH-er)
Hebrew— *Happy, blessed*

**Ashford** (ASH-ford)
Old English— *Dweller by the
ash-tree ford*
**Ash, Ashen, Ashlen,**
**Ashley, Ashlin, Ashton**

**Ashur** (ASH-er)
Swahili— *Month*

**Asiel** (Ā-sē-el)
Hebrew— *God has created him*

**Asker** (ASK-er)
Turkish— *Soldier*

**Aswad** (AS-wad)
Arabic— *Black*

**Athmore** (ATH-mor)
Old English— *From the moor*

**Atman** (AT-man)
Hindi— *The self*

**Atuanya** (a-TWAN-yuh)
Nigerian— *Unexpected*

**Aubrey** (AW-brē)
German, French— *Elf rule*
Famous: Aubrey Beardsley,
  English painter.
Literature: Oberon, elf king in *A
  Midsummer Night's Dream,* by
  Shakespeare.
**Alberik, Aube, Auberon,
Avery, Oberon**

**Audley** (AWD-lē)
Anglo-Saxon— *Unknown*

**Audric** (AWD-rik)
French— *Old and wise ruler*
**Aldrich, Aldrick**

**Audun** (AWD-un)
Norwegian— *Deserted or desolate*

**Audwin** (AWD-win)
Teutonic— *Rich or prospering friend*

**August** (AW-gust)
Latin— *Majestic dignity*
**Agosto, Aguistin, Agustin,
Augie, Auguste, Augustine,
Augusto, Augustus, Augy,
Austen, Austin, Gus, Guss**

**Augustus** (aw-GUS-tus)
Latin— *The exalted, sacred or sublime*
Famous: Augustus Caesar, Roman
  emperor.
**Aguistin, Agustin, Augie,
Augustin, Augy, Austen,
Austin, Gus**

**Aurek** (AW-rik)
Polish— *Golden-haired*
**Aureli, Elek**

**Austin** (AWS-tin)
See Augustine.
Literature: Austin Dobson,
  novelist.
**Austen**

**Avedig** (AV-dig)
Armenian— *Good news*

**Avel** (Ā-vel)
Greek— *Breath*

**Averill** (Ā-ver-el)
Anglo-Saxon— *Boarlike*
Famous: Averill Harriman, former
  Secretary of State.
**Av, Ave, Averell, Averil**

**Avery** (Ā-ver-ē)
Anglo-Saxon— *Ruler of the elves*
Sports: Avery Brundage,
  Chairman of U.S. Olympic
  Committee.

**Avi** (AW-vē)
Hebrew— *Father*
**Avidan, Avidor, Aviel,
Avital, Avner, Avniel**

**Awan** (A-wan)
North American Indian— *Somebody*

**Axel** (AKS-el)
Hebrew— *Man of peace*
**Aksel, Ax, Axe, Axie**

**Aylmer** (AL-mer)
German— *Noble fame*
**Aylmar, Aymar, Aymer**

**Azad** (A-zad)
Turkish— *Born free*

**Azim** (A-zim)
Arabic— *Defender*

**Azriel** (Ā-zrē-el)
Hebrew— *God is my help*

**Badem** (buh-DĒM)
Turkish — *Almond*

**Bailey** (BĀ-lē)
Teutonic — *Able*
French — *Bailiff or steward*
**Bail, Bailee, Bailie, Baillee, Baillie, Baily**

**Bainbridge** (BĀN-brij)
Gaelic — *Fair bridge*

**Baird** (BAIRD)
Gaelic — *Ballad singer*
**Bar, Bard, Barde, Barr, Bart**

**Balder** (BAL-der)
Scandinavian — *God of light*
**Aldur**

**Baldwin** (BALD-win)
Teutonic — *Bold friend*
**Bald, Balduin, Baudoin**

**Balfour** (BAL-for)
Scottish — *Pasture land*

**Balin** (BĀ-lin)
Hindi — *Mighty soldier*
**Baline**

**Balint** (BĀ-lint)
Hungarian, Latin — *Strong and healthy*

**Ballard** (BAL-ard)
Teutonic — *Bold or strong*
**Ball**

**Bancroft** (BAN-kroft)
Old English — *From the bean field*

**Baram** (BAIR-am)
Hebrew — *Son of a nation*

**Barclay** (BAR-klā)
Old English — *From the birch tree meadow*

**Bardo** (BAR-dō)
Danish — *Son of the earth*
**Barth, Barto, Bartoli, Bartolme, Toli**

**Barlow** (BAR-lō)
Old English — *From the bare hill*
**Bar, Barlie, Barly**

**Barnabas** (BAR-nuh-bus)
Hebrew — *Son of prophecy*
Biblical: Friend of Apostle Paul.
**Barnaba, Barnabe, Barnaby, Barnebas, Barney, Barnie, Barny, Burnaby**

**Barnaby** (BAR-nuh-bē)
See Barnabas.
Entertainment: Barnaby Jones, TV character played by Buddy Ebsen.
**Barnabas, Barney**

**Barnett** (bar-NET)
Old English — *Noble man*
**Barn, Barney, Baron, Barron, Barry**

**Barrett** (BAIR-et)
Teutonic — *Bearlike*

**Barry** (BAIR-ē)
French — *Dweller at the barrier*
Entertainment: Barry Gibb, singer; Barry Manilow, composer and singer.
**Barri, Barrie, Barris**

## Bartholomew
(bar-THAW-lo-mū)
Hebrew— *Son of the farrow*
Biblical: One of the 12 Apostles of
Jesus Christ.
**Bart, Bartel, Barth, Barthel,
Barthelemy, Bartholomeo,
Bartholomeus, Bartlet,
Bartlett, Bartley,
Bartolome, Bat**

## Baruch (ba-ROOK)
Greek— *Doer of good*
Famous: Baruch Spinoza,
philosopher.

## Basham (BA-sham)
Zodiac— *Rich soil*

## Basil (BA-zel)
Greek— *Kingly*
Entertainment: Basil Rathbone,
actor who played Sherlock
Holmes.
**Base, Basile, Basilio,
Basilius, Vasibis, Vassily**

## Basir (BA-sir)
Turkish— *Intelligent and discerning*

## Baul (BOL)
English— *Snail*

## Bavol (BA-vol)
English— *Wind*

## Baxter (BAKS-ter)
Old English— *Baker*
**Bax, Baxie, Baxy**

**BAXTER**— *Baker*

**Bayard** (BĀ-ard)
Teutonic— *Red-brown hair*
Historical: Pierre du Terrail,
  known as Chevalier de Bayard, a
  French hero.
**Bay**

**Beau** (BŌ)
French— *Handsome*
Entertainment: Beau Bridges, actor.
**Beal, Beale, Bealle,
Beaufort, Bo**

**Beauregard** (BŌ-ruh-gard)
French — *Beautiful expression*
**Beau, Bo, Gard**

**Beck** (BEK)
Swedish— *Brook*

**Bedrich** (BED-rik)
Czech, German— *Peaceful leader*
**Beda, Bedo, Bedric**

**Bela** (BE-luh)
Hebrew— *Destruction*
Biblical: Name given to a city
  destroyed by earthquakes.

**Beldon** (BEL-don)
Old English— *Child of unspoiled or
  beautiful glen*
**Belden**

**Belen** (BĀ-len)
Greek— *An arrow*
**Belan, Belon**

**Bellamy** (BEL-uh-mē)
French— *Beautiful friend*
**Belamy, Bell, Bellum**

**Bem** (BEM)
Nigerian— *Peace*

**Bemossed** (BE-mos-ed)
North American Indian— *The
  walker*
**Bemosed**

**Ben** (BEN)
Hebrew— *Son*
**Benn, Bennie, Benny, Benton**

**Benci** (BEN-se)
Hungarian— *Blessed*
**Bendek, Benedek, Benedict,
Benedik, Benedyk, Benek**

**Benedict** (BEN-e-dikt)
Latin— *Blessed*
Interesting: Benedict is a
  confirmed bachelor that finally
  marries later in life.
Historical: Benedict Arnold,
  Revolutionary War traitor.
**Ben, Bendick, Bendict, Bendix,
Benedetto, Benedick, Benedicto,
Benedikt, Bengt, Benito,
Bennie, Benny, Benoit**

**Benjamin** (BEN-ja-min)
Hebrew— *Son of the right hand*
Famous: Benjamin Harrison,
  President; Benjamin Franklin,
  statesman and inventor.
Entertainment: Benny Goodman,
  clarinet player; Benny Anderson,
  member of the pop group, ABBA.
**Ben, Beniamino, Benji, Benjie,
Benjy, Benn, Bennie, Benno,
Benny, Benson, Jamie**

**Bentley** (BENT-le)
Old English— *From the moor*
**Ben, Benn, Bennie, Benny,
Bent, Bentlee, Benton**

**Benzi** (BEN-zē)
Hebrew— *Excellent son*

**Berdy** (BER-de)
Russian, German— *Brilliant mind*
**Berdi, Berdie**

**Berg** (BERG)
Hebrew— *Mountain*

**Bergren** (BER-gren)
Swedish— *Mountain stream*

**Berkeley** (BERK-lē)
Anglo-Saxon— *From the birch
  meadow*
**Berk, Berkie, Berkley, Berkly,
Berky**

**Bern** (BERN)
Teutonic— *Bear*
**Bern, Berne, Bernie,**
**Berny, Bjorn**

**Bernard** (BER-nard)
Teutonic— *Grim bear*
Literature: George Bernard Shaw,
   playwright.
**Barnard, Barne, Barney,**
**Barny, Bear, Bearnard, Bern,**
**Bernardo, Bernarr, Bernhard,**
**Bernie, Berny, Burnard**

**Bernhard** (BERN-hard)
Swedish— *Brave as a bear*
**Bern**

**Bersh** (BERSH)
English— *One year*
**Besh**

**Bert** (BERT)
Old English— *Bright*
Entertainment: Bert Lahr, Bert
   Lancaster, actors; Burt
   Bacharach, songwriter.
Sports: Bart Starr, football
   quarterback.
**Bart, Bertie, Berty, Burt,**
**Burty, Butch**

**Berthold** (BER-tōld)
Teutonic— *Brilliant ruler*
Literature: Bertold Brecht, author
   of *The Three Penny Opera*.
**Bert, Berthoud, Bertie, Bertold,**
**Bertolde, Berty**

**Bertin** (BER-tin)
Spanish— *Distinguished*

**Berton** (BER-ton)
Teutonic— *Glorious raven*
Famous: Bertrand Russell,
   philosopher and winner of the
   Nobel Prize.
**Bart, Beltran, Bert, Bertie,**
**Bertram, Bertrand, Bertrando,**
**Berty**

**Berwin** (BER-win)
Teutonic— *Warrior friend*

**Bevan** (BE-van)
Celtic— *Youthful warrior*
**Bev, Bevon**

**Bevis** (BĒ-vis)
Teutonic— *Bowman*
**Bevus**

**Bialy** (BĒ-al-ē)
Polish— *White-haired boy*
**Bialas**

**Bildad** (BIL-dad)
Hebrew— *Beloved*

**Bill** (BIL)
See William.
Famous: Buffalo Bill Cody; Billy
   Graham, evangelist.
Literature: *Billy Budd*, by Herman
   Melville.
Entertainment: Bill Cosby, Bill
   Bixby, Billy Dee Williams, actors;
   Billy Joel, singer.
**Bil, Billee, Billie, Billy**

**Bing** (BING)
Teutonic— *Kettle-shaped hollow*
Entertainment: Bing Crosby,
   singer and actor.

**Birch** (BIRCH)
Old English— *Birch tree*
Famous: Birch Bayh, Senator.
**Birk, Burch**

**Bishop** (BI-shop)
Old English— *Bishop*
**Bish**

**Bjorn** (bē-ORN)
Norwegian— *Bear*
Entertainment: Bjorn Ulvaeus,
   member of the pop group, ABBA.
Sports: Bjorn Borg, tennis
   champion.

**Blaine** (BLĀN)
Gaelic— *Thin or lean*
**Blainey, Blane, Blayne, Blayney**

**Blair** (BLAIR)
Gaelic— *Child of the fields*

**BORIS**—*Battler*

**Blake** (BLĀK)
  Old English—*Pallid*
  Entertainment: Blake Edwards,
    film producer.

**Blaze** (BLĀZ)
  Latin—*Stammerer*
  **Biagio, Blaise, Blas, Blase,
  Blasius, Blayze, Bleasien**

**Bo** (BŌ)
  See Beauregard.

**Boaz** (BŌ-az)
  Hebrew—*Swift and strong*

**Bob** (BOB)
See Robert.
Entertainment: Bob Hope, Bob
  Newhart, actors; Bob Dylan,
  singer; Bob Fosse, choreographer
  and film director.
Sports: Bob Cousy, basketball
  player.
**Bobbie, Bobby**

**Bogart** (BŌ-gart)
French—*Strong as a bow*
**Bo, Bogery, Bogey, Bogie**

**Bohdan** (BŌ-dan)
Ukrainian—*Given by God*
**Bogdan, Bogdashka**

**Bolton** (BŌL-ton)
Old English—*Of the manor farm*

**Bond** (BOND)
Old English—*Tiller of the soil*
**Bondie, Bondon, Bondy**

**Boone** (BO̅O̅N)
French—*Good*
**Bone, Bonnie, Booney**

**Booth** (BO̅O̅TH)
Old English—*From the hut*
**Boot, Boote, Boothe**

**Borden** (BOR-den)
Old English—*From the valley of the
  boar*
**Bord, Bordie, Bordy**

**Borg** (BORG)
Norwegian—*From the castle*

**Boris** (BOR-is)
Slavic—*Battler*
Literature: Boris Pasternak, author
  of *Doctor Zhivago*.
Entertainment: Boris Karloff, actor.

**Bowie** (BO̅O̅-ē)
Gaelic—*Yellow-haired*

**Bowle** (BŌL)
English—*Snail*
**Baul**

**Bowman** (BŌ-man)
Zodiac—*An archer*

**Boyce** (BOIS)
French—*From the woodland*
**Boy, Boycey, Boycie**

**Boyden** (BOI-den)
Anglo-Saxon—*A herald*
**Boy, Boyer**

**Boynton** (BOIN-ton)
Celtic—*White-cow river*

**Brad** (BRAD)
Old English—*Broad*
**Bradley, Brady**

**Bradburn** (BRAD-bern)
Zodiac—*Broad brook*

**Braden** (BRĀ-den)
Old English—*From the wide valley*
**Bradan**

**Bradford** (BRAD-ford)
Old English—*From the broad river
  crossing*
Entertainment: Bradford Dillman,
  actor.
**Brad, Ford**

**Bradley** (BRAD-lē)
Old English—*From the broad
  meadow*

**Bradshaw** (BRAD-shaw)
English—*Large virginal forest*

**Brainard** (BRĀ-nard)
Teutonic—*Bold raven*

**Bram** (BRAM)
Gaelic—*Raven*
Old English—*Famous*
Literature: Bram Stoker, author of
  *Dracula*.
**Bran**

**Bramwell** (BRAM-wel)
Old English—*Of Abraham's well*
Entertainment: Bramwell Fletcher,
  actor.

**Brand** (BRAND)
Old English — *Firebrand*
**Bran, Brander, Brandy, Brant**

**Brandon** (BRAN-don)
Teutonic — *Flaming hill*
Anglo-Saxon — *Sword*
**Bran, Brand, Brandy**

**Brede** (BRĒD)
Norwegian, Danish — *Glacier*

**Brencis** (BREN-sis)
Latin — *Crowned with laurel*

**Brendan** (BREN-dan)
Gaelic — *Little raven*
German — *Aflame*
Literature: Brendan Behan, author
   of *The Hostage.*
**Bren, Brenden, Brendin, Brendis**

**Brent** (BRENT)
Old English — *Steep hill*
**Brentan, Brenton**

**Brett** (BRET)
Celtic — *Native of Brittany*
Literature: Bret Harte, western
   short-story writer.
Entertainment: Bret Maverick,
   character played by James
   Garner.
**Bret, Brit, Britt**

**Brewster** (BROO-ster)
Old English — *Brewer*
**Brew, Brewer, Bruce**

**Brian** (BRĪ-an)
Celtic — *The strong*
Historical: Brian Boru, heroic king
   of Ireland.
Entertainment: Brian Aherne,
   Brian Keith, actors.
**Briano, Briant, Brien, Brion,
Bryan, Bryant, Bryon**

**Brice** (BRĪS)
Celtic — *Quick moving*
**Bryce**

**Brigham** (BRI-gam)
Old English — *Dweller by the bridge*
Famous: Brigham Young, Mormon
   prophet and pioneer.
**Brig, Brigg, Briggs**

**Brock** (BROK)
Old English — *Badger*
Sports: Brock Yates, automotive
   journalist.
**Brockie, Brocky, Brok**

**Broderick** (BROD-er-ik)
Old English — *From the broad ridge*
Entertainment: Broderick
   Crawford, actor.
**Brod, Broddie, Broddy,
Broderic, Rick, Rickie, Ricky**

**Brody** (BRŌ-dē)
Gaelic — *Ditch*
**Brodie**

**Bromley** (BROM-lē)
Old English — *From the
   broom-covered meadow*
**Bromlee**

**Bronson** (BRON-sun)
Old English — *Dark-skinned*

**Brook** (BROOK)
Old English — *From the brook*
**Brooke, Brooks, Burne**

**Bruce** (BROOS)
French — *From the thicket*
Literature: Bruce Catton, author.
Entertainment: Bruce Dern, actor.
**Brucie, Bruis**

**Bruno** (BROO-nō)
Italian — *Brown-haired*
**Bruna, Bruns**

**Bryant** (BRĪ-ant)
Celtic — *Strong*
Entertainment: Bryant Gumbel,
   newscaster.
**Bryan**

## Buck (BUK)
Old English — *Buck deer*
Entertainment: Buck Henry, actor;
  Buck Rogers, space character.
**Buckie, Bucky**

## Bud (BUD)
Old English — *Herald*
Entertainment: Buddy Hollie, rock
  singer.
**Budd, Buddie, Buddy**

## Burgess (BER-jes)
Old English — *Citizen of a fortified
  town*
Entertainment: Burgess Meredith,
  actor.
**Burg, Burr**

## Burke (BERK)
French — *From the fortress*
**Bark, Berk, Berke, Bourke**

## Burl (BERL)
Old English — *Cup-bearer*
Entertainment: Burl Ives, singer.
**Burlie, Byrle**

## Burne (BERN)
Old English — *From the brook*
**Bourn, Bourne, Burn, Byrne**

## Burris (BER-ris)
Anglo-Saxon — *Of the town*
**Burr**

## Burton (BER-ton)
Old English — *From the fortress*
Entertainment: Burt Lancaster,
  Burt Reynolds, actors.
**Bert, Burt**

## Butch (BUTCH)
See Bert.
Famous: Butch Cassidy (Robert
  LeRoy Parker), Western
  bankrobber and outlaw.

## Byrd (BERD)
Old English — *Birdlike*
**Byrdie**

## Byron (BĪ-ron)
Anglo-Saxon — *Bear*
Teutonic — *From the cottage*
Literature: Lord Byron, poet.
Sports: Byron Nelson, professional
  golfer.
**Biron, Buiron, Byran,
Byrann, Byrom**

## Cadao (ka-DĀ-ō)
Vietnamese — *Folk song*

## Cadell (ka-DEL)
Celtic — *Of material spirit*
**Cadel, Cedell**

## Cadmar (KAD-mar)
Celtic — *Mighty in battle*
**Cad, Mar**

## Caesar (SĒ-zer)
Latin — *Cut down*
Historical: Julius Caesar.
Famous: Cesar Chavez, organizer
  of migrant farmworkers.
Entertainment: Cesar Auguste,
  French organist; Cesare Siepi,
  opera singer; Caesar Romero,
  actor.
**Casar, Cesar, Cesare, Kaiser**

## Cahil (KĀ-hil)
Turkish — *Young or naive*

## Calder (KAL-der)
Old English — *Stream*
**Cal, Caldwell**

**Caleb** (KĀ-leb)
Hebrew — *Dog*
**Cal, Cale**

**Calut** (KAL-ut)
Turkish — *Goliath*

**Calvert** (KAL-vert)
Old English — *Herdsman*
**Cal, Calbert**

**Calvin** (KAL-vin)
Latin — *Bald*
Famous: John Calvin, Protestant
reformer; Calvin Coolidge,
President; Calvin Klein, designer.

**Cam** (KAM)
English — *Beloved*

**Camden** (KAM-den)
Scottish — *From the winding valley*
**Camdan, Camdin**

**Cameron** (KA-mer-un)
Celtic — *Crooked nose*
Entertainment: Cameron Mitchell,
actor.
**Cam, Camero, Camey, Cammy**

**Campbell** (KAM-bel)
Scottish — *Crooked mouth*
**Cam, Camp, Campy**

**Canute** (ka-NŌOT)
Old Norse — *Knot*
**Cnut, Knut, Knute**

**Cappi** (KAP-ē)
English — *Good fortune*

**Cardew** (kar-DŌO)
Celtic — *From the black forest*

**Carew** (ka-RŌO)
Welsh — *From the fortress*

**Carey** (KAIR-ē)
Welsh — *From near the castle*
Entertainment: Cary Grant, actor.
**Care, Cary**

**Carl** (KARL)
Old English — *Farmer's town*
Literature: Carl Sandburg, poet.
Entertainment: Carl Reiner, actor;
Carl Wilson, member of the rock
group, The Beach Boys; Carlo
Ponti, film producer and
husband of Sophia Loren.
**Carl, Carleton, Carlo,
Carlton, Charlton**

**Carlin** (KAR-lin)
Gaelic — *Little champion*
**Carl, Carlie, Carling, Carly**

**Carlisle** (KAR-līl)
Old English, Latin — *From the walled
city*
**Carl, Carlie, Carly, Carlyle**

**Carmine** (KAR-mīn)
Latin — *Song*

**Carney** (KAR-nē)
Celtic — *Warrior*
**Car, Carney, Karney, Kearney**

**Carr** (KAR)
Norwegian — *From the marsh*
**Karr, Kerr**

**Carroll** (KAIR-ul)
Gaelic — *Champion*
Entertainment: Carroll O'Connor,
star of *All in the Family*; J. Carroll
Nash, actor.
**Carolus, Carrol, Cary, Caryl**

**Carson** (KAR-sun)
Old English — *Dweller by the marsh*

**Carswell** (KARS-wel)
Zodiac — *Child of the watercress
spring*
**Karswell**

**Carter** (KAR-ter)
Old English — *Cart driver*
**Cart**

**Carvel** (KAR-vel)
Old English — *From the villa by the
marsh*
**Carvell**

**CATALIN** — *Magic wizard*

**Carver** (KAR-ver)
 Old English — *Wood carver or
  sculptor*

**Casey** (KĀ-sē)
 Gaelic — *Brave*
 Sports: Casey Stengel, baseball
  manager.
 **Case**

**Casimir** (KAZ-i-mir)
 Slavic — *Proclamation of peace*
 **Casimire, Casper, Cass, Cassie,
 Cassy, Kazimir**

**Casper** (KAS-per)
Persian— *Treasurer*
Famous: Casper Weinberger, of the Reagan administration.
Entertainment: Casper the Friendly Ghost, cartoon character.
**Casimir, Caspar, Cass, Cassie, Cassy, Gaspard, Gasparo, Gasper, Jasper, Kaspar, Kasper**

**Cassidy** (KA-si-dē)
Gaelic— *Clever*
**Cass, Cassie, Cassy**

**Cassius** (KA-shus)
Latin— *Vain*
Famous: Cassius Jackson Keyser, authority on philosophy of mathematics.
Sports: Cassius Clay (Muhammad Ali), heavyweight boxing champion.
**Cash, Cass, Cassie, Cassy, Caz**

**Catalin** (KAT-lin)
Irish— *Magic wizard*

**Caton** (KĀ-ton)
Spanish, Latin— *Wise*

**Cavell** (ka-VEL)
Teutonic— *Boldly active*

**Cecil** (SĒ-sil)
Latin— *Blind*
Entertainment: Cecil Blount de Mille, film producer and director; Cecil Beaton, photographer and stage designer.
**Cece, Cecile, Cecilius**

**Cedric** (SED-rik)
Celtic— *Chieftain*
Entertainment: Sir Cedric Hardwicke, actor.

**Cemal** (SĒ-mal)
Arabic, Turkish— *Beauty*

**Chad** (CHAD)
Celtic— *Defender*
Entertainment: Chad Everett, actor.
**Chaddie, Chaddy**

**Chadburn** (CHAD-bern)
Old English— *From the wild catbrook*
**Chadbern**

**Chadwick** (CHAD-wik)
Old English— *From the warrior's town*

**Chaim** (kī-AM)
Hebrew— *Life*
**Hayyim, Hy, Hyman, Hymie, Mannie, Manny**

**Chal** (CHAL)
English— *Lad*
**Chelovik, Chiel, Childe**

**Chale** (CHĀL)
Spanish— *Strong and manly*
**Chalie**

**Chalmers** (CHAL-mers)
Scottish— *Son of the Lord*

**Cham** (CHAM)
Vietnamese— *Hard worker*

**Chandler** (CHAN-dler)
French— *Candlemaker*
**Chan, Chane**

**Chane** (SHĀN)
Swahili— *Tough leaf*
**Chene**

**Chaney** (SHĀ-nē)
French— *Oak wood*
**Cheney**

**Channing** (CHAN-ing)
Old English— *Knowing*
French— *Canon*
**Chan, Chane, Chanely**

**Chanoch** (CHA-nok)
Hebrew, Old English— *Clergyman*
**Chano**

**Chapman** (CHAP-man)
Old English— *Merchant*
**Chap, Chappie, Chappy, Mannie, Manny**

**Charles** (CHARLZ)
Teutonic—*Manly or strong*
Famous: Prince Charles of
England; Charles de Gaulle,
President of France; Charles
Schulz, cartoonist and creator of
*Peanuts;* Charles Proteus
Steinmetz, inventor.
Entertainment: Charles Boyer,
Charlie Chaplin, Charlton
Heston, Charles Bronson,
Charles Laughton, actors.
**Carl, Carlo, Carlos, Carrol,
Carroll, Cary, Caryl, Chad,
Chaddie, Chaddy, Charley,
Charlie, Charlot, Charlton,
Chic, Chick, Chicky, Chuck,
Karel, Karl, Karoly**

**Chase** (CHĀS)
French—*Hunter*

**Chatwin** (CHAT-win)
Old English—*Warlike friend*
**Chatvin**

**Chauncey** (CHON-sē)
French, Latin—*Chancellor*

**Chen** (CHEN)
Chinese—*Vast or great*

**Cheney** (SHĀ-nē)
French—*From the oak wood*
**Chen**

**Cheslav** (CHES-lav)
Russian—*Lives in a fortified camp*
**Chet**

**Chesmu** (CHES-mū)
North American Indian—*Gritty*

**Chester** (CHES-ter)
English, Latin—*From the fortified
camp*
Famous: Chester Alan Arthur,
President.
Entertainment: Chet Huntley,
newscaster; Chester, character
on *Gunsmoke.*
**Ches, Cheston, Chet**

**Chevalier** (sha-VAL-yā)
French—*Knight*
Entertainment: Chevy Chase, actor
and comedian.
**Chev, Chevy**

**Chico** (CHĒ-kō)
See Francis.

**Chilton** (CHIL-ton)
Old English—*From the farm by the
spring*
Entertainment: Chill Wills, actor.
**Chil, Chill, Chilt**

**Christian** (KRIS-chun)
Greek—*Follower of Christ*
Interesting: Kris Kringle, another
name for Santa Claus.
Famous: Christian Barnaard,
surgeon to do first heart
transplant; Christian Dior,
clothes designer.
Literature: Hero in *Pilgrim's
Progress,* by John Bunyan.
**Chretien, Chris, Chrisse,
Chrissie, Chrissy, Christiano,
Christie, Christy, Kit,
Kris, Krispin, Kristian**

**Christopher** (KRIS-tō-fer)
Greek—*Christ-bearer*
Famous: Christopher Columbus;
Kit Carson.
Literature: Christopher Robin,
character in children's books by
A. A. Milne.
Entertainment: Christopher
Willibald Gluch, composer;
Christopher Cross, singer.
**Chris, Chrisse, Chrissy,
Christoffer, Christoforo,
Christoph, Christophe,
Christophorus, Cris, Cristobal,
Cristoforo, Kit, Kristo,
Kristofer, Kristoforo**

**Cicero** (SI-ser-ō)
Latin—*Chickpea*
Famous: Cicero, Greek
philosopher.

**Ciro** (SĒ-rō)
Spanish— *The sun*

**Clare** (KLAIR)
Latin— *Famous*
**Clair**

**Clarence** (KLAIR-ens)
Latin— *Illustrious*
**Clair, Clarance**

**Clark** (KLARK)
French— *Scholar*
Entertainment: Clark Gable, actor;
 Clark Kent, Superman's real
 name.
**Clarke, Clerc, Clerk**

**Claude** (KLAWD)
Latin— *Lame*
Famous: Claude Monet,
 impressionist painter.
Entertainment: Claude Debussy,
 composer.
**Claudian, Claudianus, Claudio,
Claudius, Claus**

**Clay** (KLĀ)
Teutonic— *Born of the earth*
**Claiborn, Clayborn, Clayborne,
Claybourne, Clayton**

**Clemens** (KLEM-ens)
Danish— *Gentle or kind*

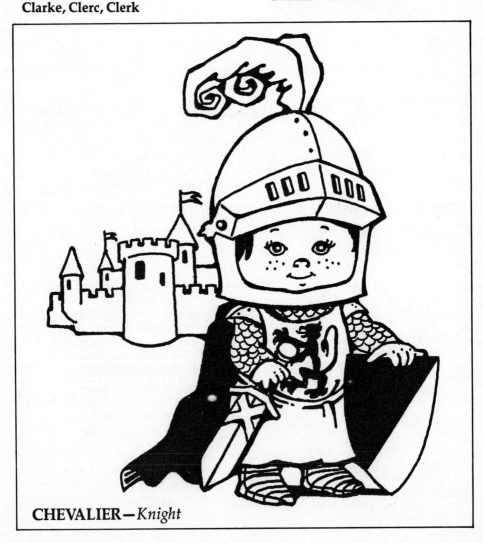

**CHEVALIER—** *Knight*

**Clement** (KLEM-ent)
Latin—*Merciful*
Literature: Clement E. Moore,
  author of *A Visit from St.
  Nicholas;* Samuel Clemens, real
  name of Mark Twain.
**Chim, Clem, Clemens, Clemente,
Clementius, Clemmie, Clemmy,
Klemens, Klement, Kliment**

**Cleon** (KLĒ-on)
Greek—*Famous*
Entertainment: Cleon
  Throckmorton, stage designer.
**Kleon**

**Cletus** (KLĒ-tus)
Greek—*Summoned*
Sports: Cletis Boyer, baseball
  player.
**Cletis**

**Cleveland** (KLĒV-land)
Old English—*From the cliffs*
Literature: Cleveland Amory,
  author of syndicated column,
  *Animal.*
**Cleve, Cleaveland, Clevey,
Clevie**

**Clifford** (KLIF-erd)
Old English—*Dweller in the ford
  near the cliff*
Literature: Clifford Odets,
  playwright.
Entertainment: Clifton Webb, Cliff
  Roberts, Clifton Fadiman, actors.
**Cliff, Clifton**

**Clinton** (KLIN-tun)
Teutonic—*From the headland farm*
Literature: Clinton Scollard,
  American poet.
Entertainment: Clint Eastwood,
  actor.
**Clint**

**Clive** (KLĪV)
Old English—*From the cliff*

**Clyde** (KLĪD)
Scottish, Celtic—*Heard from afar*
Welsh—*Warm*
**Cly, Clyd, Clyte**

**Cody** (KŌ-dē)
English—*Unknown*
**Codi**

**Colby** (KŌL-bē)
Old English—*From the black farm*
**Cole**

**Cole** (KŌL)
See Nicholas.
Literature: Old King Cole, a
  nursery rhyme.
Entertainment: Cole Porter,
  songwriter.
**Coleman, Colman**

**Colin** (KAW-lin)
Gaelic—*Child*
Sports: Colin Chapman, race-car
  designer.
**Cailean, Colan, Cole, Collin**

**Collier** (KOL-yer)
Old English—*Miner*
**Colier, Colis, Collayer, Collis,
Collyer, Colyer**

**Colton** (KŌL-ton)
Old English—*From the dark*

**Coman** (KŌ-man)
Arabic—*Noble*
**Comen**

**Conal** (KŌ-nal)
Celtic—*High and mighty*
**Conall, Conan, Conant,
Connel, Konal, Kynan**

**Conant** (KŌ-nant)
Celtic—*Wise*
**Con, Conal, Conn,
Conney, Connie, Conny**

**Conn** (KON)
Celtic—*Wise*
**Con**

**Conrad** (KON-rad)
Teutonic— *Brave counsel*
Famous: Conrad Hilton,
  hotel-chain owner.
Literature: *Conrad in Quest of His
  Youth,* by Leonard Merrick.
**Con, Conn, Conney,
Connie, Conny, Conrade,
Conrado, Cort, Koenraad,
Konrad, Kort, Kurt**

**Conroy** (KON-roi)
Irish— *Wise man*
**Commey, Con, Conn,
Connie, Conny, Roy**

**Constantine** (KON-stan-tēn)
Latin— *Firm*
Famous: Constantine the Great,
  Emperor of Rome.
**Con, Conn, Conney,
Connie, Conny, Constantin,
Constantino, Costa,
Konstantin, Konstantine**

**Conway** (KON-wā)
Gaelic— *Hound of the plain*
Entertainment: Conway Twitty,
  country-western singer.
**Con, Conn, Connie,
Conny**

**Cooper** (KOO-per)
Old English— *Barrel maker*
**Coop**

**Corbett** (KOR-bet)
Latin— *Raven*
**Corbet, Corbie, Corbin,
Corby, Cory**

**Corbin** (KOR-bin)
Latin— *The raven*
**Corwin**

**Cordell** (kor-DEL)
French— *Ropemaker*
**Cord, Cordie, Cordy,
Cory**

**Corey** (KOR-ē)
Irish— *From the hollow*
**Cori, Cory**

**Cormac** (KOR-mak)
Irish— *Charioteer*

**Cornelius** (kor-NĒL-ē-us)
Latin— *War horn*
Famous: Cornelius Vanderbilt,
  railroad tycoon.
**Conney, Connie, Conny,
Cornall, Cornell, Corney,
Cornie, Corny, Cory,
Neel, Nelly**

**Cornell** (kor-NEL)
See Cornelius.
Entertainment: Cornell Wilde,
  actor.
**Cornall, Corney, Cornie,
Corny, Cory**

**Cort** (KORT)
Teutonic— *Bold*
Norwegian— *Short*
**Cortie, Corty, Kort**

**Corydon** (KOR-i-don)
Greek— *Lark*
**Coridon, Coryden**

**Cosmo** (KOZ-mō)
Greek— *Well-ordered*
**Cos, Cosimo, Cosme,
Cozmo**

**Courtland** (KORT-land)
Anglo-Saxon— *From the enclosed
  land*
**Court, Courtley, Courtly**

**Courtney** (KORT-nē)
French— *From the court*
**Cort, Court, Courtnay,
Curt**

**Cowan** (KOW-an)
Gaelic— *Hillside hollow*
**Coe, Cowey, Cowie**

**Craig** (KRĀG)
Scottish— *Crag-dweller*
Sports: Craig Breedlove,
  land-speed record holder.
**Craggie, Craggy**

**Crandall** (KRAN-dal)
Old English— *From the crane's valley*
**Can, Carndell**

**Crawford** (KRAW-ford)
Old English— *From the ford of the crow*
**Craw, Crow, Ford**

**Creighton** (KRĀ-ton)
Old English— *From the farm*
**Creight, Crichton**

**Crispin** (KRIS-pin)
Latin— *Curly haired*

**Crofton** (KROF-ton)
Old English— *From the enclosed*

**Crompton** (KROMP-ton)
Old English— *From the winding farm*

**Cromwell** (KROM-wel)
Old English— *Dweller by the winding brook*

**Crosby** (KROZ-bē)
Norwegian— *From the shrine of the cross*
**Cross**

**Culbert** (KUL-bert)
Teutonic— *Cool and brilliant*
**Colbert, Colvert**

**Cullen** (KUL-en)
Celtic— *Young animal*
**Cull, Cullan, Cullen, Culley, Cullie, Cullin, Cully**

**Culver** (KUL-ver)
Old English— *Dove*
**Colver, Cull, Cullie, Cully, Kullen, Kullie**

**Curcio** (KER-sē-ō)
Spanish, French— *Courteous*
**Curt**

**Curran** (KER-en)
Gaelic— *Hero*
**Curr, Currey, Currie, Curry**

**Curt** (KERT)
Latin— *Short or little*
Sports: Curt Gowdy, sportscaster.
**Curtie, Curty, Kurt**

**Curtis** (KER-tis)
French— *Courteous*
**Curcio, Curt, Curtice**

**Cutler** (KUT-ler)
Old English— *Knife-maker*
**Cut, Cuttie, Cuty**

**Cyril** (SĒR-il)
Spanish, French— *Lordly one*
Entertainment: Cyril Ritchard, opera singer.
**Cirillo, Cirilo, Cy, Cyrill, Cyrille, Cyrillus**

**Cyrus** (SĪ-rus)
Persian, Greek— *Sun*
Famous: Cyrus Vance, former Secretary of State.
**Ciro, Cy, Russ**

**Dabir** (da-BĒR)
Algerian— *Teacher*

**Dacey** (DĀ-sē)
Gaelic— *Southerner*
**Dace, Dacy**

**Dag** (DAG)
Norwegian— *Day or brightness*
Famous: Dag Hammerskjold,
  former Secretary-General of the
  United Nations.
**Dagny**

**Dagaim** (da-GĪ-um)
Hebrew— *Two fishes*

**Dagan** (DĀ-gan)
Hebrew— *Corn or grain*
Entertainment: Dagwood,
  comic-strip character.
**Dagwood**

**Dale** (DĀL)
Old English— *From the valley*
Entertainment: Dale Robertson,
  actor.
**Dael, Dal**

**Dalibor** (DAL-i-bor)
Czech— *He dwells in the valley*

**Dallas** (DAL-as)
Celtic— *Wise*
**Dal, Dall, Dallis**

**Dalston** (DAL-ston)
Anglo-Saxon— *From Daegal's place*
**Dalis**

**Dalton** (DAL-ton)
Old English— *From the farm in the
  dale*
**Dal, Dalt, Tony**

**Damek** (DĀ-mek)
Czech— *Man of the earth*
**Adamec, Adamek, Adamik,
Adamok, Adham**

**Damon** (DĀ-mon)
Greek— *Tamer*
Famous: Damon and Pythias of
  Sicily.
Literature: Damon Runyon,
  journalist and storyteller.
**Dame, Damian, Damiano,
Damien**

**Dan** (DAN)
Hebrew— *Judge*
Biblical: One of the 12 tribes of
  Israel.
Entertainment: Dan Rather,
  newscaster.
Sports: Dan Gurney, race-car
  driver.
**Dannie, Danny**

**Dana** (DĀ-nuh)
Scandinavian— *From Denmark*
Entertainment: Dana Andrews,
  actor.
**Dane**

**Daniel** (DAN-yel)
Hebrew— *God is my judge*
Biblical: Hebrew prophet who was
  delivered from the lion's den.
Historical: Daniel Boone, explorer
  and Indian fighter.
Famous: Daniel Webster,
  politician and orator.
Literature: Hero in Shakespeare's
  *Merchant of Venice;* Daniel Defoe,
  author of *Robinson Crusoe.*
Entertainment: Danny Kaye, actor.
**Dan, Dani, Dannel,
Dannie, Danny, Dawnee**

**Dante** (DON-tē)
See Durante.
Literature: Dante Alighieri, poet.

**Danya** (DAN-yuh)
Ukrainian— *Given by God*
**Bohdan, Dania**

**Dar** (DAR)
Hebrew— *Pearl*

**Darby** (DAR-bē)
Gaelic— *Free man*
Norwegian— *From the deer estate*
**Dar, Darb, Darbee, Darby**

**Darcy** (DAR-sē)
Gaelic— *Dark*
**D'Arcy, Dar, Darce**

**Dario** (DAIR-ē-ō)
Spanish, Greek— *Wealthy*
**Darin**

**DAN**—*Judge*

**Darius** (DAIR-ē-us)
  Persian—*Wealthy*
  Entertainment: Darius Milhaud,
    French composer.
  **Dare, Dario, Derry**

**Darnell** (dar-NEL)
  Old English—*From the hidden place*
  **Dar, Darn, Darnall**

**Darrel** (DAIR-el)
  French—*Beloved or dear*
  Entertainment: Daryl Dragon, also
    known as Captain Tennille;
    Darryl F. Zanuck, film director
    and producer.
  **Dare, Darrell, Darrill,**
  **Darryl, Daryl, Daryle**

**Darren** (DAIR-en)
Gaelic—*Great*
**Dare, Daren, Daron,
Darrin**

**Darrick** (DAIR-ik)
Teutonic—*Ruler of the people*
**Dare, Darick**

**Darton** (DAR-ton)
Old English—*From the deer park*
**Dart, Dartan, Darten**

**Dasan** (DĀ-san)
Pomo Indian—*Leader of bird clan*

**Daudi** (DAW-dē)
Swahili—*Beloved one*
**Daudy**

**David** (DĀ-vid)
Hebrew—*Beloved*
Biblical: David, boy who killed
   Goliath and became king.
Historical: Admiral David
   Glasgow Farragut, explorer and
   leader.
Literature: *David Copperfield,* novel
   by Dickens; David Herbert
   Lawrence, author of *Lady
   Chatterley's Lover.*
Entertainment: David Niven,
   David Carradine, actors; David
   Crosby, member of Crosby, Stills
   and Nash singing group; David
   Bowie, rock star; David Brinkley,
   newscaster; David Hartman,
   anchorman; David Frost,
   talk-show host.
**Dav, Dave, Daven, Davey,
Davidde, Davide, Davie,
Davin, Davis, Davy, Dewey,
Dov**

**Davis** (DĀ-vis)
Scottish—*David's son*
**Dave, Davie, Davy**

**Dean** (DĒN)
Old English—*From the valley*
Entertainment: Dean Jones, Dean
   Jagger, actors; Dean Martin,
   singer.
**Deane, Dene, Dino**

**Dearborn** (DĒR-burn)
Old English—*Beloved child*

**Dedrick** (DĒ-drik)
Teutonic—*Ruler of people*
**Dedric**

**Delbert** (DEL-bert)
Old English—*Bright as day*
Entertainment: Delbert Mann,
   director.
**Bert, Bertie, Berty, Del**

**Delmar** (DEL-mar)
French, Latin—*Mariner*
**Del, Delmer**

**Delmore** (DEL-mor)
French—*At a marsh*
Literature: Delmore Schwartz,
   poet.
**Del, Delmar, Delmer,
Delmor**

**Delsin** (DEL-sin)
North American Indian—*He is so*
**Delsen**

**Delwin** (DEL-win)
Teutonic—*Valley friend*
**Del, Delwyn**

**Demetrius** (de-MĒ-trē-us)
Greek—*Of the earth*
Biblical: Silversmith of Ephesus.
Entertainment: Dmitri
   Shostakovich, Dmitri Tiomkin,
   composers.
**Demetri, Demetria, Demetris,
Demitry, Demmy, Dimetre,
Dimitri, Dmitri**

**Dempsey** (DEM-sē)
Gaelic—*Proud*
**Demp, Dempsey, Dempster,
Dempstor**

**Denby** (DEN-bē)
Norwegian—*From the village of the
Danes*
**Danby, Den, Denney,
Dennie, Denny**

**Deniz** (DEN-ez)
Turkish— *Sea*
**Denyz**

**Dennis** (DEN-is)
French, Latin— *Of Dionysus*
Entertainment: Dennis Wilson,
    member of The Beach Boys
    singing group; Dennis the
    Menace, comic character; Dennis
    Day, Dennis Weaver, actors.
**Den, Denis, Dennett,
Denney, Dennie, Dennison,
Denny, Denys, Denzil, Dion,
Dionisio, Dionysus**

**Denton** (DEN-tun)
Old English— *From the valley farm*
**Dent, Denten**

**Denys** (DEN-is)
Russian, Greek— *God of wine*
**Denis, Dennis, Denya**

**Derek** (DAIR-ik)
Teutonic— *Ruler of people*
**Darrick, Derick, Derk,
Derrick, Dirk**

**Dermot** (DER-mot)
English, Gaelic— *Free from envy*
**Der, Dermott, Diarmaid,
Diarmid**

**Derry** (DER-rē)
Gaelic— *Red-haired*

**Desmond** (DES-mund)
Celtic— *Man from South Munster*
Literature: Desmond Young,
    author.
**Des, Desi, Desmund**

**Devin** (DEV-in)
Celtic— *A poet*
**Dev, Devy**

**Devlin** (DEV-lin)
Gaelic— *Brave or fierce*
**Dev, Devlen**

**Dewey** (DOO-ē)
Welsh— *Prized*
**Dew, Dewie**

**Dewitt** (de-WIT)
Dutch— *White*
**DeWitt, Dewit, Dwight,
Wit, Wittie, Witty**

**Dexter** (DEKS-ter)
Latin— *Dexterous*
**Decca, Deck, Dex**

**Dichali** (dī-KĀL-ē)
North American Indian— *He speaks
often*
**Dichaly**

**Dick** (DIK)
See Richard.
Entertainment: Dick Cavett,
    talk-show host; Dick Clark, host
    of *American Bandstand;* Dick
    Powell, actor; Dick Tracy,
    comic-strip detective.
**Dickie, Dicky**

**Diego** (dē-Ā-gō)
Spanish— *The supplanter*
Famous: Diego Rivera, Mexican
    painter.
**Jaime, James, Jayme, Jaymie**

**Dieter** (DĒ-ter)
See Theodoric.

**Dietrich** (DĒ-trik)
See Theodoric.

**Dillon** (DIL-on)
Gaelic— *Faithful*
**Dill, Dillie, Dilly**

**Dima** (DĒ-muh)
Russian— *Powerful warrior*
**Vladimir**

**Dinos** (DĒ-nōs)
Greek, Latin— *Firm and constant*
**Costa, Kastas, Konstandinos,
Konstantions, Kostas, Kostis,
Kotsos**

**Dinsmore** (DINZ-mor)
Celtic— *From the great hill fort*
**Dins, Dinzmore**

**DOANE**—*Dweller of the sand dune*

**Dion** (DĒ-on)
See Dionysos.
Entertainment: Dion, singer.

**Dirk** (DIRK)
Teutonic—*Ruler of the people*
Famous: Dirk J. Struik,
mathematician.
Entertainment: Dirk Bogarde,
actor.
**Derek**

**Diverous** (DĪ-ver-us)
English—*Unknown*
**Diver**

**Doane** (DŌN)
Celtic—*Dweller of the sand dune*

**Dobry** (DŌ-brē)
Polish—*Good*
Entertainment: *Doby Gillis* comedy
show.
**Doby**

**Dodek** (DŌ-dek)
Polish—*Noble hero*
**Adek, Adolf, Adolph,
Dolf, Dolfa, Dolfi**

**Dodley** (DOD-lē)
Old English — *From the people's meadow*
Entertainment: Dudley Moore, actor.
**Dudley**

**Dohosan** (dō-HŌ-san)
North American Indian — *Small bluff*
**Dohosun**

**Dolf** (DOLF)
See Adolph.
**Dolph**

**Domingo** (dō-MING-gō)
Spanish — *Born on Sunday*
**Dom, Domingio, Dominic**

**Dominic** (DOM-i-nik)
Latin — *The Lord's*
Entertainment: Dom Deluise, actor.
**Dom, Dominick, Dominy, Nic, Nick, Nicky**

**Don** (DON)
Celtic — *Dark or brown*
Latin — *Lord*
Entertainment: Don Knotts, actor; Donny Osmond, singer.
Sports: Don Drysdale, baseball pitcher; Don Meredith, football quarterback.
**Donn, Donnee, Donnie, Donny**

**Donahue** (DON-a-hū)
Gaelic — *Dark warrior*
**Don, Donn, Donnie, Donny, Donohue**

**Donald** (DON-ald)
Celtic — *Dark-haired stranger*
Entertainment: Donald Sutherland, Donald Pleasance, actors; Donald Duck, Walt Disney character.
**Don, Donal, Donalda, Donall, Donalt, Donn, Donnell, Donnie, Donny**

**Donnelly** (DON-el-lē)
Gaelic — *Brave, dark man*
**Don, Donn, Donnie, Donny**

**Donovan** (DON-a-van)
Gaelic — *Dark warrior*
**Don, Donny**

**Doran** (DOR-an)
Celtic — *Stranger*
**Dorran, Dorren**

**Dorian** (DOR-ē-an)
Greek — *From the sea*
Literature: *The Picture of Dorian Gray,* novel by Oscar Wilde.
**Darren, Dore, Dorey, Dorie, Dory**

**Dorjan** (DOR-jan)
Hungarian, Latin — *Dark man*
**Adorjan, Adrian**

**Dory** (DOR-ē)
French — *Golden-haired*
**Dore**

**Dotan** (DŌ-tan)
Hebrew — *Low*
**Dothan**

**Douglas** (DUG-las)
Scottish — *From the dark water*
Famous: Douglas MacArthur, Army general.
Entertainment: Douglas Fairbanks, Douglas Campbell, Doug McClure, actors.
**Doug, Dougie, Douglass, Dougy, Dugald**

**Dovev** (DŌ-vev)
Hebrew — *To whisper*

**Doyle** (DOIL)
Celtic — *Dark stranger*
**Doy**

**Drake** (DRĀK)
English — *Male duck or swan*

**Dreng** (DRENG)
Norwegian — *Hired farmhand*

**Drew** (DROO)
German, French — *Trusty*
**Dru, Drud, Drugi**

**Driscoll** (DRIS-kol)
Celtic — *Interpreter*

**Druce** (DROOS)
Celtic - - *Wise man*

**Dryden** (DRĪ-den)
Old English — *From the dry valley*
**Dry, Drydan, Drydon**

**Duane** (DWĀN)
Celtic — *Song*
**Dewain, Dwayne**

**Dude** (DOOD)
English — *Moon*

**Duer** (DOO-er)
Celtic — *Heroic*

**Duke** (DOOK)
French — *Leader*
**Dukey, Dukie, Dukker, Duky**

**Duncan** (DUN-kan)
Scottish — *Dark-skinned warrior*
Literature: King of Scotland in
Shakespeare's *Macbeth*.
**Dun, Dunc, Dunn**

**Dunham** (DUN-am)
Celtic — *Dark man*
**Dun**

**Dunstan** (DUN-stan)
Old English — *From the brown, stone
hill*
**Dun**

**Dur** (DER)
Hebrew — *To pile up*

**Durant** (der-ANT)
Latin — *Enduring*
**Dante, Dunte, Durand, Durante**

**Durriken** (DER-i-ken)
English — *Fortune telling*

**Durward** (DER-ward)
Old English — *Gate-keeper*
Entertainment: Durward Kirby,
announcer on *The Garry Moore
Show*.

**Durwin** (DER-win)
Anglo-Saxon — *Beloved friend*

**Dustin** (DUS-tin)
German — *Brave fighter*
Entertainment: Dustin Hoffman,
actor.
**Dust, Dustie, Dusty**

**Dwight** (DWĪT)
Old English — *A cutting or clearing*
Famous: Dwight David
Eisenhower, President.
**Dewit**

**Dyami** (DĪ-am-ē)
North American Indian — *An eagle*

**Dylan** (DIL-un)
Welsh — *The sea*
Literature: Dylan Thomas, poet.
**Dilan, Dill, Dillie, Dilly**

**Dyre** (DĪR)
Norwegian — *Dear or precious*

**Earl** (ERL)
Old English — *Nobleman*
Literature: Erle Stanley Gardner,
creator of *Perry Mason* series.
**Earle, Earlie, Early, Erle,
Erly, Errol, Erroll, Rollo**

**Eaton** (Ē-tun)
Old English— *From the estate on the river*
**Eatton**

**Ebenezer** (eb-e-NĒ-zer)
Hebrew— *Rock of help*
Literature: Ebenezer Scrooge, character in Dickens' *A Christmas Carol*.
**Eb, Eben, Ebeneser, Evenezer**

**Eberhard** (eb-er-HARD)
German— *Boar-strong*
**Everart, Everard, Everett, Evrard, Eward**

**Ed** (ED)
See Edward.
Entertainment: Ed McMahon, co-host of *Tonight Show;* Ed Sullivan, host of TV variety show; Ed Asner, actor.

**Eddy** (ED-ē)
Scandinavian— *Unresting*
Entertainment: Eddy Arnold, country-western singer; Eddy Fisher, Eddie Albert, actors.
**Edan, Eddie, Eden**

**Edgar** (ED-ger)
Anglo-Saxon— *Happy warrior*
Literature: Edgar Allen Poe, poet and short-story writer; Edgar Rice Burroughs, author of Tarzan series.
Entertainment: Edgar Bergen, ventriloquist.
**Ed, Eddie, Eddy, Edgard, Edgardo, Ned, Neddy, Ted, Teddy**

**Edik** (ED-ik)
Russian— *Wealthy guardian*
**Edward**

**Edison** (ED-i-sun)
Old English— *Son of Edward*
**Ed, Eddie, Eddy, Edson**

**Edmund** (ED-mund)
Anglo-Saxon— *Fortunate protector*
Famous: Edmund Muskie, Senator; Eamon de Valera, President of Ireland.
Literature: Edmund Spenser, author of *The Faerie Queene*.
Entertainment: Edmund O'Brien, actor.
**Eadmund, Eamon, Ed, Edd, Eddie, Edmon, Edmond, Edmondio, Edmondo, Ned, Neddie, Ted, Teddie**

**Edward** (ED-ward)
Anglo-Saxon— *Happy protector*
Historical: Name given to kings in England and Saxon.
Literature: Edward Gibbon, author of *The Decline and Fall of the Roman Empire*.
Entertainment: Edward G. Robinson, Eddie Albert, Jr. actors; Edward R. Murrow, newscaster.
**Ed, Eddie, Eddy, Edik, Edouard, Eduard, Eduardo, Edvard, Ewart, Ned, Ted**

**Edwin** (ED-win)
Anglo-Saxon— *Rich friend*
Entertainment: Edwin Thomas Booth, Ed Winn, actors.
**Ed, Eddie, Eddy, Edlin, Eduino**

**Egan** (Ē-gan)
Celtic— *Ardent*
Teutonic— *Formidable*
**Egon**

**Egbert** (EG-bert)
Anglo-Saxon— *Sword bright*
**Bert, Bertie, Berty**

**Egerton** (EG-er-tun)
Old English— *From the town on the ridge*
**Egerten**

**Einar** (Ī-nar)
German— *Chief*
**Ejnar**

**Elangonel** (e-LANG-ō-nel)
North American Indian— *Friendly*

**Elbert** (EL-bert)
Teutonic— *Nobly brilliant*
**Bert, El, Elli**

**Elden** (EL-den)
Old English— *From the valley of the elves*
**Eldo, Eldon, Elton**

**Eldred** (EL-dred)
Anglo-Saxon— *Sage counselor*
**Eldrid**

**Eldridge** (EL-drij)
German— *Wise ruler*
**Aldrich, Algridge, Eldrige**

**Eldwin** (EL-dwin)
Anglo-Saxon— *Sage friend*

**Eleazar** (el-Ē-ā-zar)
Hebrew— *God has helped*
**Elazaro, Eleazar, Eli, Elie, Eliezer, Ely**

**Eli** (Ē-lī)
Hebrew— *Highest*
Biblical: High priest who trained the prophet Samuel.
Famous: Eli Whitney, inventor of the cotton gin.
Entertainment: Eli Wallach, actor.
**Ely**

**Elijah** (e-LĪ-juh)
Hebrew— *Jehovah is God*
Biblical: Prophet of God.
**El, Eli, Elia, Elias, Elihu, Elijah, Eliot, Elliott, Ellis, Ely**

**Elisha** (e-LĪ-shuh)
Hebrew— *God is salvation*
Biblical: Successor of Elijah.
**Elish, Lisha**

**Ellard** (EL-ard)
Teutonic— *Nobly brave*

**Ellery** (EL-er-ē)
Teutonic— *Dweller by the alder tree*
Literature: Ellery Queen, fictional detective.
**Ellary, Ellerey**

**Elliott** (EL-ē-ot)
Hebrew— *Close to God*
Famous: Eliot Janeway, economist and consumer advocate.
Entertainment: Elliott Gould, actor.
**Eliot, Eliott, Elliot**

**Ellison** (EL-i-son)
Old English— *Son of Ellis*
**Elson**

**Ellsworth** (ELS-worth)
Old English— *Nobleman's estate*
Famous: Ellsworth Bunker, politician.
**Ellswerth, Elsworth**

**Elmen** (EL-men)
German— *Like an elm tree*
**Elman**

**Elmer** (EL-mer)
Anglo-Saxon— *Noble and famous*
Literature: *Elmer Gantry*, by Sinclair Lewis.
Entertainment: Elmer Fudd, cartoon character in Bugs Bunny series.
**Aylmar, Aylmer, Aymer**

**Elmo** (EL-mō)
Greek— *Friendly*
Italian— *Helmet*
Entertainment: Elmo Lincoln, silent-movie *Tarzan*.
**Elmore**

**Elrad** (EL-rad)
Hebrew— *God rules*

**Elroy** (EL-roi)
Latin, French— *Royal*
**Roy**

**ELLIOTT**—*Close to God*

**Elston** (EL-ston)
Old English—*Nobleman's town*
Sports: Elston Howard, baseball
player.
**Elton**

**Elton** (EL-ton)
Old English—*From the old town*
Entertainment: Elton John, rock
singer.
**Alden, Aldon, Alton,
Eldon**

**Elvis** (EL-vis)
Norwegian—*All wise*
Entertainment: Elvis Presley,
singer and actor.
**Al, Alvis, El**

**Elwin** (EL-win)
Anglo-Saxon—*Befriended by elves*
**Al, Alvis, El, Elven,
Elvis, Elvyn, Elwyn, Win**

**Elwood** (EL-wood)
Old English—*From the old wood*
**Ellwood, Woody**

**Eman** (Ē-man)
Czech, Hebrew — *God with us*
**Manuel**

**Emanuel** (ē-MAN-ū-el)
Hebrew — *God with us*
Famous: Immanuel Kant,
  philosopher and author of
  *Critique of Pure Reason.*
**Emmanuel, Immanuel, Mannie,
Manuel, Manny**

**Emery** (EM-er-ē)
Teutonic — *Industrious ruler*
Historical: Amerigo Vespucci,
  explorer.
**Amerigo, Amery, Amory,
Emerson, Emery, Emmerich,
Emory**

**Emil** (Ā-mēl)
Latin — *Flattering, winning*
Literature: Emile Zola, author.
**Emelen, Emile, Emilio,
Emlen, Emlyn**

**Emlyn** (EM-lin)
Welsh — *Cling to*
Sports: Emlin Tunnel, football player.
**Emlin**

**Emmet** (EM-et)
Anglo-Saxon — *Ant or industrious*
Famous: Emmet Kelly, circus
  clown.
**Em, Emmit, Emmott, Emmy**

**Eneas** (uh-NĒ-us)
Spanish, Greek — *Praised one*
Literature: Aeneas, hero of Virgil's
  epic poem.
**Aeneas**

**Engelbert** (ENG-el-bert)
Teutonic — *Bright as an angel*
Entertainment: Engelbert
  Humperdinck, singer.
**Bert, Bertie, Berty, Englebert,
Ingelbert**

**Enoch** (Ē-nok)
Hebrew — *Dedicated or consecrated*
Biblical: Father of Methusaleh.
Literature: Enoch Arden, hero of
  the poem by Tennyson.

**Enos** (Ē-nus)
Hebrew — *Man*
**Enoss**

**Enrico** (en-RĒ-kö)
See Henry.
Entertainment: Enrico Caruso,
  opera singer.

**Enyeto** (en-YĀ-tö)
Miowok Indian — *The bear's manner
  of walking*
**Enieto**

**Ephraim** (Ē-frē-um)
Hebrew — *Doubly fruitful*
Biblical: Second son of Joseph.
Entertainment: Efrem Zimbalist,
  Sr., violinist; Efrem Zimbalist, Jr.,
  actor.
**Efrem, Ephrem**

**Erasmus** (er-AS-mus)
Greek — *Loveable*
**Erasme, Erasmo**

**Erastus** (er-AS-tus)
Greek — *Beloved*
**Elmo, Eraste, Ras, Rastus**

**Eric** (AIR-ik)
Norwegian — *Ever ruler*
Historical: Eric the Red, viking
  hero.
Literature: Eric Ambler, author.
Entertainment: Eric Sevareid,
  newscaster; Eric von Stroheim,
  film director; Eric Clapton, rock
  singer; Erik Estrada, actor.
**Erek, Erhard, Erhart,
Erich, Erick, Erik, Rick,
Rickie, Ricky**

**Erin** (AIR-in)
Irish — *Peace*

**Erland** (ER-land)
Teutonic— *Stranger or foreigner*
**Arlan, Arland, Erlan**

**Ernald** (ER-nald)
Teutonic— *Noble eagle*
**Erneld**

**Ernest** (ER-nest)
Old English— *Earnest*
Literature: Ernest Hemingway,
  novelist.
Entertainment: Ernst Lubitsch,
  film director; Ernest Borgnine,
  Ernie Kovacs, actors.
**Erna, Ernestine, Ernestis,
Ernesto, Ernestus, Ernie,
Ernst, Erny**

**Errol** (AIR-ol)
Teutonic— *A nobleman*
Entertainment: Errol Flynn, actor.
**Erroll, Rolls**

**Erskine** (ER-skin)
Scottish— *From the height of the cliff*
Literature: Erskine Caldwell,
  novelist.
**Kin, Kinnie, Kinny**

**Ervin** (ER-vin)
Czech, Hungarian— *Friend of the sea*
**Erwin**

**Eshcol** (ESH-kol)
Hebrew— *A grape cluster*
**Eshkoll**

**Esmond** (ES-mond)
Anglo-Saxon— *Gracious protector*

**Este** (ES-tē)
Italian— *From the east*
**Estes**

**Ethan** (Ē-than)
Hebrew— *The strong or firm*
Historical: Ethan Allen,
  Revolutionary War hero.
Literature: *Ethan Frome,* by Edith
  Wharton.
**Etan, Ethe**

**Ethelbert** (ETH-el-bert)
Teutonic— *Of shining nobility*
Entertainment: Ethelbert Nevins,
  composer.
**Adalbert, Edelbert, Ethelberta**

**Etu** (Ē-tōō)
North American Indian— *The sun*

**Eugene** (ū-JĒN)
Greek— *Well-born*
Literature: Eugene O'Neill,
  playwright; Eugene Field,
  journalist and poet.
**Engenio, Eugen, Eugene,
Eugenius, Gene, Jean**

**Eustance** (Ū-stuns)
Greek— *Fruitful*
**Eustashe, Eustasius,
Eustatius, Eustazio, Eustis,
Stacie, Stacy**

**Evan** (E-vun)
Greek— *Well-born*
Celtic— *Young warrior*
Literature: Evan Hunter, author of
  *The Blackboard Jungle.*
**Ev, Even, Evin, Ewan,
Ewen, Owen**

**Evelyn** (E-vel-in)
French, Teutonic— *Ancestor*
Literature: Evelyn Waugh,
  novelist.
**Evelin**

**Everett** (E-ver-et)
Old English— *Strong as a boar*
Famous: Edward Everett Dirksen,
  Senator.
**Eberhard, Ev, Everard,
Evered, Eward, Ewart**

**Evers** (EV-ers)
Anglo-Saxon— *Wild boar*

**Ezekiel** (e-ZĒ-kē-ēl)
Hebrew— *Strength of God*
Biblical: Prophet of the Old
  Testament.
**Ezechiel, Ezequiel,
Eziechiele, Zeke**

**Ezhno** (EZ-nō)
North American Indian — *Solitary*

**Ezra** (EZ-ruh)
Hebrew — *Helper*
Literature: Ezra Pound, poet.
**Azariah, Azrikam, Azur, Ezer, Ezera, Ezra, Ezri**

**Faber** (FĀ-ber)
German — *Bean grower*
**Fabi, Fabian, Fabujan**

**Fabian** (FĀ-bē-un)
Latin — *Bean grower*
Entertainment: Fabian, rock singer.
**Fabe, Faber, Fabiano, Fabien, Fabio**

**Fabron** (FĀ-bron)
Latin — *Mechanic*

**Fadey** (FĀ-dē)
Ukrainian — *Stout-hearted or courageous*
**Faddeyka, Faddi, Fadeyka, Fadeyusha**

**Fadil** (FA-dil)
Arabic — *Generous*

**Fairfax** (FAIR-faks)
Anglo-Saxon — *Fair-haired*
**Fair, Fax**

**Fairleigh** (FAIR-lē)
Unknown — *From the meadow of the bull*
**Fairlay, Fairlee, Fairlie, Farlay, Farlee, Farley, Farly**

**Falkner** (FALK-ner)
Old English — *Trainer of falcons*
**Faulkner, Fowler**

**Famous** (FĀ-mus)
Old English — *Famous*
Interesting: Famous Amos, popular cookie shop in California.

**Farand** (FAIR-und)
Old English — *Attractive or pleasant*
**Farant, Farrand, Ran**

**Farley** (FAR-lē)
Old English — *From the sheep meadow*
Literature: Farley Mowat, author.
Entertainment: Farley Granger, actor.
**Fairleigh, Fairlie, Far, Farleigh, Farlie, Farly**

**Farrell** (FAIR-el)
Celtic — *The valorous*
**Farr, Farrel, Ferrell**

**Fath** (FĀTH)
Arabic — *Victory*

**Favian** (FĀ-vē-an)
Latin — *A man of understanding*

**Faxon** (FAKS-on)
Latin — *Blessed*
Entertainment: Felix Mendelssohn, composer and conductor; Felix the Cat, cartoon character.
**Fee, Felic, Felicio, Felike, Feliks, Felix, Felizio**

**Felton** (FEL-ton)
Old English — *From the estate built on the meadow*
**Felten**

**FALKNER**—*Trainer of falcons*

**Feodor** (FĀ-ō-dor)
See Theodore.
Literature: Fyodor Dostoyevsky,
    author of *Crime and Punishment*.
Entertainment: Feodor Chaliapin,
    opera singer.
**Fyodor**

**Ferdinand** (FER-di-nand)
German—*Bold venture*
Famous: Ferdinand de Lesseps,
    builder of the Suez and Panama
    canals.
Literature: Ferdinand, lover of
    Miranda in Shakespeare's *The
    Tempest*.
Entertainment: Fernando Lamas,
    actor.
Sports: Fernando Valenzuela,
    baseball pitcher.
**Ferdie, Ferdy, Fergus,
Fernando, Hernando**

**Fergus** (FER-gus)
Gaelic—*Strong man*
**Ferd**

**Fermin** (FER-min)
Spanish—*Firm and strong*

**Fernald** (FER-nald)
Teutonic—*Dweller by the alder tree*

**Ferris** (FAIR-is)
Gaelic—*Peter, the rock*
**Farris**

**Fidel** (fa-DEL)
Latin—*Faithful*
Famous: Fidel Castro, Cuban
    President.
**Fidele, Fidelio**

**Fielding** (FĒL-ding)
Old English—*From the field*
**Field**

**Filbert** (FIL-bert)
Old English — *Brilliant*
**Bert, Filberte, Filberto,
Phil, Philbert**

**Filmore** (FIL-mor)
Old English — *Very famous*
**Filmer, Phil,
Pilmer, Pilmore**

**Finlay** (FIN-lē)
Gaelic — *Little fair-haired soldier*
**Fin, Findlay, Findley,
Finley, Finn**

**Firman** (FIR-man)
Old English — *Fair man*
Anglo-Saxon — *Traveler*

**Fisk** (FISK)
Scandinavian — *The fisherman*
**Fiske**

**Fitzgerald** (fitz-JAIR-ald)
Old English — *Son of the spear-mighty*
Famous: John Fitzgerald Kennedy,
President.
**Derrie, Fitz, Gerald,
Gerry, Jerry**

**Fitzhugh** (FITZ-hū)
Old English — *Son of the intelligent
man*
**Fitz, Hugh**

**Fitzpatrick** (fitz-PAT-rik)
Old English — *Son of a nobleman*
**Fitz, Pat, Patrick**

**Fleming** (FLEM-ing)
Anglo-Saxon — *Dutchman*
**Flem**

**Fletcher** (FLE-cher)
English — *Arrow-maker*
Literature: Fletcher Knebel,
novelist.
**Fletch**

**Flint** (FLINT)
Old English — *Stream*

**Florian** (FLOR-ē-an)
Latin — *Flowering or blooming*
**Flory**

**Floyd** (FLOID)
Welsh — *Dark complexion*
Sports: Floyd Patterson, boxing
champion.

**Flynn** (FLIN)
Gaelic — *Son of the red-haired man*
**Flin, Flinn**

**Forbes** (FORBS)
Gaelic — *Prosperous or headstrong*

**Ford** (FORD)
Old English — *River crossing*
**Bradford**

**Fordel** (for-DEL)
English — *Forgives*

**Forrest** (FOR-est)
French — *Forest; woodsman*
Entertainment: Forrest Tucker,
actor.
**Forest, Forester, Forrester,
Forster, Foss, Foster**

**Fortune** (FOR-chun)
French — *Lucky*
**Fortunato, Fortune, Fortunio**

**Foster** (FOS-ter)
Latin — *Keeper of the woods*
Entertainment: Foster Brooks,
comedian.

**Fowler** (FOWL-er)
Old English — *Hunter of wild fowl*

## Francis (FRAN-sis)

Latin— *Frenchman*
Biblical: St. Francis of Assisi.
Historical: Sir Francis Drake,
   explorer.
Famous: Francis Scott Key, author
   of *The Star-Spangled Banner.*
Entertainment: Franchot Tone,
   singer; Francis X. Bushman,
   actor.
**Chico, Fran, Francais,
Francesco, Franchot, Francisco,
Franciskus, Frangois, Frank,
Frankie, Franky, Frannie, Franny,
Frans, Frants, Franz, Pancho**

## Francisco (fran-SIS-kō)

Latin— *Free man*
Entertainment: Chico Marx, actor.
**Chicho, Chico, Chilo, Chito,
Currito, Curro, Farruco, Frans,
Franz, Franzen, Frasco, Frascuelo,
Paco, Pacorro, Panchito, Pancho,
Paquito, Quico**

## Frank (FRANK)

See Francis.
Famous: Frank Lloyd Wright,
   architect.
Entertainment: Frank Sinatra,
   singer and actor; Frankie
   Avalon, Frankie Lane, singers.
Sports: Frank Howard, baseball
   player.
**Frankie, Franky**

**FRAZER**—*Curly-haired*

**Franklin** (FRANK-lin)
German — *Free man*
Famous: Franklin Pierce,
President; Franklin D. Roosevelt,
President.
Literature: Franklin Pierce Adams,
columnist and poet.
**Francklin, Francklyn, Frank,
Frankie, Franklyn, Franky**

**Frazer** (FRĀ-zer)
Old English — *Curly-haired*
French — *Strawberry*
**Fraser, Frasier, Fraze,
Frazier**

**Fred** (FRED)
See Frederick.
Entertainment: Fred Astaire,
dancer and actor; Fred Gwynn,
actor.
**Freddie, Fredie, Fredy**

**Frederick** (FRED-rik)
Teutonic — *Ruler in peace*
Historical: Frederick II of Prussia.
Famous: Frederic Remington,
western artist.
Entertainment: Frederic Francois
Chopin, composer; Fredric
March, actor.
**Eric, Erich, Erick, Erik,
Fred, Freddie, Freddy, Fredek,
Frederic, Frederich, Frederico,
Frederigo, Frederik, Fredric,
Fredrick, Friedrick, Fritz,
Rick, Rickie, Ricky**

**Fredi** (FRE-dē)
German — *Peaceful ruler*
**Frederick, Fredrik, Friedel,
Friedrick, Fritz**

**Freeman** (FRĒ-man)
Anglo-Saxon — *One born free*
**Free, Freedman, Freeland,
Freemon**

**Fremont** (FRĒ-mont)
Teutonic — *Guardian of freedom*
**Free, Monty**

**Friedrich** (FRĒ-drik)
See Frederick.
Literature: Friedrich von Schiller,
poet and dramatist.

**Fritz** (FRITZ)
See Frederick.
Entertainment: Fritz Kreisler,
composer and violinist.

**Fulton** (FUL-ton)
Anglo-Saxon — *From a field*
Famous: Bishop Fulton J. Sheen,
author and TV personality.
**Fult**

**Gabriel** (GĀ-brē-el)
Hebrew — *God is my strength*
Biblical: Archangel of the
annunciation.
Entertainment: Gabe Kaplan,
comedian.
**Gabbie, Gabby, Gabe, Gabi,
Gabie, Gabriele, Gabriello,
Gaby**

**Gadi** (GĀ-dē)
Hebrew — *My fortune*
**Gadiel**

**Gage** (GĀJ)
French — *Pledge*

**Gale** (GĀL)
Irish — *Stranger*
Scandinavian — *Ravine*
Norwegian — *To sing*
Sports: Gale Sayers, football player.
**Gael, Gail, Gaile, Gayle**

**Galen** (GĀ-len)
Gaelic — *Intelligent*
Greek — *Calm*
**Gael, Gaelan, Gail, Gale,
Gayle**

**Galeno** (ga-LĒ-nō)
Spanish — *Little bright one*

**Gallagher** (GA-luh-ger)
Gaelic — *Eager helper*

**Galt** (GALT)
Norwegian — *High ground*

**Galvin** (GAL-vin)
Gaelic — *Sparrow*
**Gal, Galvan, Galven**

**Gamaliel** (GA-ma-lēl)
Hebrew — *Lord is vengeance or
recompense*
Famous: Warren Gamaliel
Harding, President.

**Gan** (GAN)
Vietnamese — *To be near*

**Gannon** (GAN-on)
Gaelic — *Fair-complected*
**Gan, Gannie, Ganny**

**Garald** (GAR-ald)
Russian — *Spear strong*
**Garold, Garolds, Gerald**

**Gardell** (GAR-del)
Teutonic — *Guardian*

**Gardner** (GARD-ner)
Anglo-Saxon — *A gardener*
**Gar, Gard, Gardener,
Gardie, Gardiner, Gardy**

**Gareth** (GAIR-eth)
Welsh — *Gentle*
**Gar, Garth**

**Garfield** (GAR-feld)
Old English — *Battlefield*
Entertainment: Garfield the Cat,
cartoon character.

**Garibald** (GAIR-i-bald)
Old English — *A welcome addition*

**Garland** (GAR-land)
Old English — *From the battlefield*
French — *Wreath*
**Gar, Garlen**

**Garner** (GAR-ner)
Teutonic — *Protecting warrior*
Famous: Garner Ted Armstrong,
leader of the Church of God
International.

**Garnett** (GAR-net)
Old English — *Armed with a spear*
**Gar, Garnet**

**Garrett** (GAIR-et)
Anglo-Saxon — *Powerful with the
spear*
Literature: Gerard Manley
Hopkins, religious poet.
Entertainment: Garrett Morris,
actor.
**Gar, Gareth, Garrard,
Garret, Garreth, Garrot,
Garrott, Gerard**

**Garrick** (GAIR-ik)
Teutonic — *Spear king*
Entertainment: Garrick Utley,
newscaster.
**Gar, Garek, Garik,
Garrik**

**Garridan** (GAIR-i-dan)
English — *You hid*

**Garth** (GARTH)
Norwegian — *Groundskeeper*
Literature: Hero in Maxwell
Anderson's *Winterset*.
**Gar, Gareth, Gerth**

**Garvey** (GAR-vē)
Gaelic — *Rough peace*
**Garv, Garvy**

**Garvin** (GAR-vin)
Teutonic— *Befriending warrior*
**Gar, Garwin, Vin, Vinnie,
Vinny, Win, Winnie, Winny**

**Garwood** (GAR-wood)
Old English— *From the fir-tree forest*
**Gar, Wood, Woodie, Woody**

**Gary** (GAIR-ē)
Old English— *Spear carrier*
Entertainment: Gary Cooper,
Garry Moore, Gary Coleman,
actors; Gary Crosby, singer, actor
and son of Bing Crosby.
**Gare, Garey, Garry**

**Gaspar** (GAS-par)
Spanish— *Master of treasure*

**Gasper** (GAS-per)
See Jasper.
**Gaspard**

**Gaston** (ga-STON)
French— *From Gascony*

**Gavin** (GAV-in)
Scottish— *White hawk*
Literature: Gawain, nephew of
King Arthur and knight of the
Round Table.
Entertainment: Gavin McLeod,
actor.
**Gav, Gavan, Gaven,
Gawain, Gawen**

**Gavril** (GAV-ril)
Russian— *Man of God*
**Ganya, Gav, Gavrel**

**Gaylord** (GĀ-lord)
French— *Jailor*
Sports: Gaylord Perry, baseball
pitcher.
**Gallard, Gay, Gayelord,
Gayler, Gaylor**

**Gaynor** (GĀ-nor)
Gaelic— *Son of the fair-complected
man*
**Gainer, Gainor, Gay,
Gayner**

**Geber** (gē-BAIR)
Hebrew— *Strong*

**Gene** (JĒN)
See Eugene.
Entertainment: Gene Kelly, actor
and dancer; Gene Hackman,
actor.

**Geoffrey** (JEF-rē)
See Godfrey.
**Geoff, Jeff**

**George** (JORJ)
Greek— *Farmer*
Famous: George Washington, first
President; George Washington
Carver, inventor of many uses
for the peanut.
Literature: George Bernard Shaw,
playwright; George Orwell,
novelist.
Entertainment: George Harrison,
one of the Beatles; George
Benson, jazz singer and guitarist;
George C. Scott, George Segal,
actors; George Carlin, comedian;
George M. Cohan, actor,
playwright and composer.
Sports: George *(Babe Ruth)*
Herman, baseball player.
**Egor, Georas, Geordie,
Georg, Georges, Georgie,
Georgy, Giorgio, Goran,
Gorya, Jorgan, Jorge, Yurik**

**Gerald** (JER-uld)
Teutonic— *Mighty with the spear*
Famous: Gerald Ford, President.
**Garald, Garold, Gary,
Gearalt, Gearard, Gerard,
Gerrie, Gerry, Giraldo, Giraud,
Jerald, Jerrie, Jerrold, Jerry**

**Gerard** (je-RARD)
Old English— *Spearhead*
Literature: Gerard Manley
Hopkins, poet.
**Gearard, Gerardo, Geraud,
Gerhard, Gerhardt, Gerrie,
Gerry, Gherardo**

**GEORGE**—*Farmer*

**Gerhard** (GAIR-hard)
Scandinavian—*Spearbrave*
**Gerri, Gerrie, Gerry**

**Gerik** (GAIR-ik)
Polish—*Prosperous*
**Edek, Gerek, Geri,
Gerick, Gerrick**

**Gershom** (GER-shom)
Hebrew—*The expelled or exiled*

**Gervase** (jer-VĀ-sē)
Teutonic—*Honorable*
**Gervais, Jarv, Jarvey,
Jarvis, Jervis**

**Giamo** (jē-A-mō)
Italian—*The supplanter*
Entertainment: Giacamo Puccini,
   composer of *Madam Butterfly.*
**Giacamo, Giacomo, Gian,
James**

**Gibor** (gi-BOR)
Hebrew—*Strong*
**Gabor**

**Gideon** (GID-ē-on)
Hebrew—*Feller of trees or destroyer*
Biblical: Judge of Israel.

207

**Gifford** (GIF-ord)
Teutonic — *Bold giver*
**Giff, Giffard, Gifferd,
Giffie, Giffy**

**Gil** (GIL)
Spanish — *Shield bearer*
**Giles, Gill**

**Gilad** (GIL-ad)
Hebrew, Arabic — *Camel hump*
**Giladi, Gilead**

**Gilbert** (GIL-bert)
Old English — *Trusted*
Famous: Gilbert Stuart, portrait
  painter.
Literature: Gilbert K. Chesterton,
  essayist and poet.
**Bert, Bertie, Berty, Burt,
Burtie, Burty, Gib, Gibb,
Gibbie, Gibby, Gil, Gilberto,
Gilburt, Gill, Giselbert, Guilbert,
Wilbert**

**Gilchrist** (GIL-krist)
Gaelic — *Servant of Christ*
**Gil, Gill, Gilley, Gillie, Gilly**

**Giles** (JĪLS)
Greek — *Shield bearer*
Literature: *Giles Goat-Boy,* novel by
  John Barth.
**Egide, Egidio, Egidius,
Gide, Gil, Gill, Gilles,
Gilley**

**Gillie** (GIL-ē)
English — *A song*

**Gilmore** (GIL-mor)
Gaelic — *Devoted to Virgin Mary*
**Gillie, Gillmore, Gilly,
Gilmour**

**Gilroy** (GIL-roi)
Celtic, Latin — *Servant of the king*
**Gill, Gilley, Gillie,
Gilly, Roy**

**Gino** (JĒ-nō)
See Ambrogio.

**Ginton** (GIN-ton)
Hebrew — *A garden*
**Ginson**

**Giovanni** (jē-ō-VAN-ē)
See John.
Famous: Giovanni Bellini,
  impressionist artist.
**Gian, Gianni, Gioacchino,
Giovanna**

**Giuseppe** (je-SEP-ē)
See Joseph.
Historical: Giuseppe Mazzini,
  Italian liberation fighter.
Entertainment: Giuseppe Verdi,
  composer.
**Giuseppi, Seppi**

**Givos** (GĒ-vōs)
Hebrew — *Heights*

**Gladwin** (GLAD-win)
Old English — *Cheerful*
**Glad, Gladdie, Gladdy,
Win, Winnie, Winny**

**Glen** (GLEN)
Celtic — *Valley*
Entertainment: Glen Campbell,
  singer; Glen Miller, orchestra
  leader; Glenn Gould, pianist;
  Glenn Ford, actor.
**Glenn, Glyn, Glynn**

**Glendon** (GLEN-dun)
Scottish — *From the glen fortress*
**Glen, Glenden, Glenn**

**Goddard** (GOD-erd)
Teutonic — *Divinely firm*
Literature: *Waiting for Godot,*
  existentialist play.
**Godard, Godart, Goddart,
Godot, Gothart**

**Godfrey** (GOD-frē)
German — *God's peace*
Entertainment: Godfrey
  Cambridge, comedian
**Godfree, Godfry**

**Godwin** (GOD-win)
Old English — *Friend of God*
**Godewyn, Goodwin, Win**

**Goel** (JŌ-el)
Hebrew — *The redeemer*

**Gordon** (GOR-dun)
Anglo-Saxon — *From the cornered hill*
Famous: G. Gordon Liddy, of the Nixon administration.
Entertainment: Gordon Lightfoot, singer; Gordon McRae, actor.
**Gordan, Gorden, Gordie, Gordy**

**Gorman** (GOR-man)
Zodiac — *Man of clay*
**Gormen**

**Gozal** (GŌ-zal)
Hebrew — *A bird*

**Grady** (GRĀ-dē)
Gaelic — *Noble, illustrious*
**Gradey**

**Graham** (GRĀ-um)
Anglo-Saxon — *Warlike*
Famous: Alexander Graham Bell, inventor of the telephone; Graham Kerr, gourmet cook.
Literature: Graham Greene, novelist and playwright.
Sports: Graham Hill, race-car driver.
**Graeme, Ham**

**Granger** (GRĀN-jer)
Old English — *Farmer*
**Grange, Gray**

**Grant** (GRANT)
French — *Great*
Famous: Grant Wood, American Gothic painter.
Entertainment: Grant Tinker, TV producer.
Sports: Grantland Rice, football coach and benefactor.
**Gran, Grantham, Granthem, Grantland, Grantley, Granville, Grenville**

**Grayson** (GRĀ-son)
Old English — *Son of a bailiff*
**Gray, Greerson, Greyson**

**Gregory** (GRE-gor-ē)
Greek — *Vigilant*
Entertainment: Gregory Peck, actor.
**Greg, Gregg, Gregoire, Gregoor, Gregor, Gregorio, Gregorius**

**Gresham** (GRE-sham)
Old English — *From the grassland*

**Griffin** (GRI-fin)
Latin — *Griffin or mystical beast*
**Griff, Griffie, Griffy**

**Griffith** (GRI-fith)
Welsh — *Fierce chief; ruddy*
**Griff, Griffie, Griffin, Griffy**

**Griswold** (GRIS-wold)
Teutonic — *From the gray forest*
**Gris, Grisold**

**Grosvenor** (GRŌV-ner)
French, Latin — *Mighty huntsman*
**Gros, Grosner**

**Grover** (GRŌ-ver)
Anglo-Saxon — *Grove dweller*
Famous: Grover Cleveland, President.
Entertainment: Grover, character on *Sesame Street*, a children's program.
**Grove**

**Guido** (GWE-dō)
Spanish — *Life*

**Gunther** (GUN-ther)
Old Norse — *Battle army*
Entertainment: Guenther Gebel Williams, animal trainer with Barnum & Bailey Circus.
**Guenther, Gun, Gunar, Gunnar, Gunner, Guntar, Gunter**

**Gus** (GUS)
See Augustus.
**Gusten, Gustin, Guston**

**Gustave** (GOOS-tav)
Swedish — *Staff of the Gothe*
Famous: Gustaf Adolf, Swedish
  king.
Literature: Gustave Flaubert,
  French novelist.
**Gus, Gustaf, Gustav,
Gustave, Gustavo, Gustavus**

**Guthrie** (GUTH-re)
Celtic — *War serpent*
**Guthrey, Guthry**

**Guy** (GI)
Celtic — *Guide*
Literature: Guy de Maupassant,
  French novelist and short-story
  writer; *Guy Mannering,* novel by
  Sir Walter Scott.
**Guido, Guyos, Wiatt,
Wyatt**

**Guyapi** (GI-a-pe)
North American Indian — *Candid*

**Gyasi** (JI-a-se)
Ghanan — *Wonderful child*

**Habib** (ha-BEB)
Muslim — *Beloved*

**Hadden** (HAD-un)
Old English — *From the heath or moor*
**Hadan, Haddan,
Haddon, Haden**

**Hadley** (HAD-le)
Old English — *From the heath*
**Had, Hadlee, Hadleigh,
Lee, Leigh**

**Hadrian** (HA-dre-un)
See Adrian.
Literature: *The Memoirs of Hadrian,*
  by Marguerite Yourcenar.
**Adok, Adorjan, Adrian,
Adrik, Andrian, Andryan**

**Hadwin** (HAD-win)
Teutonic — *Friend in war*

**Hahnee** (huh-NE)
North American Indian — *Beggar*

**Haidar** (HA-dar)
Indian — *Lion*
**Asad, Hirsuma**

**Haines** (HANZ)
Teutonic — *Dweller in the hedged
  enclosure*

**Hakeem** (ha-KEM)
Arabic — *Wise*

**Hakem** (HA-kem)
Arabic — *Ruler*

**Hakon** (HA-kon)
Norwegian — *Of the chosen race*
**Haakon, Hak, Hakan,
Hako**

**Hal** (HAL)
See Harold.
Entertainment: Hal Linden, Hal
  Holbrook, actors.

**Halbert** (HAL-bert)
Teutonic — *Gem*
**Bert, Hal, Hulbert**

**Halden** (HAL-den)
Teutonic — *Half-Dane*
**Dan, Dannie, Hal,
Haldan, Halfdan**

**Hale** (HAL)
Old English — *From sturdy stock*
**Hail, Hal, Heal**

**HAMILTON**—*From the mountain hamlet*

**Haley** (HĀ-lē)
Gaelic—*Ingenious*
**Hal, Hale, Lee, Leigh**

**Halford** (HAL-ford)
Old English—*From the hall or manor*
**Hal, Halford, Halstead, Halsted**

**Hall** (HAWL)
See Halford.

**Hallam** (HAL-um)
Teutonic—*From the hillside*
**Halam**

**Halsey** (HAWL-sē)
Old English—*From Hal's Island*
Entertainment: *Little Fauss and Big Halsey,* movie starring Robert Redford.
**Hal, Hallsy, Halsy**

**Hamal** (HAM-al)
Arabic—*Lamb*

**Hamilton** (HAM-il-tun)
Old English—*From the mountain hamlet*
Famous: Hamilton Jordan, politician in the Carter administration.
**Ham, Hamel, Hamil**

**Hamish** (HĀM-ish)
See James.

**Hamlet** (HAM-let)
French, German — *Little home*
Literature: Hamlet, one of
Shakespeare's most famous
characters.
**Ham, Hamnet**

**Hamlin** (HAM-lin)
Teutonic — *Ruler of the home*
**Ham, Hamlen, Lin, Lyn,
Lynn**

**Hanan** (HĀ-nan)
Hebrew — *Gracious*
**Hanen, Hanin**

**Hanif** (HA-nif)
Arabic — *True believer*
**Hanef**

**Hank** (HANK)
See Henry.
Sports: Hank Aaron, baseball
player and home-run record
holder.

**Hanley** (HAN-lē)
Anglo-Saxon — *Of the high meadow*
**Hanleigh, Henleigh, Henley,
Henry**

**Hans** (HONS)
See John.
Literature: Hans Christian
Andersen, author of *The Silver
Skates.*

**Hansel** (HAN-sel)
Scandinavian — *Gift from God*
Literature: Hansel and Gretel,
characters in a children's story.

**Harb** (HARB)
Arabic — *War*

**Harcourt** (HAR-kort)
French — *Fortified dwelling*
**Harry, Court, Courtney**

**Harden** (HAR-den)
Old English — *From the hare valley*
**Hardan, Hardin**

**Hardy** (HAR-dē)
Teutonic — *Strong or hardy*

**Harel** (HAIR-el)
Hebrew — *God's mountain*
**Haral, Haril**

**Harim** (HAIR-im)
Hebrew — *Flat-nosed*
**Harem**

**Harlan** (HAR-lun)
Teutonic — *From the land of the
warriors*
Famous: Harlan F. Stone, Chief
Justice of the Supreme Court;
Harlan Sanders, founder of
Kentucky Fried Chicken
restaurants.
Literature: Harlan Ellison, science
fiction author.
**Harland, Harlen, Harlin**

**Harley** (HAR-lē)
Old English — *The stag's meadow*
**Arleigh, Arley, Arlie,
Harden, Harl, Harleigh,
Hart, Hartley**

**Harlow** (HAR-lō)
Old English — *Army hill*
Famous: Harlow Shapely,
astronomer.

**Harod** (HAIR-ud)
Hebrew — *The loud terror*
Biblical: Jewish king at time of
Christ's birth.
**Hared, Harrod**

**Harold** (HAIR-uld)
Anglo-Saxon — *Army power*
Historical: Last Saxon king of
England.
Famous: Harold C. Urey,
discoverer of heavy hydrogen.
Literature: Harold Robbins,
novelist.
Entertainment: Harold Lloyd,
comedian.
**Araldo, Hal, Harald, Harry,
Herald, Hereld, Herold, Herrick**

**Harper** (HAR-per)
Old English, German—*Harp player*
**Harp, Harpor**

**Harrison** (HAIR-i-sun)
Old English—*Son of Harry*
Entertainment: Harrison Ford,
actor.
**Harris**

**Harry** (HAIR-ē)
Old English—*Soldier*
Famous: Harry S. Truman,
President.
Entertainment: Harry Guardino,
actor; song *I'm Just Wild About
Harry.*
**Har, Harald, Hareld,
Harold, Hereld**

**Hart** (HART)
Old English—*Hart-deer*
Literature: Hart Crane, poet.
**Hart, Hartley, Hartwell,
Harwell, Harwill**

**Harvey** (HAR-vē)
Teutonic—*Army warrior*
Literature: Harvey Cheyne, hero of
*Captains Courageous,* by Rudyard
Kipling; *Harvey,* play by Mary C.
Chase.
Entertainment: Harvey Korman,
actor and comedian.
**Harv, Harve**

**Hasad** (ha-SOD)
Turkish—*Harvest*
**Hassad**

**Hashim** (ha-SHĒM)
Arabic—*Broker*

**Hasin** (ha-SĒN)
Indian—*Laughing*
**Hasen, Hassin**

**Haskel** (HAS-kel)
Hebrew—*Understanding*
**Haskell**

**Haslett** (HAS-let)
Old English—*From the hazel-tree
land*
**Hassal, Hassel, Hassell,
Haze, Hazel, Hazlet, Hazlett**

**Hassan** (ha-SON)
Arabic—*Handsome*
**Hasain, Hasan, Husseini,
Muhassan**

**Hastin** (HĀ-stin)
Hindi—*Elephant*

**Hastings** (HĀ-stings)
Old English—*Son of the stern man*
**Hastie, Hasty**

**Havelock** (HA-ve-lok)
Norwegian—*Sea battle*

**Hayden** (HĀ-den)
Old English—*From the hedged hill*
**Haydon, Hayes, Hayward**

**Haywood** (HĀ-wood)
Old English—*From the hedged forest*
**Heywood, Woodie, Woody**

**Heath** (HĒTH)
English—*From the hearth*

**Hector** (HEK-tor)
Greek—*Steadfast*
Literature: Hector, a hero of
Homer's *Iliad.*
**Ettore, Heck**

**Henry** (HEN-rē)
Teutonic— *Ruler of an estate*
Historical: Henry Hudson,
  navigator and explorer.
Famous: Henry Kissinger, former
  Secretary of State and winner of
  Noble Peace Prize.
Literature: Henry James, Henry
  Thoreau, novelists; Henry
  Wadsworth Longfellow, poet.
Entertainment: Henry Winkler,
  actor known as the Fonz; Henry
  Morgan, Henry Fonda, actors.
**Enrico, Enrique, Hal,
Hamlin, Hank, Harry, Heindrick,
Heinrich, Heinrik, Hendrick,
Hendrik, Henri, Henrik**

**Herbert** (HER-bert)
Teutonic— *Glorious soldier*
Famous: Herbert C. Hoover,
  President; Herbert Spencer,
  English philosopher.
**Bert, Bertie, Berty, Eberto,
Habert, Havert, Hebert, Herb,
Herbie, Herby, Heriberto**

**Hercules** (HER-kū-lēz)
Greek— *Glorious gift*
**Herc, Herculie, Herculies,
Hersule**

**Herman** (HER-man)
Teutonic— *War man*
Famous: Armond Hammer,
  businessman.
Literature: Herman Melville,
  author of *Moby Dick;* Herman
  Hesse, author of *Steppenwolf.*
**Armand, Armando, Armin,
Armond, Armyn, Ermanno,
Ermin, Harman, Harmon,
Herm, Hermann, Hermie,
Hermon, Hermy**

**Hernando** (her-NAN-dō)
See Ferdinand.

**Herrod** (HAIR-ud)
Hebrew— *Heroic conqueror*
**Herod**

**Hersh** (HERSH)
Hebrew— *A deer*
**Hersch, Herschel, Hershel,
Herzl, Hirsch**

**Hervey** (HER-vē)
See Harvey.
Literature: Hervey Allen, author of
  *Israfel,* biography of Edgar Alan
  Poe.

**Herwin** (HER-win)
Teutonic— *A friend*

**Hewett** (HŪ-et)
French— *Little and intelligent*
**Hew, Hewet, Hewie, Hewitt**

**Heywood** (HĀ-wood)
Anglo-Saxon— *Forest enclosure*
Entertainment: Heywood Hale
  Broun, newspaper columnist and
  humanitarian.
**Haywood, Hey, Wood, Woodie**

**Hezekiah** (he-ze-KĪ-uh)
Hebrew— *God is my strength*
**Hesketh**

**Hilary** (HIL-a-rē)
Latin— *Cheerful*
**Hi, Hilaire, Hilario,
Hilarius, Hill, Hillary,
Hillery, Hillie, Hilly,  Ilario**

**Hillel** (HIL-el)
Hebrew— *Greatly praised*
Biblical: Hillel, renowned Jewish
  scholar.
**Hill, Hillier, Hilly, Hillyer**

**Hilliard** (HIL-yard)
Teutonic— *War guardian*

**Hilton** (HIL-ton)
Old English— *From the house on the
  hill*

**Hinun** (HĪ-nun)
North American Indian— *God of
  clouds and rain*
**Hunon**

**Hiram** (HĪ-ram)
Hebrew — *Exalted*
**Hi, Huran, Hy**

**Hiroshi** (hir-RŌ-shē)
Japanese — *Generous*

**Hisoka** (hi-SŌ-kuh)
Japanese — *Reserved*

**Ho** (HŌ)
Chinese — *The good*

**Hobart** (HŌ-bart)
Teutonic — *Bright mind*
**Hobard, Hobe, Hobey, Hobie, Hoebart**

**Hod** (HOD)
Hebrew — *Vigorous*

**Hogan** (HŌ-gan)
Gaelic — *Youth*

**Holbrook** (HŌL-brook)
Old English — *From the brook in the hollow*
**Brook, Holbrooke**

**Holden** (HŌL-den)
Teutonic — *Kind*

**Holleb** (HOL-ub)
Polish, German — *Peace*
**Hollub, Holub**

**Hollis** (HOL-is)
Anglo-Saxon — *Dweller by the holly tree*

**Holman** (HŌL-man)
Teutonic — *From the river island*

**Holt** (HŌLT)
Ecological — *Son of the unspoiled forest*

**Homer** (HŌ-mer)
Greek — *Pledge*
Literature: Homer, author of *The Iliad* and *The Odyssey*.
**Homere, Homerus, Omero**

**Honovi** (hō-NŌ-vē)
North American Indian — *Strong*

**Horace** (HOR-is)
Latin — *Keeper of the hours*
Famous: Horace, Greek philosopher; Horatio Alger, rags-to-riches success story; Horace Mann, innovator of teaching methods.
Literature: Horace Gregory, poet.
**Horacio, Horatio, Horatuis, Orazio**

**Horton** (HOR-ton)
Old English — *From the gray estate*
**Hort, Horten, Orten, Orton**

**Hosea** (ho-SĀ-uh)
Hebrew — *Salvation*
**Hoseia**

**Houston** (HŪ-ston)
Anglo-Saxon — *Hill town*

**Howard** (HOW-ard)
Old English — *Watchman*
Famous: Howard Hughes, aviator and businessman.
Literature: Howard Lindsay, author of *Life with Father*.
Entertainment: Howard Barlow, conductor.
Sports: Howard Cosell, sportscaster.

**Howe** (HOW)
Teutonic — *High*
**Howey, Howie**

**Howin** (HOW-in)
Chinese — *A loyal swallow*

**Howland** (HOW-land)
Old English — *Of the hills*
**Howey, Howie, Howlan**

**HOWARD** — *Watchman*

**Hubert** (HŪ-bert)
  Teutonic — *Bright mind*
  Historical: Hubert Wilkins, polar
    explorer.
  Famous: Hubert H. Humphrey,
    Senator and candidate for
    President; Hubert de Givenchy,
    designer.
  **Bert, Bertie, Berty, Hobard,
  Hobart, Hube, Huberto, Hubey,
  Hubie, Hugh, Hugibert, Hugo,
  Ugo, Ulberto**

**Hugh** (HŪ)
  Old English — *Intelligence*
  Literature: Hugh Hefner, founder
    of *Playboy* magazine.
  Entertainment: Hugo Wolf,
    Austrian composer; Hugh
    O'Brien, actor.
  **Hugo, Ugo**

**Humbert** (HUM-bert)
  German — *Giant; brilliant*
  Literature: Humbert Wolfe,
    English poet.
  **Bert, Bertie, Berty, Hum**

**Humphrey** (HUM-frē)
Teutonic — *Peaceful Hun*
Famous: Sir Humphrey Davis, inventor of the miner's safety lamp.
Literature: *Humphrey Clinker*, novel by Tobias Smollett.
Entertainment: Humphrey Bogart, actor.
**Hum, Humfredo, Humfrey, Humfrid, Humfried, Hump, Humph, Onfoi, Onfre, Onofredo**

**Hunter** (HUN-ter)
Old English — *Huntsman*
Literature: Hunter Thompson, novelist.
**Hunt**

**Huntington** (HUN-ting-ton)
Old English — *Hunting estate*
**Hunt, Huntingdon, Huntingston**

**Huntley** (HUNT-lē)
Old English — *Hunter's meadow*
**Hunt, Huntlee, Lee, Leigh**

**Hurd** (HERD)
Anglo-Saxon — *Hard, strong*

**Hurley** (HER-le)
Gaelic — *Sea tide*
**Hurlee**

**Husain** (hōō-SĀN)
Muslim — *Little beauty*
**Hussein**

**Hussein** (hōō-SĀN)
Arabic — *Little and handsome*
Famous: King Hussein of Syria.
**Husein**

**Hute** (ŪT)
North American Indian — *Star*

**Hutton** (HUT-ton)
Old English — *From the house on the jutting ledge*
**Hut, Hutt, Huttan**

**Hyatt** (HĪ-at)
Old English — *From the high gate*
**Hy, Hyat**

**Hyman** (HĪ-mun)
Hebrew — *Life*
Masculine form of Eve.
Literature: Admiral Hyman G. Rickover, author of *Education and Freedom;* Hy Gardner, syndicated columnist.
**Chaim, Hayyim, Hy, Hymen, Hymie, Mannie, Manny**

**Iago** (Ē-a-gō)
See James.
Literature: Villain in Shakespeare's *Othello.*
**Iagio**

**Ian** (Ē-an)
See John.
Literature: Ian Fleming, creator of James Bond.

**Innis** (IN-is)
Celtic — *From the island*
**Innes, Inness**

**Inteus** (in-TĀ-us)
North American Indian — *He shows his face*

**Ioakim** (Ē-ō-kim)
Russian, Hebrew — *God will establish*
**Akim, Iav, Jov, Yov**

**Ira** (Ī-ruh)
Hebrew— *Descendants or watchful one*
Famous: Ira Hays, one of the flag-raisers on Iwo Jima.

**Irvin** (IR-vin)
Anglo-Saxon— *Sea friend*
**Ervin, Ervine, Erwin, Irv, Irving, Irwin, Marv, Marvin, Merv, Mervin, Merwin**

**Irving** (IR-ving)
Gaelic— *Beautiful*
Old English— *Sea friend*
Famous: Irving Langmuir, Nobel Prize winner for chemistry.
Literature: Irving Wallace, Irving Stone, authors.
Entertainment: Irving Berlin, Irving Caesar, composers.
**Earvin, Erv, Ervin, Erwin, Irv, Irvin, Irvine, Irwin**

**Irwin** (IR-win)
Anglo-Saxon— *Lover of the sea*
Entertainment: Irwin Allen, film producer; Professor Irwin Corey, actor and comedian.
**Irwinn, Irwon**

**Isaac** (Ī-zak)
Hebrew— *Laughing*
Biblical: Son of Abraham and Sarah.
Famous: Isaac Newton, discoverer of the law of gravity.
Literature: Isaac Asimov, science fiction author.
Entertainment: Isaac Stern, violinist; Isaac Hayes, singer and actor.
**Ike, Ikey, Isaak, Isac, Isacco, Izaak, Izak**

**Isaiah** (ī-ZĀ-uh)
Hebrew— *God is my helper*
Biblical: Hebrew prophet.
**Isa, Isak**

**Isas** (Ī-sas)
Japanese— *Meritorious*

**Isidore** (IZ-i-dor)
Greek— *A gift of Isis*
Famous: Isidor Isaac Rabi, atomic scientist.
**Dore, Dorian, Dory, Isador, Isadore, Isidor, Isidoro, Isidro, Issy, Iz, Izzy**

**Israel** (IZ-rē-ul)
Hebrew— *Ruling with the Lord*
Biblical: One of the 12 Hebrew tribes; another name for Jacob.
**Isa**

**Ivan** (Ī-van)
Hebrew— *Gracious gift of God*
Famous: Ivan Mestrovic, sculptor.
Literature: Ivan Turgenv, novelist.
**Vania, Vanya**

**Ivar** (Ī-var)
Scandinavian— *Military archer*
Famous: Ivor Novello, composer.
**Ive, Iver, Ivers, Ives, Ivo, Ivon, Ivor, Yvon, Yvor**

**Iye** (Ī-yuh)
North American Indian— *Smoke*

**Jabez** (yuh-BEZ)
Hebrew— *Cause of sorrow*
**Jabe**

**Jacinto** (ha-SEN-tō)
Spanish— *Hyacinth*

**Jack** (JAK)
 See John.
 Entertainment: Jackie Cooper, Jack
   Paar, Jackie Gleason, Jack Benny,
   Jack Klugman, Jack Lemmon,
   Jack Nicholson, actors; Jackson
   Brown, singer.
 Sports: Jackie Robinson, baseball;
   Jack Nicklaus, golf champion;
   Jack Brabham, race-car driver.
 **Jackie, Jackson, Jacky,**
 **Jock, Jocko**

**Jacob** (JĀ-kub)
 Hebrew — *Supplanter*
 Biblical: Son of Abraham and
   brother of Esau.
 **Cob, Cobb, Cobbie, Cobby,**
 **Giacobo, Giacomo, Giacopo,**
 **Hamish, Iago, Jack, Jackie,**
 **Jacky, Jacobo, Jacques,**
 **Jaime, Jake, Jakie, Jakob,**
 **James, Jamesy, Jamey,**
 **Jamie, Jay, Jayme, Jim,**
 **Jock, Seamus, Seumas, Shamus**

**Jacques** (ZHOK)
 See James.
 Masculine form of Jacqueline.
 Historical: Jacques Cartier,
   discoverer of the St. Lawrence
   River.
 Famous: Jacques Cousteau,
   oceanographer and explorer.
 Literature: Philosopher in
   Shakespeare's *As You Like It.*
 Entertainment: Jacques Offenbach,
   light-opera singer.

**Jael** (JĀ-el)
 Hebrew — *Mountain goat*

**Jafar** (YAW-far)
 Muslim — *A little stream*

**Jagger** (JA-ger)
 Unknown — *To carry in a cart*
 **Jaggar**

**Jahi** (ya-HĒ)
 Swahili — *Dignity*

**Jaime** (JĀ-mē)
 See James.
 **Diego, Jayme, Jaymie**

**Jake** (JĀK)
 See Jacob.

**Jal** (JAWL)
 English — *He goes*

**James** (JĀMZ)
 Hebrew — *The supplanter*
 Biblical: Disciple of Jesus Christ.
 Famous: James Madison, James
   Monroe, James Polk, James
   Buchanan, James Garfield,
   Presidents; James Watt, inventor
   of the steam engine.
 Entertainment: James Garner,
   James Cagney, James Caan,
   James Stewart, James Coburn,
   actors.
 **Diego, Giacomo, Hamish,**
 **Iago, Jacques, Jaime, Jakie,**
 **Jamesy, Jamey, Jamie, Jay,**
 **Jayme, Jemmy, Jim, Jimmie,**
 **Jimmy, Jock, Jocko, Seamus,**
 **Seumas, Shamus**

**Jamil** (ja-MĒL)
 Arabic — *Handsome*
 **Jamill**

**Jan** (JAN)
 See John.
 Entertainment: Jan Peerce, opera
   singer; Jan, singer in group, Jan
   and Dean.
 **Janek, Janko, Jano, Janos,**
 **Jenda**

**Jared** (JAIR-ed)
 Hebrew — *Descending*
 **Jarad, Jordan**

**Jarek** (JAIR-ek)
 Polish — *January*
 **Janiuszck, Januarius,**
 **Januisz, Jarek**

**Jarlath** (JAR-lath)
 Latin — *Man of control*

**JARON** — *To sing*

**Jaron** (JAIR-un)
Hebrew — *To sing*

**Jaroslav** (JAR-ō-slav)
Czech — *Glory of spring*

**Jarvis** (JAR-vis)
Teutonic — *Keen as the spear*

**Jascha** (YAW-shuh)
See James.
Entertainment: Jascha Heifetz,
  violinist.

**Jason** (JĀ-sun)
Greek — *Healer*
Mythological: Leader in search of
  the Golden Fleece.
Entertainment: Jason Robards, Jr.,
  actor.
**Jasun, Jay**

**Jasper** (JAS-per)
Persian — *Treasurer*
**Caspar, Cass, Gaspar, Kaspar**

**Javas** (JA-vas)
Indian — *Quick*

**Javier** (ha-VĒR) or (ha-VE-ar)
Spanish — *Owner of the new house*
**Xavier**

**Jay** (JĀ)
French — *Blue jay*
Literature: Jay Gatsby in F. Scott
  Fitzgerald's *The Great Gatsby.*
Entertainment: Jay Gorney,
  composer.
**Jaye**

**Jean** (JĒN)
See John.
Literature: Jean Valjean, hero of
  *Les Miserables,* by Victor Hugo.
Entertainment: Jean Gabin, actor.

**Jeconiah** (je-KŌ-ne-uh)
  Hebrew — *Gift of the Lord*

**Jed** (JED)
  Hebrew — *Beloved of the Lord*
  **Jedd, Jeddy, Jedediah,
  Jedidiah**

**Jedrek** (JED-rek)
  Polish — *Manly*
  **Jedrus**

**Jeff** (JEF)
  See Godfrey.
  Entertainment: Jeff Bridges, actor.
  **Jefferson, Jeffy, Jeffie**

**Jeffrey** (JEF-re)
  French — *Heavenly peace*
  Entertainment: Jeffrey Hunter,
    actor.
  **Geoff, Geoffrey, Godfrey,
  Gottfried, Jeff, Jefferey,
  Jeffie, Jeffy**

**JASON** — *Healer*

**Jegar** (YĀ-gar)
Hebrew— *Witness our love*
**Jeggar, Jegger**

**Jeremiah** (JER-uh-mī-uh)
Hebrew— *God is high*
Biblical: One of the great Hebrew
prophets.
Famous: Jeremy Bentham, political
philosopher.
**Germaine, Jer, Jere,
Jereme, Jeremias, Jeremy,
Jermyn, Jerry**

**Jerome** (je-RŌM)
Latin— *Holy name*
Entertainment: Jerome Kern,
composer; Jerome Robbins,
choreographer.
**Gerome, Gerri, Gerrie,
Gerry, Hieronymus, Jere,
Jereme, Jerrome, Jerry**

**Jerry** (JAIR-ē)
See Gerald.
Famous: Jerry Brown, governor of
California.
Entertainment: Jerry Lewis, actor
and comedian; Jerry Lee Lewis,
rock singer; Jerry of *Tom and
Jerry* comic strip and movies.
**Gerald, Gerard, Jere, Jerey,
Jerrald, Jerrold, Jerri, Jerry**

**Jesper** (JES-per)
French— *Jasper stone*
**Jasper**

**Jesse** (JES-ē)
Hebrew— *Grace or gift of God*
Biblical: Father of David.
Famous: Jessie Helms, Senator;
Jessie James, outlaw.
Sports: Jesse Owens, Olympic
champion; Jesse Jackson, football
player and preacher.
**Jess, Jessey, Jessie**

**Jethro** (JETH-rō)
Hebrew— *Pre-eminence*
Biblical: Father-in-law of Moses.
**Jeth, Row**

**Jibben** (JIB-en)
English— *Life*
**Jibvel**

**Jim** (JIM)
See James.
Famous: Jim Bowie, frontiersman;
Jim Bludso, inventor of the
steamboat.
Literature: *Lord Jim*, novel by
Joseph Conrad.
Entertainment: Jim Henson,
creator of The Muppets; James
Earl Jones, Jimmy Durante,
Jimmy Stewart, actors; Jimmy
Dean, singer and actor.
Sports: Jimmy Connors, tennis
champion; Jim Clark, race-car
driver.
**James, Jimmie, Jimmy**

**Jin** (JIN)
Chinese— *Gold*

**Jivin** (JIV-in)
East Indian— *To give life*
**Jivanta**

**Joab** (JŌ-ab)
Hebrew— *Praise the Lord*

**Joachim** (wah-KĒM)
Hebrew— *The Lord will judge*
**Akim, Joaquin**

**Job** (JŌB)
Hebrew— *The afflicted*
Biblical: Book in the Holy Bible

**Joe** (JŌ)
See Joseph.
Entertainment: Joey Bishop, actor;
Joe Cocker, singer.
Sports: Joe Louis, heavyweight
boxing champion; Joe DiMaggio,
baseball star; Joe Garagiola,
sportscaster; Joe Namath,
football player and actor.
**Jo, Joey**

**Joel** (JŌ-el)
Hebrew— *God is willing*
Entertainment: Joel Gray, actor.

## John (JON)

Hebrew — *God is gracious*
Biblical: John the Baptist.
Historical: John Paul Jones, naval hero; Johnny Appleseed, who planted apple trees.
Famous: John Adams, John Quincy Adams, John Fitzgerald Kennedy, Presidents; John Dewey, modern educational practitioner.
Literature: John Milton, John Keats, authors.
Entertainment: John Ritter, John Belushi, John Travolta, actors; Johnny Cash, country-western singer; John Denver, singer and actor; Johnny Carson, *Tonight Show* host; John Barrymore, actor and director.
Sports: Johnny Bench, baseball catcher.
**Eoin, Evan, Ewan, Ewen, Gian, Giavanni, Hanan, Hanas, Hansel, Iaian, Iain, Ian, Ivan, Jack, Jackie, Jacky, Jan, Janos, Jean, Jens, Jevin, Jock, Jocko, Johan, Johann, Johannes, Johnnie, Johnny, Johnston, Johny, Jon, Jone, Juan, Owen, Sean, Shane, Shaughn, Shaun, Shawn, Zane**

## Jonah (JO-nuh)

Hebrew — *Dove*
Biblical: Prophet swallowed by a whale.
**Jonas**

## Jonathan (JON-a-thun)

Hebrew — *Jehovah gave*
Biblical: A friend of David.
Literature: Jonathan Swift, author of *Gulliver's Travels*; Richard Bach's *Jonathan Livingston Seagull*.
Entertainment: Jonathan Winters, comedian.
**Jon, Jonathon**

## Jordan (JOR-dun)

Hebrew — *Descending*
**Giordano, Jared, Jerad, Jori, Joudain**

## Jose (hō-SĀ)

Hebrew — *God will increase*
Famous: Che Guevara, Cuban Revolutionary War fighter.
Entertainment: Jose Ferrer, actor; Jose Feliciano, singer; Jose Greco, dancer.
**Che, Chepe, Chepito, Jose, Josecito, Joseito, Pepe, Pepillo, Pepito, Sodeph**

## Joseph (JŌ-sef)

Hebrew — *He shall add*
Biblical: Husband of Mary, Jesus' mother; Joseph was a ruler of Egypt.
Famous: Joseph Lister, discoverer of antiseptic.
Literature: Joseph Addison, poet; Joseph Conrad, novelist.
**Che, Giuseppe, Iosep, Jo, Joe, Joey, Jose, Jozef**

## Joshua (JO-shoo-uh)

Indian — *Satisfaction*
Hebrew — *Jehovah saves*
Biblical: Led Israelites to the promised land after the death of Moses.
Entertainment: Joshua Logan, film director and producer.
**Josh, Josha, Joshia**

## Josiah (jo-SĪ-ah)

Hebrew — *Jehovah supports*
**Josias**

## Jotham (JŌ-tham)

Hebrew — *Jehovah is perfect*

## Juan (WAHN)

See John.

## Judah (JOO-duh)

Hebrew — *Praise*
Biblical: Judah was the son of Jacob.
**Judas, Judd, Jude**

## Jude (JOOD)
Hebrew — *Praise*
Biblical: Jude, one of the 12 apostles, also known as Thaddeus.
Literature: *Jude the Obscure*, novel by Thomas Hardy.
Entertainment: Song *Hey Jude*, by the Beatles.
**Juda, Judas, Judd, Judson**

## Julian (JOO-lē-un)
Spanish — *Belonging to Julius*
**Halian, Julio**

## Julius (JOO-lē-us)
Greek — *Youthful and downy bearded*
Historical: Julius Caesar, Roman emperor.
Sports: Julius Erving, also known as *Dr. J*, basketball star.
**Giulio, Joliet, Jule, Jules, Juley, Julian, Julie, Julio**

## Jumah (JOO-mah)
Muslim — *Friday*
**Jimoh**

## Jun (JOON)
Chinese — *Truth*
Japanese — *Obedient*

## Junius (JOO-nē-us)
Latin — *Born in June*

## Juri (JOO-rē)
Estonian — *Farmer*
**Juris, Juritis, Jurka, Jurkan, Juss**

## Justin (JUS-tin)
Latin — *The just*
**Giustino, Giusto, Just, Justinian, Justino, Justis, Justus**

## Kadar (KĀ-dar)
Arabic — *Powerful*
**Kedar**

## Kadin (KĀ-din)
Arabic — *Companion*

## Kalig (KĀ-lik)
Arabic — *Creative*

## Kalil (ka-LIL)
Arabic — *Good friend*
**Kahaleel, Kahlil**

## Kalman (KAL-man)
See Karl.
**Karcsi, Kari, Karoly**

## Kane (KĀN)
Celtic — *Bright or radiant*
**Kayne**

## Kaniel (KAN-yel)
Hebrew — *Stalk*

## Karl (KARL)
See Charles.
Famous: Karl Marx, founder of Marxism.
Entertainment: Karl Malden, actor.
**Charles, Chuck, Kale, Karel, Karlens, Karlik, Karlis, Karol, Karolek**

## Karsten (KAR-sten)
Greek — *Anointed*

**Kasim** (ka-SĒM)
Muslim—*Divided*
**Kaseem**

**Kasimir** (KAS-mir)
Slavic—*Commands peace*

**Kass** (KAS)
German—*Like a black bird*

**Kay** (KĀ)
Latin—*Rejoiced in*
Entertainment: Kay Kaiser, band leader.

**Keahi** (KĒ-a-hē)
Polynesian—*Fire*

**Keane** (KĒN)
Old English—*Sharp or keen*
**Kean, Keen, Keene**

**Kearney** (KER-nē)
See Carney.
**Karney**

**Kedar** (KĀ-dar)
Hindi—*Mountain lord*
**Keady, Kedd, Keddie, Keddy**

**Keegan** (KĒ-gun)
Gaelic—*Little and fiery one*
**Kegan**

**Keenan** (KĒ-nun)
Gaelic—*Little and ancient*
Entertainment: Keenan Wynn, actor.
**Keen, Kienan**

**Keir** (KĒR)
Celtic—*Dark-skinned*
Entertainment: Keir Dullea, actor.

**Keith** (KĒTH)
Scottish—*From the battle place*
Entertainment: Keith Carradine, actor, composer and singer.
**Kenneth**

**Kelby** (KEL-bē)
Teutonic—*From the farm by the spring*
**Keelby, Kelbee, Kellby**

**Keleman** (KEL-man)
Hungarian—*Gentle*
**Kellman**

**Kelly** (KEL-ē)
Gaelic—*Warrior*
**Kele, Kelley**

**Kelsey** (KEL-sē)
Norwegian—*From the ship-island*

**Kelvin** (KEL-vin)
Celtic—*From the narrow river*

**Kendall** (KEN-dul)
Old English—*From the bright valley*
**Ken, Kendal, Kendell, Kenn, Kennie, Kenny**

**Kendrick** (KEN-drik)
Anglo-Saxon—*Royal ruler*
**Ken, Kendricks, Kenric, Rick, Rickie**

**Kenelm** (ka-NĒL-em)
Anglo-Saxon—*Brave helmet*
**Ken**

**Kenley** (KEN-lē)
Old English—*From the king's meadow*
**Kenleigh**

**Kenn** (KEN)
Welsh—*Clear water*
**Ken, Kennie, Kenny**

**Kenneth** (KEN-eth)
Celtic—*Handsome*
Literature: Ken Kesey, author of *One Flew Over the Cuckoo's Nest*.
Entertainment: Kenny Loggins, singer; Kenny Rogers, composer and country-western singer.
**Ken, Kennet, Kennett, Kenny, Kent**

**Kenton** (KEN-tun)
Old English—*From the king's estate*
**Ken, Kenn, Kennie, Kenny, Kent**

**KEEGAN**—*Little and fiery*

**Kenway** (KEN-wā)
Anglo-Saxon—*The brave soldier*
**Ken, Kenny**

**Kenyon** (KEN-yun)
Celtic—*Fair-haired*
**Ken, Kenny**

**Kerel** (KAIR-el)
African—*Young man*

**Kerem** (ke-RĒM)
Turkish—*Nobility and kindness*

**Kerey** (KAIR-ē)
English—*Homeward bound*
**Ker, Keri**

**Kermit** (KER-mit)
Celtic—*Free*
Entertainment: Kermit the Frog,
star of *The Muppet Show.*
**Dermont, Ker, Kermie,
Kermy, Kerr, Kerry**

**Kerr** (KER) or (KAR)
Celtic—*Dark or mysterious*
**Kerrie, Kerrin, Kerry, Kieran**

**Kerry** (KAIR-ē)
Gaelic—*The dark*
**Keary**

**Kersen** (KER-sen)
Indonesian—*Cherry*

**Kerwin** (KER-win)
Gaelic—*Little jet-black one*
**Kerwinn**

**Kevin** (KEV-un)
Gaelic—*Handsome*
Interesting: St. Kevin is the patron
saint of Dublin.
**Kev, Kevan, Keven**

**Khalil** (ka-LIL)
Arabic—*Friend*

**Kieran** (KĒR-an)
Gaelic—*Little and dark-skinned*
**Kierman, Kiernan**

**Kilby** (KIL-bē)
Teutonic — *From the farmstead by the spring*
**Kerby, Kirby**

**Killian** (KIL-ē-un)
Gaelic — *Little and warlike*
**Kilian, Killie, Killy**

**Kim** (KIM)
Old English — *Chief or ruler*
**Kimmie, Kimmy**

**Kimball** (KIM-bul)
Old English — *Warrior chief*
Literature: Kimball O'Hara, hero of Kipling's *Life in India.*
**Kim, Kimball, Kimble, Kimmie, Kimmy**

**King** (KING)
Anglo-Saxon — *Wise or ruler*

**Kingdon** (KING-dun)
Old English — *From the king's hill*

**Kingsley** (KINGZ-lē)
Old English — *From the king's meadow*
**King, Kingsly, Kinsley**

**Kingston** (KING-ston)
Old English — *From the king's manor*
**King, Kingsten**

**Kipp** (KIP)
Old English — *From the pointed hill*
**Kippar, Kipper, Kippie, Kippy**

**Kiral** (KĒR-al)
Turkish — *King*

**Kiril** (KIR-il)
Greek, Bulgarian — *Lordly one*
**Cirilo, Cyrek, Cyryl, Keereel, Kirila, Kirill, Kiryl, Kyrillos**

**Kiritan** (KIR-i-tan)
Hindi — *Wearing a crown*

**Kirk** (KIRK)
Scottish — *Church*
Entertainment: Kirk Douglas, actor.
**Kerk**

**Kistur** (KIS-ter)
English — *A rider*

**Kit** (KIT)
See Christopher.
Famous: Kit Carson, pony-express rider and frontiersman.

**Kliment** (KLIM-ent)
Russian, Latin — *Gentle*
**Klemenis, Klemens, Klemeny, Klemet, Klim, Klyment**

**Knoton** (NOT-un)
North American Indian — *The wind*
**Nodin**

**Knox** (NOKS)
Old English — *From the hills*

**Knud** (NŌŌD)
Danish — *Kind*

**Knut** (NŌŌT)
Norwegian — *Knot*
Sports: Knute Rockne, football coach.
**Canute, Cnut, Knute**

**Konrad** (KON-rad)
Teutonic — *Able in counsel*
**Conrad**

**Kontar** (KON-tar)
Akan — *An only child*

**Kris** (KRIS)
Latvian — *Christian*
Famous: Kris Kringle, another name for Santa Claus.
Entertainment: Kris Kristofferson, singer and actor.
**Kristafa, Krisus**

**Krister** (KRIS-ter)
Swedish — *Anointed one*
**Krist, Kristian**

**Kruin** (KR$\overline{OO}$-in)
Afrikaans— *Mountain peak*

**Kumar** (K$\overline{OO}$-mar)
Indian— *Prince*

**Kurt** (KERT)
German— *Bold counselor*
Entertainment: Kurt Weill,
    composer of *The Three Penny
    Opera;* Kurt Russell, actor.

**Kyle** (K$\overline{I}$L)
Gaelic— *Fair and handsome*
Sports: Kyle Rote, football player.
**Kile, Ky**

**Kynan** (KI-nan)
See Conal.
**Ky, Kyn**

**Laban** (L$\overline{A}$-ban)
Hebrew— *White*

**Lachlan** (LAK-lan)
Celtic— *Warlike*

**Ladd** (LAD)
English— *Attendant*
**Lad, Laddey, Laddie, Laddy**

**Laird** (LAIRD)
Celtic— *Proprietor*

**Lambert** (LAM-bert)
Teutonic— *Land bright*

**Lamont** (luh-MONT)
Norwegian— *Lawyer*
**Lammond, Lamond, Monty**

**Lancelot** (LAN-suh-lot)
Anglo-Saxon— *Spear*
Literature: Greatest of King
    Arthur's knights.
**Lance, Lancelot, Lancey,
Lancy, Launce, Launcelot**

**Landers** (LAN-derz)
French— *From the long hill*
**Langson**

**Landry** (LAN-dr$\overline{e}$)
Anglo-Saxon— *Ruler of the place*

**Lane** (L$\overline{A}$N)
English— *From the narrow road*
**Laney, Lanie**

**Lang** (LANG)
Teutonic— *Tall man*

**Langdon** (LANG-don)
Old English— *From the long hill*
**Landon, Langsdon, Langston**

**Langley** (LANG-l$\overline{e}$)
Old English— *From the long meadow*

**Langundo** (lan-GUN-d$\overline{o}$)
North American Indian— *Peaceful*

**Lani** (la-N$\overline{I}$)
Polynesian— *Sky*

**Lanny** (LAN-$\overline{e}$)
See Roland.
Entertainment: Lennie Bruce,
    comedian.
Sports: Lanny Watkins, golf
    champion.
**Lannie, Lennie**

**Lashi** (LA-sh$\overline{e}$)
English— *Famous warrior*
**Lajos, Lasho, Laszlo, Lazlo,
Lesley**

**LAWTON**—*Man of refinement*

**Lathrop** (LĀ-throp)
Old English—*From the
barn-farmstead.*
**Lathe, Lathrope, Lay**

**Latimer** (LA-ti-mer)
English—*Interpreter*
**Lat, Latie, Latiner, Lattey, Latty**

**Lavi** (LĀ-vē)
Hebrew—*Lion*
**Leib, Leibel**

## Lawrence (LOR-ens)
Latin—*Crowned with laurel*
Famous: Lawrence of Arabia.
Entertainment: Larry Hagman, Sir
Lawrence Olivier, actors;
Lawrence Welk, band leader.
**Larry, Lars, Lauren
Laurence, Laurens, Laurent,
Laurie, Lauritz, Lawry,
Lenci, Lon, Lonnie, Lonny,
Lorant, Loren, Lorens,
Lorenzo, Lori, Lorin,
Lorrie, Lorry, Lowrance, Rance**

## Lawton (LAW-ton)
Old English—*Man of refinement*
**Law, Laughton**

## Lazarus (LA-zuh-rus)
Hebrew—*God will help*
Biblical: Lazarus was raised from
the dead by Christ.
**Eleazar, Lazare, Lazaro, Lozar**

## Leander (lē-AN-der)
Greek—*Lionlike*
**Ander, Leander, Leandro,
Lee, Leigh, Leo**

## Learoyd (LER-oid)
Teutonic—*From the cleared meadow*

## Leben (LĒ-ben)
Hebrew—*Life*

## Ledyard (LED-yard)
Teutonic—*The nation's guardian*
Entertainment: Led Zeppelin, rock
group.
**Led**

## Lee (LĒ)
Old English—*From the meadow*
Entertainment: Lee J. Cobb, Lee
Majors, Lee Marvin, actors.
**Leigh, Leo**

## Leif (LĒF)
Norwegian—*Beloved*
Famous: Leif Erickson, Nordic
explorer.
**Lief**

## Leighton (LĀ-ton)
Old English—*From the herb garden*
**Lay, Layton, Leigh**

## Leland (LĒ-lund)
Old English—*Meadow land*
Famous: Leland Stanford, founder
of Stanford University.
**Lee, Leeland, Leigh**

## Lemar (luh-MAR)
Teutonic—*Close to the sea*
**Lemar**

## Lemuel (LEM-ū-el)
Hebrew—*Consecrated to God*
Literature: Lemuel Gulliver, hero
of *Gulliver's Travels*.
**Lem, Lemmie, Lemmy**

## Leo (LĒ-ō)
Latin—*Brave as a lion*
Entertainment: Leo Sayer, singer.
Sports: Leo Durocher, baseball
coach.
**Lee, Len, Lennie, Lenny,
Leon, Leonard, Leonardo, Lev,
Lion, Lionel, Lyon**

## Leonard (LEN-erd)
Teutonic—*Bold lion*
Famous: Leonardo da Vinci,
Renaissance inventor and
painter of the *Mona Lisa* and *The
Last Supper*.
Entertainment: Leonard Nimoy,
actor; Leonard Bernstein,
conducter and composer.
**Lee, Len, Lenard, Lennard,
Lennie, Lenny, Leo, Leon,
Leonardo, Leonerd, Leonhard,
Leonid, Leonidas, Lonnard,
Lonnie, Lonny, Lonya**

## Leopold (LĒ-uh-pōld)
Teutonic—*Bold for the people*
Entertainment: Leopold
Stakowski, conductor; Leopold
Auer, violinist.
**Leo, Leupold, Leupool**

**Leron** (LAIR-un)
Hebrew—*Song is mine*
**Lerone, Liron, Lirone**

**Leroy** (LĒ-roi)
French—*King*
**Elroy, LeRoy, Lee, Leigh,
Leroi, Regis, Rex, Roi, Roy**

**Leslie** (LEZ-lē)
Celtic—*From the gray fort*
Entertainment: Leslie Howard,
actor.
**Lee, Leigh, Les, Lesley,
Lester, Lezlie**

**Lester** (LES-ter)
Latin—*From the chosen camp*
**Leicester, Les**

**Levi** (LĒ-vī)
Hebrew—*Joined in harmony*
Biblical: Son of Jacob and Leah.
**Lev, Levey, Levy, Lewi**

**Lewis** (LOO-is)
Teutonic—*Renowned in battle*
Famous: Clovis Ruffin, designer.
Sports: Lew Alcindor, now known
as Kareem Abdul Jabbar.
**Aloysius, Clovis, Lew,
Lewes, Lewie, Lou, Louie,
Louis, Ludovick, Ludvig,
Luigi, Luis**

**Liam** (LĪ-am)
See William
Literature: Liam O'Flaherty,
author of *The Informer.*

**Liang** (LĒ-ang)
Chinese—*Excellent*

**Lincoln** (LINK-un)
Old English—*From the place by the
pool*
Historical: Lincoln Ellsworth,
polar explorer.
Famous: Abraham Lincoln,
President.
**Linc, Link**

**Lindsay** (LIND-sē)
Old English—*From the linden-tree
island*
**Lind, Lindsey**

**Linfred** (LIN-fred)
German—*Gentle peace*

**Linus** (LĪ-nus)
Hebrew—*Flaxen-haired*
Entertainment: Linus, friend of
Charlie Brown in *Peanuts* comic
strip.
**Lionello**

**Livingston** (LIV-ing-stun,
Old English—*From Lyfing's place*
Literature: *Jonathan Livingston
Seagull,* by Richard Bach.

**Liwanu** (li-WAN-oo)
Miowok Indian—*Bear growling*

**Llewellyn** (loo-EL-en)
Welsh—*Lionlike or lightning*
**Lew, Lewis, Llywellyn**

**Lloyd** (LOID)
Celtic—*Gray hair*
Famous: David Lloyd George,
Prime Minister of England
during World War I.
Entertainment: Lloyd Nolan,
Lloyd Bridges, actors.
**Floyd, Loy, Loydie**

**Locke** (LOK)
Old English—*From the forest*
**Lock, Lockwood**

**Logan** (LŌ-gun)
Gaelic—*From the hollow*
Literature: Logan Clendening,
author of *The Human Body.*

**Lombard** (LOM-bard)
Latin—*Long-bearded*
**Brad, Lem, Lomberd**

**Lon** (LON)
See Alonso.
Entertainment: Lon Chaney, actor.
**Lonnie, Lonny**

**Lorant** (LOR-ant)
Hungarian, Latin — *Crowned with laurel*
**Lenci, Lorencz, Lorincs**

**Loren** (LOR-en)
See Lawrence.
Entertainment: Lorin Maazel, conductor; Lorin Hollander, pianist.
**Larin, Lauren, Lorin**

**Lorenzo** (lor-EN-zō)
See Lawrence.
**Loring, Lorry**

**Lorimer** (LOR-i-mer)
Latin — *Harness-maker*
**Lorrie, Lorrimer, Lorry**

**Lot** (LOT)
Hebrew — *Veiled*
Biblical: Jewish patriarch whose wife was turned to a pillar of salt.

**Lothar** (LŌ-thar)
German — *Famous warrior*

**Loudon** (LOW-dun)
Teutonic — *From the low valley*
**Lowdon**

**Louis** (LOO-is)
German — *Renowned warrior*
Interesting: Name used for 18 French kings.
Famous: Louis Pasteur, French scientist and developer of method to purify milk.
Literature: Louis L'Amour, western writer.
Entertainment: Lou Rawls, singer; Louis Armstrong, jazz musician.
Sports: Lou Gehrig, baseball player.
**Lew, Lewis, Lou, Louie, Loysius, Ludvig, Ludwig, Luigi, Luis**

**Lowell** (LŌ-el)
French — *Little wolf*
Famous: Lowell Thomas, journalist and newscaster.
**Lovell, Lowe**

**Lucius** (LOO-shus)
Latin — *Bringer of light*
Literature: Lucius Morris Beebe, author of western folklore.
**Luca, Lucais, Lucas, Luce, Lucian, Luciano, Lucias, Lucien, Lucio, Lukas, Luke**

**Ludlow** (LUD-lō)
Old English — *From the prince's hill*

**Ludwig** (LUD-wig)
See Louis.
Famous: Ludwig van Beethoven, composer.
**Luis**

**Luister** (LOO-is-ter)
Afrikaans — *A listener*

**Luke** (LOOK)
Greek — *A person from Lucania.*
Biblical: Book in the Bible.
**Lucais, Lucas, Lukas**

**Luther** (LOO-ther)
Teutonic — *Famous warrior*
Famous: Martin Luther, religious reformer; Martin Luther King, civil rights leader.
Entertainment: Luther Adler, actor.
**Lothaire, Lothario, Lutero**

**Lutherum** (LOO-ther-um)
English — *Slumber*

**Lyle** (LĪL)
French — *From the island*
**Lisle, Lothar, Lothario, Ly, Lyel, Lyell**

**LUISTER**—*A listener*

**Lyman** (LĪ-man)
Old English—*Man from the valley*

**Lyndon** (LIN-dun)
Teutonic—*From the linden-tree hill*
Famous: Lyndon B. Johnson,
  President.
**Lin, Lindon, Lindy,
Lyn, Lynn**

**Lynn** (LIN)
Anglo-Saxon—*From the waterfalls*
**Lin, Linn, Lyn**

**Lyron** (LĪ-ron)
Hebrew—*Lyrical*
**Liron**

**Lysander** (lī-SAN-der)
Greek—*Liberator*
**Sander, Sandra**

**Mac** (MAK)
Scottish—*Son of*
Entertainment: Mac Davis, singer.
**Mack, Max**

**Mackenzie** (ma-KEN-zē)
Gaelic—*Son of the wise leader*
**Mac, Mack**

**Macnair** (mak-NAIR)
Gaelic—*Son of the heir*
**Macknair**

**Maddox** (MAD-oks)
Celtic—*Beneficent*
**Madoc, Maddock**

**Madison** (MAD-i-son)
Old English—*Son of the powerful
soldier*
**Maddie, Maddy, Son,
Sonnie, Sonny**

**Magnus** (MAG-nus)
Latin—*Great one*
**Manus**

**Mahir** (MA-ir)
Hebrew—*Industrious*
**Mahira**

**Mahlon** (MĀ-lun)
Hebrew—*Sickness*
Biblical: First husband of Ruth.

**Maimun** (MĀ-mun)
Arabic—*Lucky*

**Major** (MĀ-jer)
Latin—*Greater*
**Maje, Mauer, Mayor**

**Makis** (MĀ-kis)
Greek—*Who is like God*
**Mahail, Maichail, Mikhail,
Mikhalis, Mikhos**

**Malachi** (MAL-uh-kī)
Hebrew—*My messenger*
Biblical: Last book of the Old
Testament.
Entertainment: Malachi Throne,
actor.
**Mal, Malachy**

**Malcolm** (MAL-kom)
Celtic—*Dove*
Literature: Malcolm, son of King
Duncan in Shakespeare's
*Macbeth.*
**Mal**

**Malik** (MĀ-lik)
Muslim—*Master*

**Mallory** (MAL-ō-rē)
Teutonic—*Army counselor*
**Mal, Mallery**

**Malvin** (MAL-vin)
Celtic—*Chief*
**Mal, Melvin**

**Manco** (MAN-kō)
Peruvian—*King*

**Mandek** (MAN-dek)
Polish—*Army man*
**Arek, Armand, Armandek**

**Mandel** (MAN-del)
German—*Almond*
**Mandal**

**Manfred** (MAN-fred)
Old English—*Man of peace*
Entertainment: Manfred Mann,
rock singer.
**Fred, Mannie**

## Manipi (MAN-i-pē)
North American Indian — *A walking wonder*

## Manton (MAN-tun)
Anglo-Saxon — *From the king's estate*

## Manuel (man-WEL)
Hebrew — *God with us*
Entertainment: Manuel de Falla, Spanish composer.
**Emmanuel, Emmanuil, Manuil, Manuyill**

## Manvel (MAN-vel)
Latin — *From the great estate*
**Manvil**

## Marcel (mar-SEL)
Latin — *Little and warlike*
Literature: Marcel Proust, author of *Remembrance of Things Past*.
Entertainment: Marcel Marceau, pantomimist.
**Marcello, Marcellus, Marcelo**

## Marcus (MAR-kus)
See Mark.
Famous: Marcus Aurelius, Roman emperor.
Entertainment: *Marcus Welby, M.D.*, television series starring Robert Young.

## Mardon (MAR-dun)
Old English — *From the valley with the pool*
**Marden**

## Marid (muh-RID)
Arabic — *Rebellious*

## Marion (MAIR-ē-un)
See Mary.
Interesting: Name usually reserved for boys.
**Marlin**

## Mark (MARK)
Latin — *Warlike*
Biblical: One of the 12 apostles of Christ.
Famous: Marco Polo, explorer.
Literature: Mark Twain (Samuel L. Clemens), author; Mark Van Doren, critic, novelist and poet; *Marco Millions*, play by Eugene O'Neill.
Entertainment: Mark Hamill, actor in *Star Wars*.
Sports: Mark Spitz, Olympic gold medal swimmer.
**Marc, Marco, Marcos, Marcus, Mario, Marius, Markos, Markus**

## Marland (MAR-land)
Old English — *From the boundary*
**Marlan**

## Marlon (MAR-lon)
French — *Little falcon*
Entertainment: Marlon Brando, actor; Marlin Perkins, narrator and host of *Wild Kingdom*.
**Marlin, Merlin**

## Marlow (MAR-lō)
Old English — *From the hill by the lake*
**Mar, Marlo, Marlot, Marlowe, Merlot**

## Marmaduke (MAR-muh-dūk)
Celtic — *Sea leader*
**Duke**

## Marnin (MAR-nin)
Hebrew — *One who creates joy*

## Marshall (MAR-shal)
French — *Steward*
**Marsh, Marshal**

**MASON** — *Worker in stone*

**Martin** (MAR-tin)
Latin — *The warlike*
Famous: Martin Van Buren,
President; Martin Luther King,
civil rights leader.
Literature: *Martin Chuzzlewit*,
novel by Dickens.
Entertainment: Marty Feldman,
comedian.
**Mart, Martain, Marten,
Martie, Martijn, Martino,
Marty, Martyn**

**Marvin** (MAR-vin)
Teutonic — *Sea friend*
Entertainment: Marvin Hamlisch,
composer.
**Marv, Marwin**

**Maska** (MAW-skuh)
North American Indian — *Powerful*

**Mason** (MĀ-son)
Latin — *Worker in stone*
Entertainment: Mason Williams,
composer and singer.
**Maison, Mayson**

## Matthew (MA-thyoo)
Hebrew — *Gift of God*
Biblical: Matthew, one of the 12 apostles of Christ.
Famous: Matthew B. Brady, Abraham Lincoln's photographer.
Entertainment: Matt Dillon, old west hero on television series, *Gunsmoke.*
**Mata, Matei, Matek, Mateo, Mathe, Mathian, Mathias, Matias, Matt, Matteo, Matthaeus, Matthaus, Mattheus, Matthias, Matthiew, Mattias, Mattie, Matty, Matus, Matvey, Matyash, Motka**

## Maurice (mor-ES)
Latin — *Dark-skinned*
Entertainment: Maurice Chevalier, Morey Amsterdam, Maurice Evans, actors; Maurice Ravel, composer; Maurice Gibb, member of the rock group, The Bee Gees.
**Mauricio, Maurie, Maurise, Maurits, Maurizio, Maury, Morey, Morie, Moritz, Morris**

## Max (MAKS)
See Maximillian.
Famous: Max Planck, winner of Nobel Prize for physics.
Entertainment: Max Reinhardt, film director and producer; Max Baer, Jr., actor.
**Maxie, Maxy**

## Maximillian (maks-i-MIL-ē-an)
Latin — *Most excellent*
Famous: Ferdinand Maximillian Joseph, Archduke of Austria and Emperor of Mexico.
Entertainment: Maximillian Schell, actor.
**Mac, Mack, Massimiliano, Massimo, Max, Maxie, Maxim, Maximilianus, Maximilien, Maximo, Maxy**

## Maxwell (MAKS-wel)
Old English — *From the influential man's well*
Literature: Maxwell Anderson, author.
Entertainment: Maxwell Smart, character on TV show, *Get Smart.*
**Mac, Mack, Max, Maxie, Maxy**

## Mayer (MA-er)
Austrian — *Farmer*

## Maynard (MA-nerd)
Anglo-Saxon — *Mightily strong*
Entertainment: Maynard G. Krebbs, character on *Doby Gillis* TV show.

## Mead (MED)
Old English — *From the meadow*
**Meade**

## Medwin (MED-win)
Teutonic — *Strong friend*

## Melbourne (MEL-born)
Old English — *From the mill stream*
**Melborn, Melburn**

## Meldon (MEL-don)
Old English — *From the hillside mill*
**Meldan, Melden**

## Melville (MEL-vil)
Old English — *From the estate of the hard worker*
**Mel, Melbille**

## Melvin (MEL-vin)
Celtic — *Chief*
Entertainment: Melvyn Douglas, actor; Mel Brooks, actor and film director.
Sports: Mel Allen, sportscaster.
**Mal, Malvin, Mel, Melvyn**

## Mendel (MEN-del)
East Semitic — *Knowledge, wisdom*
**Mendie, Mendy**

## Mendeley (MEND-lē)
Russian — *Comforter*
Latin — *Of the mind*
**Menachem, Mendelly, Mendely**

**Mercer** (MER-ser)
French, Latin — *Merchant*

**Meredith** (MAIR-e-dith)
Welsh — *Guardian from the sea*
**Merideth, Merry**

**Merle** (MERL)
French — *Blackbird*
Entertainment: Merle Haggard,
country-western singer.
**Merlin, Merrill**

**Merlin** (MER-lin)
English — *Falcon*
Literature: Merlin, wizard in King
Arthur legend.
**Marlin, Marlon, Merle**

**Merrick** (MAIR-ik)
Teutonic — *Industrious ruler*

**Merrill** (MAIR-il)
French — *Famous*
**Merill, Merle, Merrel,
Merrell, Meryl**

**Merripen** (MAIR-i-pen)
English — *Life or death*

**Merton** (MER-ton)
Anglo-Saxon — *From the farm by the
sea*
Entertainment: Merv Griffin, TV
talk-show host.
**Merv, Merwyn**

**Merwin** (MER-win)
Teutonic — *Lover of the sea*
**Merwyn**

**Mestipen** (me-STIP-en)
English — *Life, fortune or luck*

**Meyer** (MĪ-er)
Belgian — *Farmer*
**Mayeer, Mayer, Mayor,
Meier, Meir, Myer**

**Micah** (MĪ-kuh)
Hebrew — *Like unto the Lord*
Entertainment: Mick Jagger, singer.
**Mic, Mick, Mike, Mikey**

**Michael** (MĪ-kul)
Hebrew — *Who is like the Lord*
Biblical: An archangel.
Famous: Michelangelo
Buonarrotti, painter and sculptor.
Literature: Michel Eyquem de
Montaigne, essay writer.
Entertainment: Mike Love, of the
rock group, The Beach Boys;
Michael Jackson, singer and
actor; Michelangelo Antonioni,
actor and film director; Michael
Caine, Michael Landon, Michael
Douglas, Mike Nichols, Sir
Michael Redgrave, actors;
Michael Kitt, choreographer;
Mike Douglas, host of *The Mike
Douglas Show.*
**Micah, Michael, Michail,
Micheil, Michel, Michele,
Mickey, Mickie, Micky, Mikael,
Mike, Mikel, Mikey, Mikkel,
Mikkell, Miquel, Mischa, Mitch,
Mitchel, Mitchell, Mychal**

**Milap** (MĪ-lap)
North American Indian — *He gives*

**Milburn** (MIL-bern)
Old English — *Of the stream by the
mill*
Entertainment: Melburn Stone
played Doc on TV series
*Gunsmoke.*

**Miles** (MĪLS)
Greek — *Millstone*
Latin — *Soldier*
**Mihiel, Milo, Myles**

**Millard** (MIL-ard)
Old English — *Caretaker of the mill*
Famous: Millard Fillmore,
President.
**Millward, Milward**

**Milo** (MĪ-lō)
See Miles.

**Milton** (MIL-ton)
Old English — *From the mill town*
Literature: John Milton, poet.
Entertainment: Milton Berle,
  known as Uncle Milty and Mr.
  TV.
**Milt, Miltie, Milty**

**Minor** (MĪ-ner)
Latin — *Junior or younger*
**Miner**

**Mitchell** (MITCH-el)
See Michael.
Entertainment: Mitch Miller, band
  leader.
**Mitch, Mitchel**

**Mohammed** (mō-HAW-mud)
See Muhammad.

**Mohan** (MŌ-han)
Hindi — *Delightful*
**Krishna**

**Mojag** (MŌ-hag)
North American Indian — *Never
  quiet*

**Monroe** (mon-RŌ)
Gaelic — *From the mouth of the Roe
  River*
**Monro, Munro, Munroe**

**Montague** (MON-ta-gū)
French — *From the pointed mountain*
**Monte, Monty**

**Monte** (MON-tē)
Latin — *Mountain*
Entertainment: Monte Hall, host of
  *Let's Make A Deal.*
**Montgomery**

**Montgomery** (MONT-gum-er-ē)
Old English — *From the rich man's
  mountain*
Entertainment: Montgomery Clift,
  actor.
**Monte, Monty**

**Moore** (MOR)
French — *Dark-complected*

**Mordecai** (MOR-de-kī)
Hebrew — *Belonging to Marduk*
Biblical: Cousin of Queen Esther.

**Moreland** (MOR-lund)
Old English — *From the moor*

**Morgan** (MOR-gun)
Celtic — *Born by the sea*
**Morgun**

**Morley** (MOR-lē)
Old English — *From the meadow on
  the moor*
Entertainment: Morley Safer,
  newscaster.
**Morlee, Morly**

**Morrell** (MOR-el)
Latin — *Swarthy*
**Morel**

**Mortimer** (MOR-ti-mer)
French — *Still water*
Entertainment: Mortimer Snerd,
  character created by Edgar
  Bergen, ventriloquist.
**Mort, Mortie, Morty**

**Morton** (MOR-tun)
Old English — *From the farm on the
  moor*

**Morven** (MOR-ven)
Celtic — *Mariner*
**Morvin**

**Moses** (MŌ-zes)
Hebrew — *Saved*
Egyptian — *Child*
Biblical: Prophet that gave us the
  Ten Commandments.
Famous: Moses Mendelssohn,
  philosopher known as the
  German Socrates; Moshe Dayan,
  Israeli Defense Minister.
**Moe, Moise, Moises,
Mose, Moshe, Moss, Mozes**

**Moulton** (MŌL-tun)
Old English, Latin — *From the mule
  farm*

**Muhammad** (mu-HAW-mud)
Arabic—*Praised*
Famous: Muhammad, founder of
the Muslim religion.
Sports: Muhammad Ali,
heavyweight boxing champion.
**Ahmad, Amed, Hamdrenn,
Hamdun, Hamid, Hammad,
Humayd, Mahmoud, Mahmud,
Mehamet, Mehemet, Mehmet,
Mohammad**

**Muir** (MŪR)
Celtic—*Moor*

**Muraco** (mer-AW-kō)
North American Indian—*White
moon*

**Murdock** (MER-dok)
Celtic—*Wealthy sailor*
**Murdoch, Murtach**

**Murray** (MER-ē)
Celtic—*Seaman*
**Murry**

**Musenda** (mū-SEN-duh)
African—*Nightmare*

**Myron** (MĪ-ron)
Greek—*Fragrant ointment*
Entertainment: Myron Cohen,
comedian.
**My, Ron, Ronnie, Ronny**

**Nabil** (na-BĒL)
Arabic—*Noble*

**Nagid** (na-GĒD)
Hebrew—*Ruler*

**Nahele** (na-HĒ-lē)
Polynesian—*Grove of trees*

**Nahum** (NĀ-hum)
Hebrew—*Compassion*
Biblical: Prophet who predicted
the fall of Nineveh.

**Naldo** (NAL-dō)
Teutonic—*Power*

**Namir** (nā-MĒR)
Hebrew—*Leopard or cunning
swiftness*

**Napoleon** (na-PŌ-lē-on)
Greek—*Lion of the woodland dell*
Historical: Napoleon Bonaparte,
French ruler.
**Leon, Nap, Napoleon,
Nappie, Nappy**

**Narcissus** (nar-SIS-us)
Greek—*Self-loving*

**Nathan** (NĀ-than)
Hebrew—*Gift*
Biblical: Prophet who rebuked
    David for his treachery to Uriah.
Historical: Nathan Hale,
    Revolutionary War hero.
Literature: *Nathan The Wise*, play
    by Lessing.
Entertainment: Nathan Milstein,
    violinist; Nat King Cole, singer.
**Nat, Nate**

**Nathaniel** (na-THAN-yel)
Hebrew—*Gift of God*
Biblical: Nathaniel, one of the 12
    apostles of Christ.
Literature: Nathaniel Hawthorne,
    author of *The Scarlet Letter*;
    Nathanael West, author.
**Nataniel, Nate, Nathan,**
**Nathanael, Natie, Natty**

**Neal** (NĒL)
Celtic—*Champion*
**Neale, Nealey, Nealon, Neil**

**Ned** (NED)
See Norton.

**Nehemiah** (nē-uh-MĪ-uh)
Hebrew—*Comforted by the Lord*
Biblical: Prophet who helped
    rebuild Jerusalem.
Entertainment: Nehemiah Persoff,
    actor.
**Hemiah**

**Neil** (NĒL)
Irish—*Chief*
Latin—*Dark*
Literature: Neil Simon, playwright.
Entertainment: Neil Diamond,
    actor, songwriter and singer;
    Neil Sedaka, singer.
**Neal, Neale, Neall, Nealon,**
**Neel, Neil, Neill, Neils,**
**Nels, Nial, Niall, Niels,**
**Nil, Niles, Nils**

**Nelson** (NEL-son)
English—*Son of Neil*
Entertainment: Nelson Eddy,
    singer and actor.
**Nealson, Neils, Nels,**
**Niles, Nils, Nilson**

**Neron** (NER-on)
Spanish, Latin—*Stern*
**Nero**

**Nestor** (NES-ter)
Greek—*Wisdom*
Mythological: Chieftain of the
    seige of Troy.

**Neville** (NE-vil)
French—*From the new town*
Literature: Nevil Shute, author of
    *On the Beach*.
**Nebille, Nev, Nevil,**
**Nevile, Newton**

**Nevin** (NE-vin)
Gaelic—*Worshipper of the saints*
Anglo-Saxon—*Nephew*
**Nevins**

**Newbold** (NOO-bōld)
Old English—*New building*

**Newlin** (NOO-lin)
Celtic—*From the spring*
**Newlyn, Newlynn**

**Nicholas** (NI-kō-lus)
Greek—*Victory of the people*
Interesting: St. Nicholas, another
    name for Santa Claus.
Historical: Nicholas, Czar of
    Russia.
Famous: Nikita Kruschev, Russian
    Premier.
Literature: *Nicholas Nickleby*, novel
    by Dickens.
Entertainment: Nick Nolte, actor.
**Claus, Colas, Cole, Colet,**
**Colin, Colley, Klaus,**
**Niccolo, Nichol, Nicholl,**
**Nick, Nickie, Nickolaus, Nicky,**
**Nicol, Nicolai, Nicolas, Niki,**
**Nikita, Nikki, Nikolai, Nikolas,**
**Nikolaus, Nikolos, Nikos,**
**Niles, Nixo**

**NORMAN**—*Norseman*

**Nicodemus** (ni-kō-DĒ-mus)
Greek—*The people-conqueror*
Biblical: Jewish priest and member of Sanhedrin.
**Nick, Nicky**

**Nigel** (NĪ-jel) or (NĒ-gel)
Latin—*Dark or black*
Literature: *The Fortunes of Nigel*, by Sir Walter Scott; *Sir Nigel*, novel by Arthur Conan Doyle.
Entertainment: Nigel Bruce, actor who played the part of Watson in Sherlock Holmes series.

**Niles** (NĪLS)
Danish—*Son of Neil*
Famous: Niels Bohr, scientist known for his work with atoms.
**Niel, Niels, Nils**

**Noah** (NŌ-uh)
Hebrew—*Wandering or rest*
Biblical: Noah built the ark and survived the Great Flood.
Literature: Noah Webster, author of the Webster dictionary.
Entertainment: Noah Beery, actor.

**Nobel** (NŌ-bel)
Latin — *Well-born*
**Nobe, Nobie, Noble, Noby**

**Nodin** (NŌ-din)
North American Indian — *The wind*
**Noton**

**Noel** (NŎ-ul)
French — *Born at Christmas*
Entertainment: Noel Coward,
  actor and director.
**Natal, Natale, Nowell**

**Nolan** (NŌ-lan)
Gaelic — *Famous or noble*
**Noland**

**Norbert** (NOR-bert)
Norwegian — *Brilliant hero*
Famous: Norbert Wiener, scientist
  prominent in the field of
  cybernetics.
**Norbie, Norby**

**Norman** (NOR-man)
Anglo-Saxon — *Norseman*
Historical: Norman Thomas, six
  times a Presidential candidate.
Famous: Norman Rockwell,
  painter and illustrator.
Literature: Norman Mailer, author
  of *The Naked and the Dead.*
Entertainment: Norm Crosby,
  comedian.
**Norm, Normand, Normie,
Normy**

**Norris** (NOR-is)
French — *From the north*
**Norrie, Norry, Norvin**

**Northrop** (NORTH-rup)
Old English — *From the north farm*
**North, Northrup**

**Norton** (NOR-tun)
Anglo-Saxon — *From the north place*
**Ned, Norty, Noton**

**Norward** (NOR-ward)
Teutonic — *The guard at the northern
  gate*
**Norwood, Norword**

**Noy** (NOI)
Hebrew — *Beauty*

**Nuri** (NER-ē)
Hebrew — *Fire*
**Nur, Nuriel, Nuris**

**Nye** (NĪ)
English — *Islander*

**Oakley** (ŌK-lē)
Anglo-Saxon — *From the oak-tree
  meadow*
**Oak, Oakes, Oakie,
Oaks**

**Obadiah** (ō-buh-DĪ-uh)
Hebrew — *Servant of God*
**Obadias, Obed, Obediah,
Obie, Oby**

**Octavio** (ok-TÃ-ve-ō)
Latin — *Eighth*
**Octave, Octavian, Octavius,
Octavus, Tavey**

**Odell** (Ō-del)
Norwegian — *Little and wealthy*
**Dell, Ode, Odey,
Odie, Ody**

**Odoric** (Ō-dor-ik)
Latin — *Son of a good man*

**Ogden** (OG-den)
Old English — *From the oak valley*
Literature: Ogden Nash, humorist poet.
**Ogdan, Ogdon**

**Ohanko** (ō-HAN-kō)
North American Indian — *Reckless*

**Olaf** (Ō-laf)
Norwegian — *Ancestor*
Famous: St. Olaf, first Christian King of Norway.
**Olafur, Olav, Olen, Olin**

**Olery** (Ō-ler-ē)
Teutonic — *Ruler of all*

**Oliver** (OL-i-ver)
Latin — *Olive tree*
Historical: Oliver Hazard Perry, American officer at the battle of Lake Erie.
Famous: Oliver Wendell Holmes, Supreme Court Justice.
Entertainment: Oliver Hardy, of comedy team Laurel and Hardy.
**Noll, Nollie, Nolly, Olivero, Olivier, Oliviero, Ollie, Olly, Olvan**

**Olney** (ŌL-nē)
Old English — *Unknown*

**Omar** (Ō-mar)
Arabic — *First son, highest follower of the prophet*
Entertainment: Omar Sharif, actor.
**Omer**

**Onan** (Ō-nan)
Turkish — *Prosperous*
**Onon**

**Orban** (OR-ban)
Latin, Hungarian — *City boy*

**Ordway** (ORD-wā)
Anglo-Saxon — *Spear fighter*
**Orway**

**Oren** (OR-en)
Hebrew — *Pine tree*
**Oran, Orin, Orren, Orrin**

**Orestes** (or-ES-tez)
Greek — *Mountain man*
Mythological: Son of Agamemnon, who avenged his father's murder by slaying his mother.
**Oreste**

**Orford** (OR-ford)
Old English — *From the cattle ford*

**Orion** (or-Ī-on)
Greek — *Son of fire*

**Orji** (OR-jē)
Nigerian — *Mighty tree*

**Orland** (OR-land)
Old English — *From the pointed land*
**Land, Lannie, Lanny, Orlan, Orlando**

**Orman** (OR-mun)
Teutonic — *Mariner or shipman*

**Ormond** (OR-mund)
English — *Bear or ravine mound*

**Orson** (OR-sun)
Latin — *Bearlike*
Entertainment: Orson Welles, actor and director; Orson Bean, actor; Sonny Bono, singer and actor.
**Sonnie, Sonny, Urson**

**Orton** (OR-ton)
English — *Ravine town*
**Horton**

**Orville** (OR-vil)
French — *From the golden estate*
Famous: Orville Wright, one of the inventors of the airplane.
**Orv**

**Osbert** (OZ-bert)
Anglo-Saxon — *Divinely bright*
**Bert, Bertie, Berty, Oz, Ozbert, Ozzie**

**Osborn** (OZ-born)
Teutonic — *Divine bear*
**Osborne, Osbourn, Osbourne**

## Oscar (OS-ker)
Celtic— *Leaping warrior*
Interesting: Oscar, award of the Academy of Motion Picture Arts and Sciences.
Literature: Oscar Wilde, author.
Entertainment: Oscar Hammerstein II, librettist for many of Richard Rodger's musicals.
**Oshar, Ossie, Ossy, Ozzie, Ozzy**

## Osgood (OZ-good)
Teutonic— *Gift of our Lord*
**Ozzie, Ozzy**

## Osmond (OZ-mund)
Teutonic— *Under divine protection*
**Osmund**

## Oswald (OZ-wald)
Anglo-Saxon— *Divine power*
**Ossie, Ossy, Oswell, Oz, Ozzie, Ozzy, Wald, Waldo**

## Otis (Ō-tis)
Greek— *Keen of hearing*
**Oates, Otes**

## Otman (OT-mun)
Teutonic— *Gift of our Lord*
Entertainment: Ozzie, character of *Ozzie and Harriett* TV show.
**Ozzie, Ozzy**

## Otto (OT-tō)
Teutonic— *Rich*
Literature: Othello, character in Shakespeare's play.
Entertainment: Otto Preminger, film producer and director.
**Odo, Othello, Otho**

**ORSON** — *Bearlike*

**Otway** (OT-wā)
Teutonic— *Fortunate in battle*

**Outram** (OT-ram)
Teutonic— *Prospering raven*

**Ovid** (Ō-vid)
Latin— *Shepherd*
Historical: Greek historian and chronicler.
**Ovidius**

**Owen** (Ō-wen)
Celtic— *Lamb*
Greek— *Well-born*
**Ewen**

**Oxford** (OKS-ford)
Old English— *From the river-crossing of the oxen*
**Ford**

**Pablo** (POB-lō)
See Paul.
Famous: Pablo Picasso, painter.
Entertainment: Pablo Cassals, cellist.

**Paco** (PA-kō)
North American Indian— *Bald eagle*

**Paddy** (PA-dē)
See Patrick.

**Padraic** (pa-DRĀ-ik)
See Patrick.
Literature: Padraic Colum, playwright and author.
**Padrayc**

**Page** (PĀJ)
French— *Servant to the royal court*
**Padget, Padgett, Paige**

**Paine** (PĀN)
Latin— *Country man*
**Payne**

**Pal** (PAL)
English— *Brother*

**Pallaton** (PAL-a-tun)
North American Indian— *Fighter*
**Palladin, Pallaten**

**Palmer** (POL-mer)
Latin— *The palm-bearer or pilgrim*
**Palm, Palmer**

**Parker** (PAR-ker)
English— *Guardian of the park*
**Park, Parke**

**Parlan** (PAR-lan)
Scottish— *Son of the earth*
**Parlen**

**Parnell** (par-NEL)
French— *Little Peter*
Entertainment: Pernell Roberts, actor.
**Parrnell, Pernell**

**Parrish** (PAIR-ish)
English— *From the church yard*
**Parrie, Parrisch, Parry**

**Parry** (PAIR-ē)
French— *Guardian*

**Pascal** (PAS-kal)
Hebrew— *Passover*
**Pascale, Pasquale**

**PAXTON**—*A traveler*

## Patrick (PAT-rik)

Latin—*Nobleman*

Interesting: St. Patrick, patron
saint of Ireland.

Historical: Patrick Henry,
Revolutionary War hero.

Literature: Sir Patrick Spens,
author of Scottish ballads;
Paddie Chayefsky, author.

Entertainment: Pat Boone, singer;
Pat Paulsen, comedian.

**Paddie, Paddy, Padraic, Padraig,
Pat, Paton, Patric, Patrice,
Patricio, Patrizio, Patrizius,
Patsy, Patten, Pattie, Patty, Peyton**

## Patton (PAT-tun)

Old English—*From the warrior's
estate*

**Pat, Paten, Patin,
Paton, Patten, Pattin, Patty**

## Paul (PAWL)

Latin—*Small*

Biblical: Saul, called Paul, was one
of the 12 apostles of Christ.

Historical: Paul Revere, known for
his ride to warn of the British
coming.

Entertainment: Paul Newman,
Paul Scofield, actors; Paul Anka,
singer and songwriter; Paul
McCartney, singer; Paul Lynde,
comedian.

**Pablo, Pall, Paolo,
Paulie, Pauly, Pavel, Poul**

**Paxton** (PAKS-tun)
Teutonic— *A traveler*
**Packston, Paxon**

**Payat** (PĀ-yat)
North American Indian— *He is coming*
**Pay, Payatt**

**Paz** (PAWZ)
Spanish— *Peace*

**Peder** (PĀ-der)
Danish— *Rock*
**Panos, Pedro, Peet, Pero, Petr, Petras, Petros, Piero, Pierre, Pieter, Pietrek**

**Pembroke** (PEM-brōk)
Celtic— *From the headland*

**Penn** (PEN)
Old Engish— *Enclosure*
Teutonic— *Commander*
**Pen, Penny**

**Penrod** (PEN-rod)
Teutonic— *Famous commander*
**Pen, Penn, Pennie, Penny, Rod, Roddie, Roddy**

**Percival** (PER-si-vul)
French— *Pierce the valley*
Interesting: Name invented by Chretien de Troyes.
Literature: Percival C. Wren, author of *Beau Geste;* Sir Percival, knight of King Arthur's Round Table.
Entertainment: Opera *Parsifal*, by Richard Wagner.
**Parsifal, Perce, Perceval, Percy, Purcell**

**Percy** (PER-sē)
English— *Pear tree*
French— *Little Peter*
Entertainment: Percy Grainger, pianist and composer.

**Peregrine** (PER-e-grin)
Latin— *Wander*
**Perry**

**Perrin** (PER-in)
See Peter.
**Perren, Perryn**

**Perry** (PER-ē)
French— *Pear tree*
Welsh— *Son of Harry*
Literature: Perry Mason, hero of Erle Stanley Gardner books.
Entertainment: Perry Como, singer.
**Par, Parry, Perr**

**Peter** (PĒ-ter)
Greek— *Rock*
Biblical: Simon, called Peter, was one of the 12 apostles of Christ.
Historical: Peter the Great, of Russia.
Literature: *Peter Ibbetson,* novel by George du Maurier; *Peter Pan,* by James Barrier; Peter Benchley, author of the novel *Jaws.*
Entertainment: Peter O'Toole, Peter Falk, Peter Graves, actors; Peter Ilyich Tchaikovsky, composer; Peter Duchin, orchestra leader.
**Farris, Ferris, Parry, Peador, Pearce, Pearson, Peder, Pedro, Peerson, Peirce, Perkin, Perren, Perry, Pete, Peterus, Petey, Petr, Pierce, Pierre, Pierson, Pietrek, Pietro, Piotr**

**Peyton** (PĀ-tun)
Old English— *From the warrior's estate*
**Pate**

**Phelan** (FĀ-lun)
Celtic— *Wolf or brave as a wolf*

**Philander** (FIL-an-der)
Greek— *Lover of mankind*

**Philbert** (FIL-bert)
Teutonic— *Illustriously brilliant*
**Bert, Filbert**

## Philemon (FIL-e-mon)
Greek— *Loving*
Biblical: Greek to whom Paul
wrote an Epistle.
**Philemonn, Phillemon**

## Philip (FIL-ip)
Greek— *Lover of horses*
Biblical: One of the 12 apostles of
Christ.
Historical: Father of Alexander the
Great.
Famous: Prince Philip, husband of
the Queen of England.
Literature: Philip Carey, hero in *Of
Human Bondage*, by Somerset
Maugham.
Entertainment: Phil Silvers, actor;
Phil Donahue, host of *Donahue*
talk show.
**Felipe, Filip, Filippo, Phelps,
Phil, Philipe, Philipp, Phillip,
Phillipp**

## Philo (FĪ-lō)
Greek— *Friendly*
**Philio**

## Phineas (FIN-ē-as)
Hebrew— *Oracle*
Famous: Phineas T. Barnum,
founder of Barnum and Bailey
Circus.

## Pierce (PĒRS)
See Peter.
Famous: Pierre Cardin, clothes
designer.
Literature: Pierre Corneille, author
of *Golden Age of Louis*.
**Pearce, Peirce, Pierre**

## Pierpont (PĒR-pont)
French, Latin— *Dweller by the stone
bridge*
**Pierre, Pierrepont, Pierrie,
Pierrpont**

## Pius (PĪ-us)
Latin— *Pious*
**Pyus**

## Plato (PLĀ-tō)
Greek— *Broad-shouldered*
Historical: Eminent Greek
philosopher.
**Platon**

## Pollard (POL-erd)
Teutonic— *Cropped hair*

## Pomeroy (POM-e-roi)
French— *From the apple orchard*
**Pom, Pommie, Pommy, Roy**

## Porter (POR-ter)
Latin— *Door keeper*
**Port, Portie, Porty**

## Powell (POW-el)
Celtic— *Alert*

## Prentice (PREN-tis)
Latin— *Learner or apprentice*
**Pren, Prent, Prentiss, Prentiz**

## Prescott (PRES-kot)
Old English— *From the priest's
cottage*
**Scott, Scottie, Scotty**

## Preston (PRES-ton)
Anglo-Saxon— *Of the priest's place*

## Price (PRĪS)
Welsh— *Son of Rice*
**Brice, Bryce, Phip, Pryce**

## Primo (PRĒ-mō)
Italian— *First born*

## Prince (PRINS)
Latin— *Prince*

## Prior (PRĪ-or)
Latin— *Superior*
**Prior, Pry, Pryor**

## Proctor (PROK-tor)
Latin— *Manager or leader*
**Procter**

## Putnam (PUT-nam)
Anglo-Saxon— *Dweller of the pond*
**Putmen, Putnem**

**Quartus** (KWAR-tus)
Latin — *Fourth son*

**Quentin** (KWEN-tin)
Latin — *The fifth*

**Quillan** (KWIL-an)
Gaelic — *Cub*

**Quinby** (KWIN-bē)
Scandinavian — *Of the womb of
woman*

**Quincy** (KWIN-sē)
French — *From the fifth son's estate*
Famous: John Quincy Adams,
President.
Literature: Quincy Howe,
newspaper columnist.
**Quin, Quinn, Quinzee**

**Quinlan** (KWIN-lan)
Gaelic — *Physically strong*
**Quinn**

**Quintus** (KWIN-tus)
Latin — *Fifth*

**Rabi** (RA-bī)
Arabic — *Breeze*
**Rabbi**

**Radburn** (RAD-burn)
Old English — *From the red stream*
**Rad, Radborne,
Radbourne, Raddie, Raddy**

**Radcliffe** (RAD-klif)
Old English — *From the red cliff*
**Rad, Raddie, Raddy**

**Radman** (RAD-man)
Slovak — *Joy*
**Radmen**

**Radomil** (RAD-ō-mil)
Czech — *Love of peace*
**Rad, Radomill**

**Rafael** (RA-fī-el)
Spanish — *God has healed*
**Rafe, Raphael**

**Rafferty** (RA-fer-tē)
Gaelic — *Rich, prosperous*
**Rafe, Raff, Raffarty**

**Rafi** (RĀ-fī)
Arabic — *Exalting*

**Ragnar** (RAG-nar)
Norwegian, Swedish — *Mighty army*
**Ragnor, Rainer, Rayner,
Raynor**

**Rahman** (RAW-man)
Arabic— *Compassionate*
**Abdul, Allah, Rahmet**

**Raleigh** (RAW-lē)
Old English— *Of the deer field*
**Lee, Leigh, Rawley**

**Ralph** (RALF)
Old English— *Wolf counselor*
Famous: Ralph Nader, consumer
  advocate; Ralph Lauren, clothes
  designer.
Entertainment: Ralph Bellamy,
  actor.
**Rafe, Raff, Ralf, Raoul,
Rolf, Rolph**

**Ralston** (RAL-ston)
Old English— *Of the house of Ralph*
**Ralfston, Rolfston**

**Ramon** (ra-MŌN)
See Raymond.

**Ramsay** (RAM-sē)
Teutonic— *From the ram's island*
Famous: Ramsay MacDonald,
  Great Britain's first Labor Prime
  Minister.
**Ram, Ramsey**

**Randall** (RAN-dul)
See Randolph.
Literature: Randall Jarrell, poet.
Entertainment: Randy Newman,
  songwriter and singer.
**Rand, Randal, Randell,
Randi, Randy**

**Randolph** (RAN-dolf)
Anglo-Saxon— *Protected; advised by
  wolves*
Entertainment: Randolph Scott,
  actor.
**Raff, Raffaello, Ralph,
Rand, Randal, Randall,
Randell, Randolf, Randy**

**Ranger** (RĀN-jer)
French— *Guardian of the forest*
**Rainger, Range**

**Ranon** (RĀN-on)
Hebrew— *To be joyous*
**Raman, Ranen**

**Ransom** (RAN-som)
Old English— *Son of the shield*
**Randsom, Ransum**

**Raphael** (RA-fī-el)
Hebrew— *God has healed*
Biblical: An archangel.
Famous: Raffaello Sanzio, painter
  of Madonnas.
**Rafael, Rafaelle,
Rafaello, Rafe, Ray**

**Ravi** (RA-vī)
Hindi— *Conferring*
Famous: Ravi Shankar, guru.
**Ravid, Raviv**

**Rawdon** (RAW-don)
Teutonic— *From the roe or deer hill*

**Ray** (RĀ)
French— *Kingly or king's title*
Literature: Ray Bradbury, science
  fiction writer.
Entertainment: Ray Charles,
  singer; Ray Milland, Raymond
  Massey, actors; Ray Bolger,
  dancer and actor.
**Ramon, Raymond, Raymund**

**Rayburn** (RA-burn)
Old English— *From the deer brook*
**Burn, Burnie, Burny, Ray**

**Raymond** (RĀ-mund)
Teutonic— *Wise protection*
Entertainment: Raymond Burr,
  actor.
**Raimondo, Raimund, Raimundo,
Ramon, Ray, Raymund, Reamon,
Reamonn**

**Raynor** (RĀ-nor)
Norwegian— *Mighty army*
**Ragnar, Rainer, Ray**

**Razi** (RĀ-zē)
Hebrew— *My secret*
**Raz, Raziel**

**Redford** (RED-ford)
Old English— *From the red river crossing*
Entertainment: Redd Foxx, comedian and actor.
**Ford, Red, Redd, Reddy**

**Reece** (RĒS)
Welsh— *Enthusiastic*
**Rees, Reese, Rice, Rip**

**Reed** (RĒD)
Old English— *Red-haired*
**Read, Reade, Reid**

**Reeve** (RĒV)
English— *Steward*

**Regan** (RĀ-gan)
Gaelic— *Little king*
**Reagan, Reagen, Regen**

**Reginald** (REJ-i-nald)
Teutonic— *Mighty ruler*
Literature: *Reggie Fortune,* story by H. C. Bailey.
Entertainment: Reginald de Koven, composer.
Sports: Reggie Jackson, baseball player.
**Reg, Reggie, Reggis, Reginauld, Reinald, Reinaldo, Reinaldos, Reinhold, Reinwald, Renault, Rene, Reynold, Reynolds, Rinaldo, Rinalldo, Ron, Ronald, Ronnie, Ronny**

**Remington** (RE-ming-tun)
Old English— *From the raven estate*
**Rem, Remming, Tony**

**Remus** (RĒ-mus)
Latin— *Fast-moving*
Literature: Uncle Remus, teller of *Br'er Rabbit* stories.

**Rendor** (REN-dor)
Hungarian— *Policeman*

**Rene** (re-NĀ)
French— *Reborn*
Famous: Rene Descartes, philosopher and mathematician.
**Renee**

**Reuben** (ROO-ben)
Hebrew— *Behold a son*
Biblical: Eldest son of Jacob; one of the 12 tribes of Israel.
**Reuven, Rouvin, Rube, Ruben, Rubin, Ruby**

**Rex** (REKS)
Latin— *King*
Famous: Rex Whistler, English artist.
Literature: Rex Stout, author of Nero Wolfe detective novels.
Entertainment: Rex Harrison, actor; Rex Reed, critic; Rex Allen, singer and actor.
**Rexir, Rexy**

**Reyhan** (RĀ-an)
Arabic— *Favored by God*

**Reynard** (RĀ-nard)
French— *Fox*
Teutonic— *Mighty*
**Ray, Raynard, Reinhard, Renard, Renaud, Rey**

**Rhys** (RES) or (RĪS)
Celtic— *Hero*
Welsh— *Ardor or rush*
**Rees, Rice**

**Richard** (RICH-erd)
Teutonic— *Powerful ruler*
Famous: Richard I, known as The Lion-Hearted; Richard Nixon, President.
Literature: *Poor Richard's Almanac,* by Benjamin Franklin.
Entertainment: Richard Strauss, composer; Richard Carpenter, singer; Richard Rogers, composer of musicals; Rich Little, impressionist; Richard Burton, Richard Pryor, Richard Dreyfuss, Richard Chamberlain, Richard Benjamin, actors.
**Dick, Dickie, Dicky, Ric, Ricard, Ricardo, Riccardo, Rich, Richart, Richi, Richie, Richy, Rick, Rickard, Rickert, Ricki, Rickie, Ricky, Rico, Riki, Ritch, Ritchie**

**RICHARD**—*Powerful ruler*

**Richmond** (RICH-mond)
Teutonic—*Powerful protector*
**Richmound**

**Rick** (RIK)
See Richard.
Entertainment: Ricky Nelson,
actor and singer.

**Rida** (RĒ-duh)
Arabic—*Favor*
**Rid, Ridd, Ridia**

**Rider** (RĪ-der)
Old English—*Horseman*
**Ridder, Rydder, Ryder**

**Ridgley** (RIJ-lē)
Old English—*He lives by the
meadow's edge*
**Ridley, Riddley**

**Riley** (RĪ-lē)
Gaelic—*Valiant*
**Reilly, Ryley**

**Rimril** (RIM-ril)
Chinese— *Clan's name*
**Hulen, Rimhel, Rimhen,
Rimlal, Rimnir, Rimshu**

**Ring** (RING)
Old English— *Ring*
Literature: Ring Lardner, novelist
and short-story writer.
Entertainment: Ringo Starr,
member of The Beatles.
**Ringo, Ringio**

**Riordan** (RĒ-or-dan)
Gaelic— *Bard or royal poet*
**Dan, Dannie, Danny, Rio**

**Rip** (RIP)
Dutch— *Ripe; full grown*
Literature: Rip Van Winkle,
character created by Washington
Irving.
Entertainment: Rip Torn, actor.
**Lee, Leigh, Riplee, Ripley**

**Roald** (RŌ-ald)
Teutonic— *Fame*

**Roarke** (RORK)
Gaelic— *Famous ruler*
**Rorke, Rourke**

**Robert** (ROB-ert)
Teutonic— *Of bright, shining fame*
Historical: Robert Fulton, designer
of the first successful U.S.
steamboat.
Famous: General Robert E. Lee,
Confederate general.
Literature: Robert Frost, Robert
Sherwood, Robert Stevenson,
Robert Browning, writers and
poets.
Entertainment: Robert Schumann,
composer; Robert Redford,
Robert Mitchum, Robert DeNiro,
Robert Wagner, Robert Blake,
actors.
**Bob, Bobbie, Bobby, Riobard,
Rip, Rob, Robb, Robbie,
Robby, Robers, Roberto, Robin,
Rupert, Ruperto, Ruprecht**

**Robin** (RO-bin)
See Robert.
Famous: Robin Hood of Sherwood
Forest.
Entertainment: Robby Benson,
actor; Robin Williams, actor
known as Mork; Robin Gibb,
member of the Bee Gees.
**Robby**

**Robinson** (RO-bin-sun)
English— *Son of Robert*
Literature: Robinson Jeffers, poet;
*Robinson Crusoe*, novel by Daniel
Defoe.
**Robert, Robin, Robinet,
Robers, Roberto, Ruperto**

**Rochester** (RO-ches-ter)
Old English— *From the stone camp*
Entertainment: Rochester,
character on *The Jack Benny Show.*
**Chest, Chester, Chet,
Rock, Rockie, Rocky**

**Rockwell** (ROK-wel)
Old English— *From the rocky spring*

**Rocky** (ROK-ē)
See Rochester.
Entertainment: Rock Hudson,
actor; Rocky, movie character
created by Sylvester Stallone.
Sports: Rocky Marciano,
heavyweight boxing champion.
**Rock, Rockwell, Rockey**

**Rodas** (RŌ-das)
Spanish, Greek— *Place of the roses*

**Roderick** (ROD-rik)
German— *Famous ruler*
Literature: *Roderick Hudson*, novel
by Henry James.
Entertainment: Roddy McDowall,
Rod Steiger, actors; Rod
McKuen, singer and poet; Rod
Stewart, singer.
**Rod, Rodd, Roddie, Roddy,
Roderic, Roderich, Roderigo,
Rodrick, Rodrigo, Rodrique,
Rory, Rurik, Ruy**

**Rodmann** (ROD-man)
Teutonic— *Red hair*
Old English— *One who rides with a knight*
**Rod, Rodd, Roddie, Roddy, Rodman**

**Rodney** (ROD-ne)
Teutonic— *Famous*
Anglo-Saxon— *Island clearing*
Entertainment: Rodney Dangerfield, comedian; Rodney Allen Rippy, child actor.
**Rod, Rodd, Roddie, Roddy, Rodi, Rodie**

**Roger** (ROJ-er)
Teutonic— *Famous spearman*
Historical: Rodger Williams, founder of Rhode Island.
Entertainment: Roger Daltrey, rock singer; Roger Smith, Roger Moore, actors.
Sports: Rogers Hornsby, Rodger Maris, baseball players.
**Robers, Rodge, Rodger, Rog, Rogerio, Rogers, Rudiger, Ruggiero, Rutger, Ruttger**

**Roland** (RO-lund)
German— *From the famous land*
Entertainment: Roland Petit, ballet dancer; Roland Young, actor.
**Lannie, Lanny, Rolando, Roldan, Roley, Rolland, Rollie, Rollin, Rollins, Rollo, Rolly, Rowland**

**Rolf** (ROLF)
Teutonic— *Famous wolf*
Historical: First Norman duke was the viking, Rollo.
Literature: Rolfe Humphries, poet.
**Rolfe, Rollin, Rollo, Rolph**

**Rolon** (RO-lon)
Spanish, Teutonic— *Famous wolf*

**Roman** (RO-man)
Latin— *Of Rome*
Literature: Romain Roland, author.
Sports: Roman Gabriel, football quarterback.
**Roma, Romain**

**Romeo** (RO-me-o)
Italian— *Pilgrim to Rome*
Literature: Hero in Shakespeare's *Romeo and Juliet*.
**Rome, Romie**

**Romney** (ROM-ne)
Welsh— *Curving river*

**Romulus** (ROM-u-lus)
Latin— *Citizen of Rome*
Mythological: Romulus and Remus, twins nursed by wolves and founders of Rome.
**Romulis**

**Ronald** (RON-uld)
See Reginald.
Famous: Ronald Reagan, actor and President.
Entertainment: Ronald Coleman, Ron Howard, actors.
**Ron, Ronn, Ronny**

**Rooney** (ROO-ne)
Gaelic— *Red hair*
**Rowan, Rowen, Rowney**

**Roper** (RO-per)
Old English— *Rope maker*

**Rory** (ROR-e)
Gaelic— *Red king*
Entertainment: Rory Calhoun, actor.
**Ririk**

**Roscoe** (ROS-ko)
Teutonic— *From the deer forest*
Sports: Roscoe Tanner, tennis star.
**Rosco, Ross, Rossie, Rossy**

**Rosmer** (ROS-mer)
Zodiac— *Sea horse*

**RYAN**—*Little king*

**Ross** (ROS)
French—*Red*
Scottish—*Headland*
**Rosse, Rossie, Rossy**

**Roswald** (ROZ-wald)
Teutonic—*Mighty steed*
**Roz, Rozwald**

**Roth** (ROTH)
German—*Red hair*

**Rouvin** (ROO-vin)
Greek, Hebrew—*Behold a son*
Famous: Rouvin, sculptor.

**Roy** (ROI)
Celtic—*Red-haired*
French—*King*
Entertainment: Roy Rogers, singer
and actor; Roy Clark, singer.
**Roi, Royce, Rufe, Rufo,
Rufus, Ruy**

**Royal** (ROI-ul)
French—*Kingly*
**Roy, Royall**

**Royden** (ROI-den)
French—*From the king's hill*
**Roy, Royd**

**Rudd** (RUD)
Old English — *Ruddy-complected*
**Ruddie, Ruddy, Rudy,
Rudyard**

**Rudolph** (RŌO-dolf)
Teutonic — *Famous wolf*
Entertainment: Rudolf Nureyev,
  ballet dancer; hero of Puccini's
  opera *La Boheme;* Rudolph
  Valentino, actor; Rudy Vallee,
  singer and actor.
**Raoul, Rodolfo, Rodolph,
Rodolphe, Rolf, Rolfe, Rollin,
Rollo, Rolph, Rudie,
Rudolf, Rudolfo, Rudy**

**Ruford** (RŌO-ford)
Old English — *From the red ford*

**Rufus** (RŌO-fus)
Latin — *Red-haired*
**Griffin, Griffith, Grigg,
Rufe**

**Rupert** (RŌO-pert)
Teutonic — *Of shining fame*
Historical: Prince Rupert of
  Bavaria.
Literature: *Rupert of Hentzau,* novel
  by Anthony Hope; Rupert
  Brooke, poet.

**Ruskin** (RUS-kin)
French — *Red-haired*
**Rush, Russ**

**Russell** (RUS-el)
French — *Red-haired or fox-colored*
Literature: Russell Crouse, author
  of *Life with Father.*
**Russ, Rustie, Rusty**

**Ruthford** (RUTH-ford)
Old English — *From the cattle ford*
Famous: Rutherford B. Hayes,
  President.
**Ford, Fordie, Ruther,
Rutherford**

**Rutledge** (RUT-lej)
Old English — *From the red pool*
**Rutherford, Rutter**

**Ryan** (RĪ-un)
Gaelic — *Little king*
Entertainment: Ryan O'Neal, actor.
**Ryun**

**Sabin** (SĀ-bin)
Latin — *A man of the sabine people*
Interesting: Name comes from the
  Sabines, an Italian tribe.

**Sahale** (sa-HĀL-ē)
North American Indian — *Above*

**Sahen** (SĀ-en)
Indian — *Falcon*

**Sailsbury** (SALS-bur-ē)
Old English — *From the guarded
  palace*

**Sakima** (suh-KĒ-muh)
North American Indian — *King*
**Sakim**

**Salim** (SĀ-lim)
Arabic — *Safe*

**Salvador** (SAL-va-dor)
Italian — *Savior*
Famous: Salvador Dali, surrealist
  painter.
**Sal, Sallie, Sally,
Salvidor, Sauveur**

## Sam (SAM)
See Samuel.
Interesting: Uncle Sam, symbol of the U.S. Government.
Famous: Sam Rayburn, Speaker of the House of Representatives.
Literature: Sam Weller, character in *Pickwick Papers*, by Dickens.
Entertainment: Sammy Davis, Jr., singer and actor.
**Sammie, Sammy, Shem**

## Samson (SAM-son)
Hebrew— *Like the sun*
Biblical: Samson had great strength until Delilah betrayed him.
**Sam, Sammie, Sammy, Sampson, Sanson, Sansone, Shem, Sim, Simpson, Simson**

## Samuel (SAM-ūl)
Hebrew— *Heard or asked of God*
Biblical: Prophet who anointed Saul, the first king of Israel.
Historical: Samuel Adams, Revolutionary War hero and a founder of the United States.
Famous: Samuel Finley Breese Morse, inventor of Morse code.
Literature: Samuel Butler Yeats, poet.
**Sam, Sammie, Sammy, Samuele, Samura, Shem**

## Sanat (sa-NOT)
Hindi— *Ancient*

## Sanborn (SAN-born)
Old English— *From the sandy brook*
**Sand, Sandi, Sandy**

## Sancho (SAWN-chō)
Latin— *Sanctified*
Literature: Sancho Panza, sidekick of Don Quixote.
**Sauncho, Sanjo**

## Sanders (SAN-ders)
Greek— *Son of Alexander*
Entertainment: Sander Vanocur, newscaster.
**Sander, Sanderson, Sandi, Sandor, Sandy, Saunders, Saunderson**

## Sandy (SAN-dē)
See Alexander.
**Sand, Sander, Sandi, Sandon, Sandor**

## Sanford (SAN-ford)
Old English— *From the sandy hill*
**Ford, Sand, Sandford, Sandi, Sandy**

## Sarad (sa-RAWD)
Hindi— *Autumn-born*

## Sargent (SAR-jent)
French— *Army officer*
Famous: Sargent Shriver, cabinet member in the Kennedy Administration.
**Sarge, Sergeant, Sergent**

## Sarojin (SAIR-ō-hin)
Hindi— *Lotuslike*

## Sartan (SAR-tan)
Hebrew— *House of the moon*

## Saul (SAWL)
Hebrew— *Asked for*
Biblical: King of Israel, Apostle Paul was known as Saul of Tarsus.
Literature: Saul Bellow, novelist
**Sol, Sollie, Solly, Zollie, Zolly**

## Sawyer (SOI-er) or (SAW-yer)
Old English— *Sawer of wood*
**Saw, Saxe**

## Saxon (SAKS-un)
Old English— *Swordsman*
**Sax, Saxe**

## Sayer (SĀ-er)
Welsh— *Carpenter*
**Say, Sayers, Sayre, Sayres**

SCOTT—*Scotsman*

**Schuyler** (SKĪ-ler)
Dutch—*A shelter*
**Sky, Skylar, Skyler**

**Scott** (SKOT)
Old English—*Scotsman*
Famous: Scott Carpenter,
astronaut; Francis Scott Key,
composer of *The Star-Spangled
Banner.*
Literature: F. Scott Fitzgerald,
novelist.

**Seabrook** (SĒ-brook)
Old English—*From the brook by the sea*
**Seabrooke, Brook, Brooke**

**Seadon** (SĒ-don)
Old English—*From the hill by the sea*
**Seaden, Seedon**

**Seamus** (SHĀ-mus)
See James.
**Seumas, Shamus**

**Sean** (SHAWN)
See John.
Literature: Sean O'Casey, short-story writer.
Entertainment: Sean Connery, actor.
**Shane, Shaughn, Shaun, Shawn**

**Searle** (SERL)
Teutonic—*Armed or wearing armor*
**Serle**

**Seaton** (SĒ-tun)
Old English—*From the place by the sea*
**Seton, Seeton**

**Seaver** (SĒ-ver)
Anglo-Saxon—*Victorious stronghold*
**Seever**

**Sebastian** (se-BAS-chun)
Greek—*Respected or reverenced*
Famous: Johann Sebastian Bach, composer.
Entertainment: Sebastian Cabot, actor.
**Bastian, Bastien, Sebastiano, Sebastien**

**Sedgewick** (SEJ-wik)
Old English—*From the valley of victory*
**Sedgewin, Sedgewinn, Sedgwick**

**Selby** (SEL-bē)
Teutonic—*From the manor farm*
**Selbey, Shelby**

**Seldon** (SEL-dun)
Teutonic—*From the manor valley*
**Selden, Shelden, Sheldon**

**Selig** (SĀ-lig)
German—*Blessed*
**Zelig**

**Selwyn** (SEL-win)
Old English—*Friend from the palace*
**Selwin, Winnie, Winny, Wyn, Wynn**

**Sepp** (SEP)
Hebrew—*God will increase*
Entertainment: Zeppo Marx, one of the Marx brothers.
**Josef, Jupp, Peppi, Zeppi, Zeppo**

**Serge** (SERJ)
Latin—*Attendant*
Entertainment: Sergei Rachmaninoff, composer.
**Sergei, Sergio**

**Serle** (SERL)
Teutonic—*Bearing arms*

**Seth** (SETH)
Hebrew—*The appointed*
Biblical: Son of Adam and Eve.

**Seton** (SĒ-tun)
Anglo-Saxon—*From the place by the sea*
**Seetan, Seeten, Setan**

**Sevilen** (SEV-len)
Turkish—*Beloved*

**Seward** (SOO-werd)
Old English—*Victorious defender*
**Siward**

**Sewell** (SOO-el)
Teutonic—*Victorious on the sea*
**Sewel, Suwell**

**Seymour** (SĒ-mor)
French—*Follower of St. Maur*
**Morey, Morie, Morrie**

**Shalom** (sha-LŌM)
Hebrew—*Peace*
**Sholom**

**Shandy** (SHAN-dē)
Old English—*Rambunctious*

**Shane** (SHĀN)
Hebrew — *God's gracious gift*
Literature: *Shane*, western novel by
  Zane Grey.
Entertainment: Shaun Cassidy,
  actor and pop singer.
**Sean, Shaun, Shawn**

**Shannon** (SHAN-un)
Gaelic — *Small and wise*
**Shanan, Shannan**

**Sharif** (sha-RĒF)
Arabic — *Honest*

**Shaw** (SHAW)
Old English — *From the grove*

**Sheehan** (SHĒ-an)
Gaelic — *Little and peaceful*

**Sheffield** (SHEF-fēld)
Old English — *From the crooked field*
**Field, Fields, Sheff,
Sheffie, Sheffy**

**Shelby** (SHEL-bē)
Old English — *From the ledge estate*
**Shell, Shelley, Shelly**

**Sheldon** (SHEL-dun)
Old English — *From the farm on the
  ledge*
Entertainment: Sheldon Leonard,
  producer.
**Shell, Shelley, Shelly,
Shelton**

**Shelley** (SHEL-ē)
Anglo-Saxon — *From the ledge
  meadow*
**Shel, Shell, Shelly**

**Shepherd** (SHEP-erd)
Anglo-Saxon — *Sheep tender*
Entertainment: Shepperd
  Strudwick, actor.
**Shep, Shepard, Sheply,
Sheppard, Shepperd**

**Sherard** (SHAIR-ard)
Anglo-Saxon — *Brave soldier*
**Sherrard**

**Sherborn** (SHUR-burn)
Old English — *From the clear brook*
**Sherborne, Sherburn**

**Sheridan** (SHAIR-i-dun)
Celtic — *Wild man or savage*
**Dan, Dannie, Danny,
Sherrie, Sherry**

**Sherlock** (SHUR-lok)
English — *Fair-haired*
Literature: Sherlock Holmes,
  fictional detective.
**Sherlocke, Shurlock, Shurlocke**

**Sherman** (SHUR-mun)
Anglo-Saxon — *Wool-shearer*
**Man, Manny, Sherm,
Shermie, Shermy**

**Sherwin** (SHUR-win)
English — *Swift runner*
**Sherwyn, Sherwynd, Win,
Winnie, Winny, Wyn, Wynn**

**Sherwood** (SHUR-wood)
Old English — *From the bright forest*
Interesting: Sherwood Forest in
  England.
Literature: Sherwood Anderson,
  novelist and short-story writer.
**Sher, Shurwood, Wood,
Woodie, Woody**

**Sibley** (SIB-lē)
Anglo-Saxon — *Friendly or related*
**Sibly, Sibyl**

**Sidney** (SID-nē)
French — *From Sidon*
Interesting: Sidon, oldest city of
  ancient Phoenicia.
Literature: Sydney Carlton, hero of
  Dickens' *A Tale of Two Cities;*
  Sidney Kingsley, author of *Men
  in White.*
Entertainment: Sidney Poitier,
  actor; Sid Caesar, actor and
  comedian.
**Sid, Sidnee, Syd, Sydney**

**Sidwell** (SID-wel)
Old English — *From the broad well*
**Sid, Syd, Sydwell, Well**

**Siegfried** (SIG-frēd)
German — *Glorious peace*
Literature: Siegfried Sassoon,
    satirist.
**Siffre, Sig, Sigfrid,
Sigfried, Sigvard**

**Sigmund** (SIG-mund)
Teutonic — *Victorious protector*
Famous: Sigmund Freud, father of
    psychoanalysis.
Entertainment: Sigmund
    Romberg, composer.
**Sig, Sigismondo, Sigismund,
Sigismundo, Sigsmond,
Sigsmondo, Sigurd**

**Silas** (SĪ-lus)
Latin — *Man of the forest*
Biblical: Companion of Paul on his
    missionary treks.
Literature: *Silas Marner,* novel by
    George Eliot; *The Rise of Silas
    Lapham,* novel by William Dean
    Howells.
**Silvain, Silvan, Silvanio,
Silvano, Silvanus, Silvester,
Silvie, Silvio, Sylas, Sylus,
Sylvain, Sylvan, Sylvano**

**Simen** (SĪ-men)
English — *Alike*
Interesting: Name means
    resemblance between newborn
    and parent.

**Simon** (SĪ-mun)
Hebrew — *He who hears*
Biblical: One of the 12 apostles of
    Christ.
Historical: Simon Bolívar, known
    as the George Washington of
    South America.
Literature: Simple Simon,
    character in the nursery rhyme.
**Si, Sim, Simeon, Simone,
Sy, Syman, Symen, Symon**

**Simpson** (SIMP-sun)
See Samson.
**Simpsen, Simson**

**Sinclair** (SIN-klair)
French — *From St. Clair*
Latin — *The illustrious*
Literature: Sinclair Lewis, author.
**Clair, Clare, Sinclare**

**Sion** (SĪ-on)
Hebrew — *Exalted*

**Skelly** (SKEL-ē)
Gaelic — *Storyteller*
**Skell**

**Skip** (SKIP)
Norwegian — *Shipmaster*
**Skipp, Skipper, Skippie, Skippy**

**Slade** (SLĀD)
Old English — *Child of the valley*

**Slane** (SLĀN)
Czech — *Salty*

**Slevin** (SLE-vin)
Gaelic — *Mountaineer*
**Slaven, Slavin, Sleven**

**Sloan** (SLŌN)
Celtic — *Warrior*

**Smitty** (SMIT-ē)
Old English — *Blacksmith*
**Smith**

**Sofian** (SŌ-fē-an)
Arabic — *Devoted*

**Sol** (SAWL)
Latin — *Child of the sun*
**Sollie, Solly, Zollie,
Zolly**

**Solomon** (SAWL-ō-mun)
Hebrew — *Peaceful*
Biblical: King Solomon, builder of
    great temple, known for his
    wisdom.
Literature: Sholom Aleichem,
    storyteller; Sholem Asch,
    novelist.
**Salamone, Salmon, Salomo,
Salomon, Shalom, Shlomo,
Sholem, Sholom, Sol, Sollie,
Solly, Zollie, Zolly**

**SKIP**—*Shipmaster*

**Somerset** (SOM-er-set)
Old English—*Summer place*
Literature: Somerset Maugham,
   novelist.

**Songan** (SON-gan)
North American Indian—*Strong*

**Spark** (SPARK)
English—*Happy*
**Sparke, Sparkie, Sparky**

**Spencer** (SPEN-ser)
English—*Dispenser of provisions*
Entertainment: Spencer Tracy,
   actor.
**Spence, Spense, Spenser**

**Sprague** (SPRĀG)
French—*Lively*
**Sprage**

**Stacy** (STĀ-sē)
Latin — *Stable companion*
Entertainment: Stacy Keach, actor.
**Stacee, Stacey**

**Stafford** (STAF-erd)
Old English — *Of the landing place*
**Staffard, Staford**

**Standish** (STAN-dish)
Old English — *From the stony park*

**Stanford** (STAN-ferd)
Old English — *From the rock ford*
**Standfield, Standford, Stanfield, Stanhope**

**Stanislaus** (STAN-i-slaws)
Polish — *Camp glory*
**Stan, Stanislas, Stanislaw**

**Stanley** (STAN-lē)
Old English — *From the rocky meadow*
Entertainment: Stanley Kubrick, filmmaker.
Sports: Stan Musial, baseball player.
**Stan, Stanleigh, Stanly**

**Stanton** (STAN-tun)
Old English — *From the stony dwelling*
**Stanway, Stanwood**

**Stedman** (STED-mun)
Anglo-Saxon — *Dweller at the stead*
**Steadman, Steadmen**

**Stephen** (STĒ-ven)
Greek — *Crown*
Famous: Stephen A. Douglas, Abraham Lincoln's opponent in political debates; Etienne Aigner, clothes designer.
Literature: Stephen Crane, Stephen Vincent Benet, Stefan Zweig, authors.
Entertainment: Stephen Stills, member of Crosby, Stills and Nash; Stephen C. Foster, songwriter and composer; Steve McQueen, actor.
**Etienne, Esteban, Estevan, Stefan, Stefano, Steffen, Stephan, Stephanus, Steve, Steven, Stevie, Stevy**

**Sterling** (STER-ling)
Teutonic — *Good value*
Entertainment: Sterling Hayden, actor.
Sports: Sterling Moss, race-car driver.
**Stirling**

**Sterne** (STERN)
English — *Austere*
**Stearn, Stearne, Stern**

**Steven** (STĒ-ven)
See Stephen.
Entertainment: Stevie Wonder, singer; Steve Lawrence, Steve Martin, actors; Steven Spielberg, film director.
Sports: Steve Cauthen, jockey.
**Steve, Stevie, Stevy**

**Stewart** (STŌŌ-art)
Anglo-Saxon — *Keeper of the state*
Entertainment: Stewart Granger, actor.
**Stew, Steward, Stu, Stuart**

**Stiggur** (STĒ-gur)
English — *Gate*
**Stig, Stigger**

**Stillman** (STIL-mun)
Old English — *Quiet man*
**Stillmann**

**Strephon** (STREF-un)
Greek— *One who turns*
Entertainment: Strephon, hero of
*Iolanthe,* by Gilbert and Sullivan.
**Strep, Strephonn, Strepphon**

**Stuart** (STOO-art)
Old English— *Caretaker*
Literature: Stuart Chase,
economist.
Entertainment: Stu Gallagher, actor.
**Steward, Stewart, Stu**

**Styles** (STĪLS)
Old English— *From the stiles*

**Sudi** (SOO-de̅)
Swahili— *Luck*

**Sullivan** (SUL-i-vun)
Gaelic— *Black-eyed*
**Sullie, Sully**

**Sultan** (SUL-tun)
Swahili— *Ruler.*
**Sulten**

**Sumner** (SUM-ner)
French, Latin— *A summoner*

**Sutherland** (SUTH-er-lund)
Norwegian— *Southern land*
**Sotherland, Sutherlan**

**Sutton** (SUT-un)
Anglo-Saxon— *From the south town*

**Sven** (SVEN)
Norwegian— *Youth*
**Svend, Swen**

**Swaine** (SWĀN)
Teutonic— *Boy*
**Swane, Swain, Wain**

**Sylvester** (sil-VES-ter)
Latin— *Of the woods*
Literature: *Le Crime de Sylvestre
Bonnard,* by Anatole France.
Entertainment: Sylvester Stallone,
actor; Sly Stone, singer.
**Silvester, Silvestre, Sly, Sylvestu**

**Tab** (TAB)
English— *Drummer*
Entertainment: Tab Hunter, actor.
**Tabb, Tabbie,
Tabby, Taber, Tabor**

**Tabib** (ta-BĒB)
Turkish— *Physician*

**Tabor** (TĀ-bor)
Hungary, Turkish— *Fortified camp*

**Tad** (TAD)
See Theodore.

**Tadeo** (ta-DĀ-o̅)
Spanish, Latin— *Praise*
**Tadeas, Tades**

**Tadzi** (TAD-ze̅)
Carrier Indian— *The loon*
**Tadek, Tadzio**

**Tait** (TĀT)
Scandinavian— *Cheerful*

**Tal** (TAL)
Hebrew— *Dew or rain*
**Talor**

**Talbot** (TAL-but)
Teutonic, French— *Valley shining*
**Talabert, Talbert, Tallie,
Tally**

**Tales** (TĀLS)
Spanish, Greek— *Flourishing*
**Thales**

**Talman** (TAL-mun)
Hebrew, Aramaic— *To oppress*
**Talmon**

**Taman** (TĀ-mun)
Serbo-Croatian— *Dark or black*

**Tamas** (TĀ-mas)
Hungarian, Greek— *Twin*
**Tammen, Thoma, Thomas,
Thumas, Tomasek, Tomasko,
Tomasso, Tomcio, Tomek,
Tomi, Tomislaw, Toms, Tonie**

**Tammy** (TAM-ē)
See Thomas.
Literature: *Tam O'Shanter,* by
Robert Burns.
**Tam, Tammany, Tammie**

**Tanek** (TAN-ek)
Polish, Greek— *Immortal*
**Ateck, Tanis**

**Tanner** (TAN-er)
Old English— *Leatherworker*
**Tan, Tann, Tanney,
Tannie, Tanny**

**Taro** (TAIR-ō)
Japanese— *First-born male*

**Tarrus** (TAR-us)
Zodiac— *Bull*
**Tari, Taurin, Taurus, Tawrin**

**Tate** (TĀT)
Teutonic— *Cheerful*
**Tait, Taite**

**Tavish** (TAV-ish)
Gaelic— *Twin*
**Tav, Tavis, Tevis**

**Tawno** (TAW-nō)
English— *Small*

**Tayib** (TA-ēb)
Indian— *Good or delicate*

**Taylor** (TĀ-lor)
Latin— *The tailor*

**Teague** (TĒG)
Celtic— *Poet*

**Ted** (TED)
See Theodore.
Famous: Teddy Roosevelt,
President; Ted Kennedy, Senator
Sports: Ted Williams, baseball
player.
**Tedd, Teddey, Teddie,
Teddy, Tedman, Tedmund**

**Temp** (TEMP)
Old English— *From the town of the
temple*
**Temple, Templeton**

**Terence** (TAIR-ens)
Latin— *Smooth*
Literature: Terence Mulvaney,
hero in Kipling's *Soldiers Three·*
Terence Rattigan, playwright.
Entertainment: Terry Thomas,
actor.
**Terencio, Terrence, Terry**

**Terrill** (TAIR-il)
Teutonic— *Belonging to Thor or
martial*
**Tirrell**

**Terry** (TAIR-ē)
See Terence.

**Tertius** (TER-shus)
Latin— *The third*
**Tertius, Tertus**

**Thaddeus** (THAD-ē-us)
Greek— *Courageous*
Latin— *Praiser*
Biblical: One of the 12 apostles of
Christ.
Historical: Thaddeus Stevens
brought impeachment
proceedings against President
Andrew Johnson.
Literature: *Thaddeus of Warsaw,*
novel by Jane Porter.
**Tad, Tadd, Taddeo,
Taddeuss, Tadeo, Tadio,
Thad, Thaddaus**

**THOMAS**—*Twin*

**Thaine** (THĀN)
Old English—*A roofer*
**Thacher, Thackeray, Thatch, Thaxter**

**Thayer** (THĀ-er)
Teutonic—*Of the nation's army*
**Thay**

**Theobald** (THĒ-uh-bald)
German—*Bold for the people*
**Ted, Tedd, Teddie, Teddy, Thebault, Theo, Thibaud, Thibaut, Tiebold, Tiebout, Toiboild, Tybalt**

**Theodore** (THĒ-uh-dor)
Greek—*God's gift*
Literature: Theodore Dreiser, author of *An American Tragedy*.
Entertainment: Theodore Bikel, actor and folk singer; Ted Knight, actor.
**Teador, Ted, Tedd, Teddie, Teddy, Teodoor, Teodoro, Theo, Theodor, Theodore, Tudor**

267

**Theodoric** (thē-uh-DOR-ik)
Teutonic— *The people's ruler*
Historical: Theodoric the Great,
    king of the Ostrogath, an ancient
    civilization in Italy.
**Derek, Derk, Derrick, Dieter,
Dietrich, Dirk, Ted, Tedd,
Teddy, Teodorico. Thedric,
Thedrick, Theo**

**Theron** (THAIR-on)
Greek— *Hunter*

**Thomas** (TOM-as)
Hebrew— *Twin*
Biblical: One of the 12 apostles of
    Christ; referred to as Doubting
    Thomas.
Famous: Thomas Edward
    Lawrence, known as Lawrence
    of Arabia; Thomas Jefferson,
    Thomas Woodrow Wilson,
    Presidents; Thomas A. Edison,
    inventor of the electric light bulb.
Literature: Thomas Hardy,
    Thomas Paine, Thomas Wolfe,
    authors.
Entertainment: Tommy Smothers,
    actor and singer.
**Tam, Tamas, Tammie, Tammy,
Thom, Thoma, Thomkin, Tom,
Tomas, Tomaso, Tome, Tomlin,
Tommie, Tommy**

**Thor** (THOR)
Norwegian— *The thunderous one*
Mythological: Thor, the thunder
    god.
**Thorbjorn, Thorin, Thorlief,
Thorvald, Tore, Tove, Tyrus**

**Thornton** (THORN-tun)
Anglo-Saxon— *From the thorny place*
Literature: Thornton Wilder,
    author and playwright.
**Thorn, Thorndike, Thornie,
Thorny**

**Thorpe** (THORP)
Teutonic— *From the small village*

**Thurlow** (THUR-lō)
Old English— *From Thor's hill*

**Thurston** (THUR-stun)
Scandinavian— *Thor's jewel*

**Tilden** (TIL-den)
Old English— *From the fertile valley*
**Tildan**

**Tilford** (TIL-ford)
Old English— *From the good or
    fertile ford*
**Tillford**

**Timothy** (TIM-ō-thē)
Greek— *Honoring God*
Biblical: Timothy, one of the 12
    apostles of Christ.
Famous: Timothy Leary,
    counterculture philosopher.
Literature: Tiny Tim, character in
    *A Christmas Carol,* by Dickens.
**Tim, Timmie, Timmy, Timofei,
Timoteo, Timothee, Timotheus,
Tymon**

**Titus** (TĪ-tus)
Latin— *The saved*
**Tito, Titos**

**Tivon** (TĪ-von)
Hebrew— *Naturalist*

**Tobias** (tō-BĪ-as)
Hebrew— *God is good*
Literature: Tobias Smollett, author.
**Tobe, Tobiah, Tobie,
Tobin, Tobit, Toby**

**Todd** (TOD)
Scottish— *Fox*
**Toddie, Toddy**

**Tom** (TOM)
See Thomas.
Literature: *Tom Jones,* novel by Henry Fielding; *Uncle Tom's Cabin,* by Harriet Beecher Stowe, *The Adventures of Tom Sawyer,* by Mark Twain; *Sentimental Tommy,* by James M. Barrie.
Entertainment: Tom Jones, pop singer; Tom Tryon, actor.
Sports: Tom Seaver, baseball player.

**Tony** (TŌ-nē)
See Anthony.
Entertainment: Tony Perkins, Tony Randall, actors; Tony Orlando, Tony Bennett, singers.
**Toni, Tonnie**

**Torbert** (TOR-bert)
Teutonic— *Glorious as Thor*
**Bert, Bertie, Berty, Torebert**

**Torin** (TOR-in)
Irish— *Chief*
**Thorfinn, Thorstein**

**Torrance** (TOR-uns)
Gaelic— *From the knolls*
**Tore, Torey, Torr, Torrence, Torrey, Torry**

**Townsend** (TOWN-send)
Old English— *From the town's end*
Literature: Townsend Hope, columnist.
**Town, Towney, Townie, Towny**

**Tracey** (TRĀ-sē)
Anglo-Saxon— *The brave defender*
**Trace, Tracey, Tracie**

**Trahern** (TRĀ-ern)
Celtic— *Stronger than iron*
**Tray**

**Travis** (TRAV-is)
French— *At the crossroads*
Literature: Travis McGee, hero of John MacDonald mystery novels.
Entertainment: Travis Edmondson, singer.
**Traver, Travers, Travus**

**Tremain** (tre-MĀN)
Celtic— *From the town of stone*
**Tremayne**

**Trent** (TRENT)
Latin— *Torrent*
**Trant, Trante, Trenton**

**Trevor** (TRE-vor)
Gaelic— *Prudent*
Entertainment: Trevor Howard, British actor.
**Trefor, Trev, Trevar**

**Tristan** (TRIS-tun)
Welsh— *Sorrowful*
Literature: *Tristan and Isolde,* epic poem by Thomas Malory; Tristan, knight in King Arthur legends.
Sports: Tristram E. Speaker, baseball player.
**Tris, Tristam, Tristram**

**Troy** (TROI)
Gaelic— *Foot soldier*
Entertainment: Troy Donahue, actor.

**Truman** (TROO-mun)
Old English— *Faithful man*
Literature: Truman Capote, author.
**Trueman, Trumann**

**Tucker** (TUK-er)
Old English— *Tucker of cloth*
**Tuck, Tuckie, Tucky**

**Tully** (TUL-ē)
Gaelic— *He who lives with peace of God*
**Tull, Tulley**

**Turner** (TER-ner)
Latin— *Worker of the lathe*

**Tyee** (TĪ-ē)
North American Indian— *Chief*
**Tyonek**

**Tyler** (TĪ-ler)
Old English — *Maker of tiles*
Sports: Tyrus Raymond Cobb,
baseball player.
**Tiler, Ty**

**Tymon** (TĪ-mun)
Polish, Greek — *Honoring God*
**Tymek**

**Tyrone** (TĪ-rōn)
Greek — *Sovereign*
Gaelic — *Land of Owen*
Entertainment: Tyrone Power,
actor; Tyrone Guthrie, director
and playwright.
**Tie, Tynan, Tyrus**

**Tyson** (TĪ-sun)
Teutonic — *Son of the Teutonic or
German*
**Tie, Ty, Tye**

**Udell** (Ū-del)
Old English — *From the yew-tree
valley*
**Del, Dell, Udale, Udall**

**Uland** (Ū-land)
Teutonic — *From the noble land*

**Ulric** (UL-rik)
Teutonic — *Ruler of all*
German — *Wolf ruler*
**Alaric, Ric, Rick, Rickie,
Ricky, Ulrich, Ulrick**

**Ulysses** (ū-LIS-ēs)
Latin, Greek — *Angry or wrathful*
Famous: Ulysses S. Grant,
President.
Literature: Ulysses, hero of
Homer's *Odyssey;* novel *Ulysses,*
by James Joyce.
**Ulick, Ulises, Ulixes, Ulyzes**

**Unni** (UH-nē)
Hebrew — *Modest*

**Upton** (UP-tun)
Anglo-Saxon — *From the hill town*
Literature: Upton Sinclair, novelist.

**Urban** (ER-bun)
Latin — *From the city*
**Urbain, Urbane, Urbano, Urbanus**

**Uriah** (ū-RĪ-uh)
Hebrew — *Jehovah is my light*
Biblical: Husband to Bathsheba.
Literature: Uriah Heap, character
in Dickens' *David Copperfield.*
**Urias, Uriel**

**Urian** (ū-RĪ-un)
Greek — *From heaven*
**Urien**

**Uriel** (UR-ē-el)
Hebrew — *Flame of God*
**Uri**

**Uziel** (ū-ZĒ-el)
Hebrew — *A mighty force*
**Uzziel**

**VACHEL** — *Cowkeeper*

**Vachel** (VĀ-chel)
French — *Cowkeeper*
Literature: Vachel Lindsay, poet.
**Vachell, Vachil**

**Vadin** (va-DĒN)
Hindi — *Scholarly speaker*

**Vail** (VĀL)
Anglo-Saxon — *From the valley*
**Bail, Bale, Vale, Valle**

**Valdis** (VAL-dis)
Teutonic — *Spirited in battle*
Literature: Valdis Fisher, novelist

**Valentine** (VAL-en-tīn) or
(VAL-en-tēn)
Latin— *Strong, valorous or healthy*
Interesting: St. Valentine, patron
saint of lovers.
**Val, Valente, Valentin,
Valentino, Valerian,
Valerius, Valetijn, Valiant**

**Valin** (VĀL-in)
Hindi— *Monkey king*

**Van** (VAN)
Dutch— *From*
Entertainment: Van Johnson, Van
Heflin, actors; Van Cliburn,
pianist.

**Vance** (VANS)
Dutch— *Son of a famous family*
Literature: Vance Packard, author.
**Van**

**Vancel** (VAN-sel)
Hungarian— *Wreath or garland*

**Vasilis** (va-SIL-is)
Greek— *Kingly or magnificent*
**Vasileior, Vasos**

**Vasin** (va-SĒN)
Indian— *Ruler*

**Vassily** (VAS-i-lē)
Russian, German— *Unwavering
protector*
**Vas, Vasilek, Vasya, Vasyuta**

**Vaughan** (VAWN)
Celtic— *The small*
**Vaughn, Von**

**Vere** (VAIR)
Latin— *True or faithful*
**Vered**

**Vernon** (VER-nun)
Latin— *Growing green*
**Lavern, Vern, Verne, Verney**

**Victor** (VIK-tor)
Latin— *The conqueror*
Literature: Victor Hugo, novelist
and poet.
Entertainment: Victor Herbert,
composer; Victor Borge, pianist
and comedian; Victor Mature,
Vic Tayback, actors.
**Vic, Vick, Victoir, Vittorio**

**Vidor** (VĒ-dor)
Hungarian, Latin— *Cheerful*

**Vigor** (VĒ-gor)
Latin— *Vigor*

**Vincent** (VIN-sent)
Latin— *Conquering*
Famous: Vincent van Gogh,
painter.
Entertainment: Vincent Price,
actor; Vincent Minelli, film
producer.
Sports: Vince Lombardi, football
coach.
**Vin, Vince, Vincents,
Vincenty, Vincenz, Vinnie,
Vinny**

**Vinson** (VIN-sun)
Anglo-Saxon— *The conqueror's son*

**Virgil** (VIR-jul)
Latin— *Strange or flourishing*
Literature: Virgil, author of *The
Aeneid.*
Entertainment: Virgil Thomson,
composer and critic.
**Verge, Vergil, Virg,
Virge, Virgie, Virgilio,
Virginius, Virgy**

**Vito** (VĒ-tō)
Latin— *Alive*
**Vite, Vivien**

**Vladimir** (VLA-duh-mēr)
Old Slavic— *Powerful prince*
Literature: Vladimir Nabokov,
author.
Entertainment: Vladimir
Horowitz, pianist.
**Vladamir, Vladlan, Vladlen,
Waldemar, Wladimir**

**Volney** (VOL-nē)
Teutonic — *Most popular*
**Volny**

**Waban** (WAW-ban)
North American Indian — *The east wind*

**Wade** (WĀD)
Old English — *Advancer from the river crossing*
**Wadsworth**

**Wainwright** (WĀN-rīt)
Old English — *Wagon maker*
**Wain, Wayne, Wright**

**Waite** (WĀT)
English — *Guard*

**Wakefield** (WĀK-fēld)
Old English — *From the wet field*
**Field, Wake**

**Wakiza** (wa-KĒ-zuh)
North American Indian — *Desperate fighter*

**Walbridge** (WAL-brij)
Old English — *From the walled bridge*

**Walcot** (WAL-kot)
Old English — *Dweller in the walled cottage*

**Waldemar** (WAL-de-mar)
Teutonic — *Powerful and famous*
**Valdemar, Wald, Waldo, Walley, Wallie, Wally**

**Walden** (WAL-den)
Teutonic — *Mighty*

**Waldo** (WAL-dō)
Teutonic — *Ruler*
Literature: Ralph Waldo Emerson, essayist and poet.
**Wald, Wallie, Wally**

**Waldon** (WAL-dun)
Old English — *From the wooded hill*
**Waldron**

**Walker** (WOK-er)
Old English — *Thickener of cloth, fuller*
**Walley, Wallie, Wally**

**Wallace** (WAL-is)
Old English — *Welshman*
Literature: Wallace Stegner, novelist.
**Wallache, Wallas, Wallie, Wallis, Wally, Walsh, Walt, Welch, Welsh**

**Walter** (WAL-ter)
German — *Powerful warrior*
Famous: Walter Reed, discoverer of the cause of yellow fever.
Literature: Sir Walter Raleigh, Sir Walter Scott, authors.
Entertainment: Walter Cronkite, newscaster; Walt Disney, producer of children's movies; Walter Winchell, Walter Lippmann, Walter Matthau, actors.
Sports: Walter Camp, founder of All-American selection in football; Walter Johnson, baseball player; Walter Hagen, golfer.
**Gauthier, Gualterio, Gualtiero, Wallie, Wally, Walt, Walther, Wat**

**Walton** (WAL-tun)
  Old English—*From the walled town*
  **Wallie, Wally, Walt**

**Ward** (WARD)
  Old English—*Guardian*

**Ware** (WAIR)
  Anglo-Saxon—*Prudent, astute and wary*
  **Warfield, Warford**

**Waring** (WAIR-ing)
  Latin—*True*
  Teutonic—*Heedful*

**Warner** (WAR-ner)
  Teutonic—*Guarding warrior*
  Famous: Warner Erhard, ESP theorist.

**Warren** (WAR-un)
  German—*Protecting friend*
  Famous: Warren G. Harding, President.
  Entertainment: Warren Beatty, actor and director.
  Sports: Warren Spahn, baseball player.
  **Ware, Waring**

**WARREN**—*Protecting friend*

**Warrick** (WAR-ik)
Teutonic — *Strong ruler*
**Aurick, Vareck, Varick,
Warwick**

**Warton** (WAR-tun)
Old English — *From the poplar-tree
farm*

**Washburn** (WASH-bern)
Old English — *From near the
overflowing brook*
**Burn, Burnie, Burny, Wash**

**Washington** (WASH-ing-tun)
Teutonic — *The acute or smart*
Famous: George Washington
 Carver, inventor of many uses
 for the peanut.
Literature: Washington Irving,
 author.
**Wash**

**Watson** (WAT-sun)
Anglo-Saxon — *Warrior's son*

**Waverly** (WĀ-ver-lē)
Old English — *From the meadow of
quaking aspen trees*
**Lee, Leigh, Waverley**

**Wayland** (WĀ-lund)
Teutonic — *From the land by the
highland*
Entertainment: Waylon Jennings,
 country-western singer.
**Land, Way, Waylen, Waylon**

**Wayne** (WĀN)
Anglo-Saxon — *Wagoneer*
Entertainment: Wayne Newton,
 singer and entertainer.
**Waine**

**Webb** (WEB)
Old English — *Weaver*
**Weber, Webster**

**Welby** (WEL-bē)
Scandinavian — *From the farm by the
spring*

**Weldon** (WEL-dun)
Teutonic — *From the hill by the well*

**Wells** (WELZ)
Old English — *From the springs*

**Wendell** (WEN-dul)
German — *Wanderer*
Anglo-Saxon — *Dweller by the
passage*
Famous: Wendell Phillips,
 abolitionist; Oliver Wendell
 Holmes, Chief Justice of the
 Supreme Court.
Sports: Wendell Scott, race-car
 driver.
**Wendel**

**Wescott** (WES-kot)
Teutonic — *Dwells at west cottage*
**Wes**

**Wesley** (WES-lē)
Old English — *From the western
meadow*
**Lee, Leigh, Wellesley,
Wes, West, Westleigh, Westley**

**Westbrook** (WEST-brook)
Old English — *From the western brook*
**Brook, Brooke, Wes,
West, Westbrooke, Westley**

**Weston** (WES-tun)
Old English — *From the western estate*

**Weylin** (WĀ-lin)
Celtic — *Son of the wolf*
**Waylan, Waylin**

**Wheeler** (WĒL-er)
Old English — *Wheel maker*

**Whitby** (WIT-bē)
Scandinavian — *From the white
dwellings of settlements*

**Whitelaw** (WĪT-law)
Old English — *From the white hill*
**Whitford, Whitman**

**Whitney** (WIT-nē)
Old English — *From the white island*
**Whit**

**Whittaker** (WI-tuh-ker)
Old English — *From the white field*
**Whit**

**Wicent** (WĪ-sent)
Polish, Latin — *Conqueror*
**Vincenty, Wicek, Wicenty,
Wicus, Wincenty**

**Wichado** (wi-CHA-dō)
North American Indian — *Willing*

**Wilbur** (WIL-ber)
Anglo-Saxon — *Beloved stronghold*
Famous: Wilbur Wright, inventor
of the airplane.
**Wilbert, Wilburt**

**Wildon** (WIL-dun)
Old English — *From the wooded hill*
**Wilden, Willdon**

**Wiley** (WĪ-lē)
Old English — *From the water*
Sports: Willie Mays, baseball
player.
Entertainment: Willie Nelson,
country-western singer.
**Willey, Willie, Wully,
Wylie**

**Wilfred** (WIL-fred)
Old English — *Resolute for peace*
Literature: Wilfred, hero in
*Ivanhoe,* by Sir Walter Scott.
**Wilford, Wilfrid, Will,
Willie, Willy**

**William** (WIL-yum)
Teutonic — *Determined guardian*
Historical: William Penn, founder
of Pennsylvania; William Tell,
Swiss national hero; William the
Conqueror, military leader.
Famous: William Henry Harrison,
William McKinley, William
Howard Taft, Presidents;
William Harvey, discoverer of
circulation of the blood.
Literature: William Blake, William
Wordsworth, William Butler
Yeats, William Faulkner, William
Buckley, Jr., authors.
Entertainment: William Holden,
actor; William Friedkin, director.
Sports: Willie McCovey, baseball
player.
**Bill, Billie, Billy,
Guglielmo, Guillaume,
Guillermo, Wilek, Wilhelm,
Will, Willem, Willi, Willie,
Willis, Willy, Wilmar, Wilmer**

**Wilton** (WIL-tun)
Old English — *From the farm by the
spring*
Sports: Wilt Chamberlain,
basketball player.
**Will, Willie, Willy, Wilt**

**Winfield** (WIN-feld)
Old English — *From the friendly field*
**Field, Win, Winfred,
Winfrid, Winifield, Winnie**

**Winslow** (WINZ-lō)
Old English — *From the friend's hill*
**Win, Winn, Winnie, Winny**

**Winston** (WIN-stun)
Anglo-Saxon — *Friend or friendly
town*
Famous: Winston Churchill,
British Prime Minister.
**Win, Winn, Winnie,
Winny, Winstonn**

**Winthrop** (WIN-thrup)
Old English — *From the wine village*
Entertainment: Winthrop Ames,
producer.

**Winward** (WIN-werd)
Unknown — *My brother's keeper*

**Wolcott** (WAWL-kot)
Unknown — *Cottage in the woods*
Literature: Wolcott Gibbs,
   playwright.
**Walcot, Walcott, Wolcot**

**Wolfgang** (WULF-gang)
Teutonic — *Advancing wolf*
Famous: Wolfgang Amadeus
   Mozart, composer.
**Wolf, Wolfe, Wolfie,
Wolfram, Wolfy**

**Woodrow** (WOOD-rō)
Old English — *From the passage in
   the woods*
Famous: Thomas Woodrow
   Wilson, President.
**Wood, Woodie, Woodley,
Woodman, Woodward, Woody**

**Worth** (WERTH)
Old English — *From the farmstead*
**Worthington, Worthy**

**Wright** (RĪT)
Old English — *Carpenter*

**Wuliton** (WOOL-i-tun)
North American Indian — *To do well*

**Wyatt** (WĪ-at)
French — *Little warrior*
Famous: Wyatt Earp, old west
   lawman and gunfighter.
**Wiatt, Wyat, Wye**

**Wylie** (WĪ-lē)
Old English — *Charming*
**Lee, Leigh, Wiley, Wye**

**Wyman** (WĪ-mun)
Anglo-Saxon — *Warrior*

**Wyndham** (WIN-dum)
Old English — *From the windy village*

**Wynn** (WIN)
Welsh — *Fair*
**Winnie, Winny**

**Xanthus** (ZAN-thus)
Latin — *Golden-haired*

**Xavier** (ZĀ-vē-er)
Spanish, Arabic — *Brilliant*
Entertainment: Xavier Cugat, band
   leader.
**Jaberri, Javier, Xever**

**Xenophon** (ZĒ-nō-fon)
Greek — *Strange voice*
**Xeno, Zennie**

**Xenos** (ZĒ-nōs)
Greek — *Stronger*
**Xenoz**

**Xerxes** (ZER-sēz)
Persian — *King*
Interesting: Many Persian
   emperors were named Xerxes.
**Zerk**

**Ximenes** (ZĪ-me-nēz)
See Simon.
**Ximenez, Ximenia, Xymenes**

**Xylon** (ZĪ-lon)
Greek — *From the forest*

**Yadid** (yuh-DĒD)
Hebrew — *Friend*

**Yadin** (yuh-DĒN)
Hebrew — *God will judge*
**Yadon**

**Yakecen** (YAK-sen)
Indian — *Sky or song*

**Yakez** (YAK-ez)
Carrier Indian — *Heaven*

**Yale** (YĀL)
Teutonic — *Payer; yielder*

**Yancy** (YAN-sē)
North American Indian —
*Englishman*
**Ioammis, Yance, Yancey,
Yank, Yankee, Yannakis**

**Yarin** (YAR-in)
Hebrew — *To understand*

**Yasah** (YĀ-zuh)
Arabic — *Wealth*

**Yazid** (yuh-ZĒD)
See Joseph.
**Yusef, Zaid**

**Yeates** (YĀTS)
Anglo-Saxon — *At the gates*

**Yehudi** (yuh-HOO-dē)
Hebrew — *Praise of the Lord*
Entertainment: Yehudi Menuhin,
violinist.

**Yemon** (YĀ-mon)
Japanese — *Guarding the gate*

**Yeremy** (YER-e-mē)
Russian, Hebrew — *Appointed by
God*
**Yarema, Yaremka, Yerik**

**York** (YORK)
Old English — *Estate of the boar*
**Yorke, Yorker**

**Yucel** (Ū-sel)
Turkish — *Sublime*

**Yule** (ŪL)
Old English — *Born at yuletide*
Entertainment: Yul Brynner, actor.
**Ewel, Ewell, Yul**

**Yuma** (Ū-muh)
North American Indian — *Son of a
chief*

**Yvan** (Ī-van)
See Ivan.

**Yves** (ĒVS)
French — *Little archer*
Famous: Yves Saint Laurent,
designer.
Entertainment: Yves Montand,
actor.
**Ives**

**Zachariah** (zak-uh-RĪ-uh)
Hebrew — *The Lord's remembrance*
Biblical: Zacharias, father of John
the Baptist.
Famous: Zachary Taylor,
President.
Entertainment: Zachary Scott,
actor.
**Zacarias, Zaccaria, Zach,
Zacharias, Zacharie, Zachary,
Zak, Zakarias, Zechariah, Zeke**

**Zahur** (ZĀ-hur)
Swahili — *Flower*

**Zak** (ZAK)
Czech — *Schoolboy*
**Zaki**

**Zamir** (za-MĒR)
Hebrew — *A bird or a song*
**Zemer**

**Zane** (ZĀN)
Hebrew — *Ambush*
Literature: Zane Grey, author.

**Zarek** (ZAR-ek)
Polish, Greek — *May God protect the
king*
**Balte**

**Zebadiah** (zeb-uh-DĪ-uh)
Hebrew — *Gift of the Lord*
Biblical: Zebedee, husband of
Solome and father of apostles
James and John.
**Zebedee**

**Zebulon** (ZEB-ū-lon)
Hebrew — *Dwelling place*
Historical: General Zebulon M.
Pike, for whom Pike's Peak was
named.
**Zeb, Zebulen**

**Zedekiah** (zed-e-KĪ-uh)
Hebrew — *God is mighty and just*
Biblical: Last king of Judah.

**Zeke** (ZĒK)
See Ezekiel.

**Zelig** (ZĀ-lik)
Teutonic — *Blessed*
**Selig, Zelix**

**Zelimir** (ZEL-i-mēr)
Slavic — *He wishes peace*

**Zenas** (ZĒ-nas)
Greek — *Jupiter's gift*
**Zenos**

**Zephaniah** (zef-uh-NĪ-uh)
Hebrew — *Hidden by the Lord*
Biblical: Prophet that lived at the
time of Jeremiah.
**Jeremiah, Zeph, Zephan**

**Zion** (ZĪ-un)
Hebrew — *Fortress*

**Ziven** (ZIV-en)
Czech, Russian — *Vigorous and alive*
**Ziv, Zivon**

**Zollie** (ZAWL-ē)
See Saul.
**Zolly**

**Zorya** (ZOR-yuh)
Ukrainian — *Star*

# INDEX

# BABY-NAME WORKSHEET

|  | First | Middle | Last |
|---|---|---|---|
| 1. | | | |
| 2. | | | |
| 3. | | | |
| 4. | | | |
| 5. | | | |
| 6. | | | |
| 7. | | | |
| 8. | | | |
| 9. | | | |
| 10. | | | |

## RANK NAMES IN ORDER OF PREFERENCE:

First: _____

Second: _____

Third: _____

# BABY-NAME WORKSHEET

| First | Middle | Last |
|-------|--------|------|

1. _____
2. _____
3. _____
4. _____
5. _____
6. _____
7. _____
8. _____
9. _____
10. _____

## RANK NAMES IN ORDER OF PREFERENCE:

First: _____

Second: _____

Third: _____

# BABY-NAME WORKSHEET

| First | Middle | Last |
|-------|--------|------|

1. _____
2. _____
3. _____
4. _____
5. _____
6. _____
7. _____
8. _____
9. _____
10. _____

# RANK NAMES IN ORDER OF PREFERENCE:

First: _____

Second: _____

Third: _____